MR. CALAMITY

THE STORY OF DWAINE SIMPSON, BOXINGS CLOWN PRINCE

BY
LAURA BROWN
AND JOHN GREENBURG

WITH POETRY
BY LAURA BROWN

TO BUTCH AND KATHY FLANSBURG –

THANK YOU FOR MY BEING INDUCTED IN THE 2011 FLORIDA BOXING HALL OF FAME AND BEING ABLE TO PARTICIPATE IN THE FESTIVITIES FOR THE PAST SEVEN YEARS. THE FBHOF AND YOUR FRIENDSHIP HAS BEEN THE HIGHLIGHT OF MY BOXING LIFE.

– YOURS IN THE GREAT SPORT OF BOXING –

Dwaine Simpson

A CHAMP

Have mercy on me,
A man of calamity,
I have come with wit,
So don't call me nitwit.

Inside the ring,
I will prance,
I will dance,
I will entertain,
For certain.

I will be a star,
As I spar
And come out
Without a scar.

I will swing
My boxing sting,
Giving his face
A leather taste.

I will charm
And people disarm,
As I feel like a colt
With a lightning bolt.

I punched him with force.
Down he went.
I heard the count of ten.
The fight came to an end,
And my third title I'll defend.

As I awakened,
I realized it was nothing but a dream.

PART ONE:

THE LEGEND IS BORN

DWAINES WINDFALL

It was a beautiful mid September day in 1955. Dwaine Simpson was headed for work in his 1949 Ford coupe. As he drove along NW 27th Boulevard in Opa-Locka, Florida, a toothpick hung from his lips that he would chew on until it was reduced to a soggy mess. He had enjoyed the simple pleasure for years. For a while, he also put bottle caps in his mouth as a change of pace. That ended when he almost choked on one. His face turned blue and his wife, Ramona, had to pound him on the back until he coughed up the obstruction. After saving her husband's life, she said, "You're not gonna put any more of them in your mouth, are you?"

"Nope, I'll stick with toothpicks."

"Good, honey, those are perfectly safe. Just don't clean your fingernails with 'em and then put 'em in your mouth."

The yellow Ford with pea green interior was a wedding present from his father in law. Prior to the nuptials, Russell Carter offered Dwaine the choice of a car and a down payment on a home or a job with his firm, East Coast Paving. Simpson asked, "Do I get to wear a white shirt and tie and have a secretary to dictate to?"

"No, you'll start out as part of a work crew and learn the business from the ground up."

"How much'll I make?"

"A dollar twenty five an hour, just like the rest of my men."

Not being completely sold on the idea, Dwaine rubbed his chin reflectively for a moment before nodding his head and saying, "Okay, I'll take the job."

On his first day, he was told to take the wheel of a fourteen yard dump truck hitched to a ten ton trailer loaded with huge paving rollers. There was enormous risk involved because Dwaine had never driven anything larger than a panel truck, wasn't offered training and didn't ask for any. Simpson was very careful as he pulled a heavy load swinging back and forth and managed to arrive at the work site in one piece. He then faced the challenge of positioning one hundred fifty pound runways so the rollers could be unloaded. They weighed ten pounds more than he did, but other members of the paving crew came to his aid. The next four days found him hauling rollers from one job site to another. Things went well until Friday. It suddenly began raining hard while he was taking a roller off a trailer, and the huge piece of equipment slid off the runway and nearly turned him into a human pancake. When he told his wife about it that night, he said, "I swear the roller had it in for me. It was on my heels for a good hunnert yards and I had to become a long jumper to escape."

His take home pay for fifty hours of grueling work came to a little over fifty dollars. Dwaine and Ramona talked it over, and she asked her dad if they could change their minds and take the car and the down payment instead of the job. Russell Carter went along with their request and gave them a five year old Ford he had been using for business that came without a radio. The eight hundred dollar down payment went toward the purchase of a seven thousand dollar house in Carol City. It had three bedrooms, a bathroom and a half, a gas wall heater, but no air conditioning. To their way of thinking, they made the right choice.

Simpson reflected upon his first year of married life as he drove to work. "Sure glad I'm not workin' for that pavin' company. Ya gotta be drunk, a degenerate or dumb as a horse turd to do dangerous stuff like that and not get paid much." He stopped for one of the town's few traffic signals. The light changed and he pulled away, smoothly shifting the gears of the Ford's manual transmission. Without a radio to listen to, he entertained himself by singing aloud.

"DOWN IN NEW ORLEANS WHERE EVERTHIN'S FINE, ALL THOSE CATFISH DRINK IS WINE."

He drummed on the steering wheel with his fingers and continued singing until he arrived at his job. He parked his car, left it unlocked with the windows down and walked briskly to the locker room for employees of the Opa-Locka Parks and Recreation Department. His employer oversaw facilities which were once part of a Marine air base.

The city employing Dwaine had been incorporated only thirty years before by Glenn Curtiss, an aviation pioneer whose vision of Opa-Locka was inspired by a fantasy portrayed in the book One Thousand and One Arabian Tales. Curtiss supervised construction of a hundred and five buildings with an array of domes, minarets and outside staircases that became the largest collection of Moorish architecture in the Western hemisphere. Street names included Sultan Avenue, Ali Baba Avenue, Sharazad Boulevard and Sesame Street. Thief of Baghdad, a widely popular 1924 silent movie starring Douglas Fairbanks, helped spur the development, and the town sustained the Arabian Nights theme by holding an annual festival. Each September, streets were blocked off and local merchants masqueraded as Aladdins, sultans, sheiks and desert princes. Large tents suited for desert royalty were put up and Arabian stallions and camels brought in as added attractions.

Opa-Locka's history and annual celebration were of little interest to the young family man. A more immediate concern was the lack of folding money in his wallet. His weekly take home pay was forty five dollars and thirty seven cents, less than what he made at the paving company. Gas was twenty five cents a gallon, a bottle of Coca Cola cost sixteen cents and a carton of cigarettes went for two dollars, but his salary wasn't enough to keep the lanky blonde, his wife and their baby girl afloat. They were constantly faced with too much month at the end of their money. His additional income from mowing lawns, painting houses and other side jobs kept them solvent.

The sack lunch Dwaine placed in his locker reminded him the week was not quite over and payday still hadn't arrived. On Mondays, the brown paper bag held cold roast beef or ham sandwiches on rye and fresh fruit. By Wednesday, he was eating peanut butter, banana and mayonnaise sandwiches on white bread. As the week drew to a close, the contents of his lunch bag were reduced to mustard and ketchup sandwiches and a Moon Pie. He thought, "Sure would be nice to find a few extra bucks somewhere."

His thoughts of money and food were interrupted by Bill Graves, who headed Parks and Recreation. The gray haired department head walked up to him and said, "I want you to help set up a boxing ring and put chairs in place for ringside seating."

"Whah fo'?"

"You'd talk better if you took the lumber out," said the supervisor clad in cuffed trousers, a white shirt and tie. "Did you have a toothpick in your mouth when they took your wedding pictures?"

Dwaine removed the toothpick, tossed it in a waste can and said, "I can't remember. Come to think of it, I can't recall seein' any wedding pictures. I'll ask Ramona about that tonight... if I can remember to do it."

Simpson's boss had known Dwaine long enough not to be surprised by his off the wall remarks. He asked his employee, "You didn't forget about the Arabian Nights Festival, didja? It happens every year."

"Oh, ya know me. Every day's a new day. One day I'm a goose, one day I'm a duck." The supervisor chuckled at the response. Simpson said, "Thanks for remindin' me, boss. Where they settin' up?"

"At the basketball courts."

"Who's in charge?"

"Ask for Dick Lee. He's state chairman of AAU boxing. Maybe I should write the man's name down for you."

"Ya don't hafta to do that. I learned how to remember names in college. Just associate 'em with famous people. I'll keep thinkin' 'bout Vice President Nixon and Robert E. Lee."

"I don't care how you do it. Just get over there and help the man out."

Simpson headed to the lighted outdoor basketball courts he knew so well. He spent much of his free time sharpening his shooting eye on the concrete surfaces of the two regulation size courts laid out side by side. Dwaine was 5'11" and a slender 141 pounds, but his long range shooting ability earned him a scholarship to Western Carolina College and later, the role of player-coach for an Opa-Locka All-Stars team in a very competitive Miami recreation league. When he arrived at the courts, he was momentarily taken aback to see his second home being transformed into a forbiddingly huge outdoor boxing arena. A short, stocky man with wavy hair was directing a small crew of men. The wavy haired man noticed Dwaine and without bothering to introduce himself asked, "You from Parks and Recreation?"

"That's right."

"Go help the guy settin' up chairs."

After three hundred chairs were placed to form ringside seating, Simpson returned to the man giving orders and asked, "Is your name Robert E. Nixon?"

The short, stocky man shook his head and looked at Dwaine in an odd manner.

Simpson realized he'd misspoken and quickly corrected himself. "Uh... I mean are you Dick Lee?"

"Yeah."

"Ya gonna have boxing like the Gillette Friday Night Fights they put on TV at ten o'clock?"

Lee folded his arms across his chest and replied with irritation in his voice, "Nope, amateur bouts. Florida AAU champs are gonna be fightin' Puerto Rican champs."

"How many rounds they fight?" asked Dwaine.

"Three three-minute rounds."

Dick Lee took a moment to eye the parks and recreation worker's physique as if evaluating a race horse. He briefly placed a hand on the round portion of Dwaine's shoulder, like a master butcher examining a piece of meat. Simpson appeared to be in good condition. The promoter asked, "Ya ever box?"

"Ma bought my brother'n me boxing gloves when I was five. Useta box with my cousins and kids in the neighborhood, but never did nothin' in a real ring."

Lee didn't respond, so Dwaine decided to keep talking until told to stop. "I learned a lotta 'bout it from the movie Gentleman Jim. You remember it, doncha? Errol Flynn played Gentleman Jim Corbett and Ward Bond was John L. Sullivan."

Dwaine wasn't sure the promoter heard a word he said. Dick Lee seemed to have something on his mind and was waiting for the right moment to bring it up. When the parks and recreation employee stopped talking, Lee said, "Ya look like you're in pretty good shape."

Simpson patted his chest and replied, "Yeah, I play basketball all the time. I played college ball." The remark brought a frown to his listener's face. "Now I'm in a men's league," Simpson added. "Guys on my team played in college and some of 'em played in the pros."

Lee's response was a derisive "Hummph!" Dwaine was unaware the promoter looked upon college men and basketball players as no better than insects. As far as Dick Lee was concerned, real men went toe to toe and pounded each other until one ended up on the floor and unconscious, and they learned that in gyms, not colleges. Still, the promoter apparently thought Simpson could be useful because he asked him, "Howdja like ta box tonight? A guy couldn't make it and I'm short a fighter."

Dwaine's first thought was, "It'd be somethin' different. Kinda like to see how I'd do in a real boxing ring." Taking on a daring adventure appealed to his sense of bravado. He nodded his head and said, "Okay."

"Fine, be ready to go at six o'clock."

The promoter was about to turn and walk away when Dwaine asked, "Uh... am I gonna get trunks and shoes to wear?"

Dick Lee became impatient with the raw newcomer and replied in a firm tone, "I'll getcha a corner man, but ya fetch your own equipment."

Dwaine was not put off by the response. He nodded and said, "Awright." The lanky blonde family man thought, "I've never backed down before, and I'm not gonna start now. I got some stuff I can wear." As he walked back to the rec department office, he thought, "Hey, no big deal. It's amateur boxing. They'll prolly put me in with 'nother guy who's never fought before."

When his morning's work was done, Simpson had his usual day before payday lunch of two mustard and ketchup sandwiches, a Moon Pie and an RC Cola. He hoped it would hold him until after the fight, and then he could go home to share leftovers with Ramona.

The afternoon flew by and before he knew it, it was almost time for the boxing match. Dwaine went to his locker and took out the basketball trunks and jock strap he always kept there. The only footwear he had was a pair of white tennis shoes. He didn't have a robe like boxers usually wore, and was lucky to have a towel for his corner man to use. He had no idea he should have also had a mouth guard to protect his jaw and a metal cup to guard his balls from punches below the belt.

Wearing a white t-shirt, basketball trunks and tennis shoes, Simpson walked to the boxing ring and looked for Dick Lee. When he found the promoter, he asked, "Who's gonna be in my corner?"

Lee turned to a man in his early twenties and said, "Jack, take care of this guy."

The other man shook Dwaine's hand and said, "Hi, I'm Jack McKiernan." While Jack went to a trainer's kit for supplies, Dick Lee handed Dwaine a small metal cup and said, "Slip this in your jock strap. It'll protect ya from low blows."

Simpson replied, "Isn't it kinda small?"

The promoter laughed and said, "It'll fit alright. Ya got small hands and small feet." Dwaine felt Dick Lee was making fun of him and decided not to use the protective device. He thought, "If I'm gonna fight somebody who's never done it before, a jock strap should be enough."

Jack wrapped Dwaine's hands in white bandages, helped him put on a pair of boxing gloves and laced them up. He seemed to know something about the sport. Simpson thought, "'Least he knows more'n I do, which is damn little."

When it came time for Dwaine to fight, Jack stepped on the bottom rope and held up the middle one so the novice could enter the ring. There was a smattering of polite applause from the large crowd for the unknown, ill prepared boxer.

While standing in his corner waiting for his opponent to arrive, Dwaine stripped off his t-shirt. Just as he removed the garment, the man he was going to fight jumped into the ring. He was sharply attired in a classy robe, boxing trunks and leather soled boxing shoes. His body squirmed inside his robe while he warmed up by fiercely throwing combinations of punches. His fans screamed and whistled in pure elation. Simpson thought, "Why'd they put me in with him? This guy's done it before, and I can tell he's got bad intentions."

Dwaine asked McKiernan, "What do I need to do?"

Jack replied, "How many fights ya had?"

"None."

McKiernan appeared stunned. He asked, "Don't you know who that is?"

"Nope."

"That's Robert Morale. He's the state AAU welterweight champion."

Dwaine's brow wrinkled as he asked, "What should I do?"

Jack shrugged and said, "Get outta the ring or run and hope ya don't get hit."

Dwaine replied, "Feet don't fail me now!"

While walking to the middle of the ring for the referee's final instructions, a terrifying realization came to Dwaine: "I might get smashed in the face!" He suddenly recalled scenes from the Gentleman Jim movie and thought, "If I move around like Jim Corbett, this guy might not be able to hit me." His only hope was to keep away from his opponent. Lucky for him, he had always been a very good dancer. He could move backward as fast as he could move forward, possessed excellent balance and moved in a fluid, graceful way.

At the opening bell, Morale advanced aggressively to test the mettle of his unknown opponent. Dwaine avoided the state champion by sometimes moving backwards and other times side to side. His feet gave the illusion of floating off the floor, and his elusiveness frustrated any attempt by the champ to land a blow. None of this impressed Dick Lee. He muttered, "The college boy's no fighter. He looks like he's dancin' to swing music."

While the first time fighter sat on a stool between rounds, took a drink of water and spit it into a bucket, Jack McKiernan said, "I don't know what you're doin'. It looks strange, but seems to work. Morale hasn't hit ya with anything solid, so keep it up."

As the bout continued and the state AAU champ failed to lay a glove on the boxer in the strange attire, the fans began to warm up to the underdog. More and more of them began cheering loudly for Dwaine. They enjoyed the novelty of a boxer who danced around the ring and successfully avoided being hit. Some thought he was hilarious and laughed as if watching a comedy routine. Simpson's ability to entertain the crowd made Dick Lee think, "I could make some dough with this guy. He don't know what he's doin', but he's like a sideshow freak people'll pay ta see."

Simpson lasted the full three rounds and even though his much more experienced opponent was awarded the decision, Dwaine was pleased. He was grateful to have gone the distance and best of all, avoid being hit in the face, injured or knocked out. While changing back into his street clothes, he saw Dick Lee stride into the employees' locker room as if he owned the place. Lee said, "Ya know, Simpson, we got somethin' in common."

"What's that?"

"My middle name is Duane, just like yours."

Simpson noticed Lee was holding a pencil and a pad of paper, and "Moose Lodge... Duane Simpson" was written on the pad. The novice boxer said to the promoter, "Ya didn't spell my first name right. It's D-W-A-I-N-E."

"Guess we got nothin' in common after all. Well, forget it. By the way, I'm promotin' shows at the Moose Lodge in Coral Gables. Know where Flagler and 27th Avenue is?"

"Yeah."

"Well, I can arrange for ya to fight there every week. How 'bout it, college boy?"

Simpson's head was down as he tied his shoes. He asked, "Why should I? What's in it for me?"

"Ya said ya play basketball. Do they pay ya for that?"

"No."

"Well," said Lee in an officious tone, "the fights at the Moose Lodge are sanctioned by the AAU and promoted as amateur bouts, so everyone gets an honorarium."

Dwaine thought, "Gee, that'd be great. Might help me get a better job." He had a wide eyed look as he asked, "Ya mean I can I hang my honorarium on a wall like a regular degree?"

The promoter rolled his eyes and replied in an exasperated tone. "That's not what I said. I'm talkin' 'bout payin' ya five bucks to box in a main event and three for a preliminary. Oh yeah, here's three dollars for tonight." Dick Lee reached into a pants pocket, pulled out a thick roll of dollar bills with a rubber band around it, peeled off three singles and handed them to Simpson.

It was the windfall Dwaine had been hoping for. His stomach was growling and he was hungry enough to eat bark off a tree but with three bucks in his pocket, he thought, "I'm gonna have a good dinner tonight!"

He headed for Watson's Restaurant, famous for its "All You Can Eat Fried Spring Chicken Dinner." The meal cost him a dollar forty five. He left a quarter tip and still had enough for a takeout order to bring to his family. Dwaine thought, "Lawdy, Miss Clawdy, this is a terrific day!"

WHEN DWAINE MET RAMONA

The largest monthly expense for Dwaine, his beautiful wife and their daughter Sheree was a sixty nine dollar mortgage payment. Thanks to the salary from his Parks and Recreation job and part time employment, they had a home, a car, a television set, were keeping up with the bills and doing far better than his parents had in the early years of their marriage. His father had been a coal miner in West Virginia. He lived in towns where men rented company owned housing, traded at company stores and spent most of their waking hours with their faces smudged by coal dust. Dwaine's mother had married at fifteen and had him when she was seventeen. She worked as a bookkeeper for the coal company at their combination general merchandise store and restaurant, which took up an entire block. It was the only place in town to shop. She put in ten hours a day, six days a week for twenty five cents an hour and instead of a paycheck, was given scrip redeemable only at her employer's businesses.

Simpson had attended college on a basketball scholarship and came to Florida after finishing five semesters. He applied for a solid, secure position with the U.S. Postal Service paying a dollar eighty five an hour. Veterans were given first priority and since Dwaine had not served in the military, he found himself near the end of a long waiting list. When finally interviewed, he was asked, "What are two days of the week that begin with 'T'?"

He appeared in deep thought for a moment before replying, "Today and tomorrow."

The interviewer gave him a chance at another question. "How many feet are in a mile?"

Dwaine's brow furrowed as he thought for a moment before giving his final answer. "Guess it depends on whose feet we talkin' about."

The man conducting the interview said, "Hmmm, you put on your application you went to college for two and a half years."

"Yeah, I had a high school diploma and could hear thunder and see lightnin'. That was good enough to get me into Western Carolina College."

Dwaine was told, "We'll keep your application on file," but never heard from the Postal Service again. He settled for a spot with Opa-Locka's Parks and Recreation Department paying twenty dollars a week less. Other than six weeks during his college years when he worked as a combination doorman, bellhop and elevator operator at a small hotel and made a total of two hundred dollars, it was the first job he ever had. When his college pals asked him how he liked working at the hotel, he replied, "The work's okay, but I don't like havin' to work at night."

"You're just not a nocturnal person," one of them said.

"Oh no, I'm definitely dayturnal."

Simpson's talents lay in other fields. From his earliest high school years, he had been an excellent dancer, especially when fast songs were played. He first learned to clog from girls living in the hill country and then picked up rhythm and blues steps in Myrtle Beach, South Carolina, the hot bed of up tempo dancing. He loved to talk about his Myrtle Beach experiences. "It's where ya fall in love every week and get married every Saturday night, but not in the eyes of the Lord. The dance I learned was first called the Jitterbug, then later the Be Bop... 'Ya gotta look bop, feel bop and be bop.'"

The Be Bop was known as either the Shag or Swing Dance when the lanky blonde twenty year old arrived in Miami. The first big dance Dwaine attended was held in Miami's Bayfront Auditorium. Three thousand kids showed up, but Simpson wasn't impressed with the local talent. He met Charlene, a sixteen year old from New York City who could really tear up the floor, and she complimented him on his style of dancing. He replied, "Nobody 'cept me and you knows how to dance. The guys are doin' some Elvis Presley, heel toe, rubber leg hill jack garbage and you're the best of all the girls." When a dance contest was announced, they entered as partners. One hundred couples competed, but Dwaine and the girl from the Big Apple won a twenty five dollar first prize, the equivalent of half his weekly pay. They split the money, but he didn't ask her for a date because he didn't want to be going out with someone so young.

Three days later, Dwaine received a phone call from a television station and was asked to appear on a local variety show. A ballet dancer leaving Miami to embark on a career in New York City wanted Simpson to dance with her as a way of showcasing her versatility. He gladly accepted and his appearance was a hit with the viewers. After that, he was treated like a celebrity at local dances.

While attending a record hop, he saw a gorgeous young blonde woman jitterbugging with a man in his early twenties. Bill Haley and the Comets' Shake Rattle and Roll boomed over the loudspeaker system, and the man was moving feverishly. He was so caught up in the music he danced with his eyes closed and didn't notice when his partner slipped away and walked up to Dwaine. She asked, "Didn't I see you on TV dancing with the ballerina?"

He was pleasantly surprised a girl so naturally stunning would recognize him. She was lightly made up, using only eyebrow pencil, mascara and lipstick. She wore an open neck jumper, short sleeve blouse and dance slippers.

He smiled and nodded his head, then replied, "The guy you're dancin' with looks like he's tryin' out for a scholarship. Is he your steady boyfriend?"

"No." she said with a twinkle in her eye. There was instant chemistry. He asked, "What's your name?"

"Ramona Carter," she answered with a sultry tone to her voice.

He asked her to dance, and she said, "All right." Another Bill Haley song was being played, but he wasn't listening to the words. His mind was focused on the beat and the way Ramona moved. When the record ended, they stayed on the dance floor and continued moving their feet to the throbbing rhythms. Before the night was over, he asked her out and she accepted.

For their first date, he took her to the Frank "N Bun drive in restaurant for hot dogs and frosty mugs of birch beer. He was driving a 1941 Ford business coupe he had owned for several years. The transmission had gone out on it while he was moving to Florida, and he found himself in Jacksonville, Georgia with only sixty five dollars to his name. The town consisted of a garage with two gas pumps in front and a combination general store and restaurant. Both businesses were owned by the same man, Jethro Beam. When Dwaine first met the wide spot in the road's leading entrepreneur, he was wearing grease stained coveralls with a strong odor of oil. The young traveler noticed Beam carried a stethoscope in his back pocket. He pointed to the medical instrument and asked, "What's that for?"

"Oh, I'm also the doctor 'round these parts."

Dwaine thought, "Hope I get outta this place 'fore I get sick."

Jethro took pity on Dwaine and agreed to partially rebuild the Ford's transmission for fifty dollars. He patiently explained, "I can get you back on the road, but you'll only have second and third gear." Dwaine made do and continued using the old Ford, even though he couldn't drive in reverse.

He didn't dare mention any of this to Ramona until it was time to leave the restaurant. After a car hop removed a metal tray from the driver's window, Dwaine got out, walked to the front of the Ford and began pushing it from the parking space. Ramona put her head out the passenger window and asked, "What are you doing?"

"Don't have reverse and hafta push it into position to get outta the parking lot."

He was surprised to hear her ask, "Can I help?" and thought, "She must really like me." Dwaine replied, "It'd be great if you'd get behind the wheel and steer." They made a good team with him pushing and her steering, and continued using the Ford with the faulty transmission on all their dates.

Dwaine thought she was the same age as him or maybe a little older. She used a cigarette holder to smoke her Chesterfields and most of her girl friends were out of high school. Some were older than him. She also mentioned winning beauty contests and showed him copies of Eye, Brief and Modern Male containing pin up photos of her. He wasn't aware she was fifteen years old when chosen Miss Bikini USA and Miss Army, Navy and Air Force and was underage when her photos appeared in the widely circulated men's magazines.

It wasn't until they had gone out a few times when she finally told him how young she was. He was put off by this and tried to stop seeing her, but she was so beautiful he couldn't get her out of his mind. She wasn't going to allow him to end their relationship after becoming romantically connected to him. She decided he was the man she wanted and wasn't about to take no for an answer. When she didn't hear from him for two days, she paid him a surprise visit.

Dwaine answered the door and saw Ramona staring at him with admiring goo goo eyes. She said, "Don't even try to hide from me. You can run, but you can't hide."

He remembered his mom had married when she was fifteen and thought, "What's the big deal 'bout a twenty year old guy goin' with a sixteen year old girl?" They started seeing each other again, and he learned she had a good heart, was very trustworthy and a faithful person.

One evening, they sat in a booth of a luncheonette and each of them talked about how they had been brought up. Ramona said, "My mom and dad are divorced. She lives in Washington, D.C. and he lives in Miami. I came down here to visit him and ended up staying for good."

Dwaine replied, "My birth father had a slight problem with alcohol. He only drank when he was with somebody or by himself. Ma divorced him when I was a year old. I have an older brother named Harmon, and we grew up poor but didn't know it. We always had clean clothes. They weren't new clothes, but Ma made sure they were clean."

She tapped her cigarette holder against an ashtray, flicked off an ash and listened closely as he continued to describe his upbringing. "We had plenty to eat. Six days a week, we ate pinto beans, mashed potatoes, greens Ma picked out in the woods and corn bread. Sundays, we had meatloaf, unless a neighbor killed a hog. Harmon and I walked a mile to school and got hot lunches every day, even though the school had no cafeteria. There was a restaurant nearby. Ma would give us a quarter each, and they'd sell us plates of fried squares made outta cornmeal mush for twenty five cents." He paused and asked, "Are ya really interested in this?"

She replied, "I am. Please go on."

"I was eleven years old and got my first pair of hard toe shoes when Ma married her best friend's brother, who she had dated a few times. He was a lifetime Marine mess sergeant, and we moved to Camp Lejeune, North Carolina. Thank God for him. It started a whole new life for me, and my stepfather became my first father figure. After he got transferred to the Marine air base in Opa-Locka, I came down here to live with Ma and him."

Dwaine added, "When they moved, I pitched in to help. I even took the house numbers off the ol' place so they wouldn't hafta change their address. Didn't work out the way I thought it would. My stepdad was surprised when I showed him the numbers. He said, 'They gave us different numbers here in Florida. Your idea wasn't so good, but I can't deny your heart was in the right place.' The way he said it, I didn't know if I'd done somethin' wrong or not."

"Intentions are very important," replied Ramona, "but you also have to think about the consequences. I think you should have asked him if he needed the old numbers before you took them off the house."

He sat awestruck for a moment before responding. "You're amazin'! I've been wonderin' for years what I did wrong, but ya figured it out right away. You're smart!"

Simpson had two and a half years of college but even though she had dropped out of high school, Ramona possessed common sense, which he lacked, and was much wiser in the ways of the world than Dwaine. The first time they made love, he insisted on turning the lights off, and she asked, "Don't you think I'm attractive?"

He replied, "You're beautiful, but I look like death eatin' a cheese cracker. If I was naked in a room, only thing I could turn on would be the light switch. If I tried to enter a Mr. America contest, I'd get my citizenship taken away."

After going steady for four months, he said to her, "Honey, you're above normal in intelligence and I'm way below normal. What am I gonna do if you wanna have intelligent conversation?"

"I wouldn't worry about that. You've got other wonderful qualities."

"But whatta we do when I get old and can't do the horizontal tango no more?"

Within less than a year, she became pregnant. When she told him the news, he was genuinely surprised. He asked, "How can that happen? Why do ya think we been doin' it standin' up? 'Cuz ya can't get pregnant that way."

She gave him a kiss and whispered, "I hate to tell you this, honey, but women can and I did."

Dwaine wanted to do the right thing and proposed marriage. After meeting his prospective son in law, Ramona's dad said to her, "I'll getcha on the first plane to Cuba. You can get an abortion there. You'll stay in a nice hotel, and it'll be a good trip." Ramona and her mother, Lola Carter, nixed the idea. She told her father, "I love him, Daddy, and I want to have our baby." Russell Carter had a man to man talk with Dwaine and asked his future son in law, "How do you plan to support my daughter and grandchild?"

Simpson confidently replied, "I'll burn that bridge when I come to it." This drew a strange look from his fiancée's dad. Dwaine added, "Uh... that didn't come out the way I thought it would."

Russell Carter thought, "When they handed out brains, he must've thought they said 'trains,' and wound up late for both. He's the first man I've met who goes through life with one hand tied behind his pea brain."

Ramona's dad tried to persuade her to reconsider marrying Dwaine Simpson, but she wouldn't budge. She said, "Oh, Daddy, Dwaine just needs someone to show they have faith in him and make him feel confident."

"You're wrong. He doesn't have an inferiority complex. He's just plain inferior."

Russell was not at all impressed with his daughter's choice in a husband, but realized there wasn't much he could do about it. Dwaine and Ramona were married at a small ceremony, and he willingly shouldered the responsibilities of a family man, but it left him on a treadmill, constantly chasing money.

WHAT THE WELL DRESSED BOXER WEARS

It was a hot Florida day with few clouds in the sky. While laboring in the heat, painting a house for a buck an hour, Dwaine remembered the money Dick Lee handed him. He thought, "I got three dollars for boxing nine minutes. Wonder how much an hour that is? Gotta be a lot more than I'm makin' here." He took a break for some water and while drinking from a garden hose, decided, "I'm gonna go down to that Moose Lodge the guy talked about."

When he got home from work, he went to a coffee can where he stashed money from his part time jobs. He took out twenty dollars in ones, fives and coins and went to a sporting goods store to purchase boxing trunks, a pair of leather soled boxing shoes and a metal protective cup. When he asked about the fighting trunks, the clerk said, "We carry only the best... Everlast."

"How much are they?"

"Silk trunks are six dollars and fifty cents a pair, and ones made from celanese are five bucks."

"Lemme have the ones from the foreign country."

The salesman slowly shook his head and replied, "Celanese isn't from a foreign country. It's made in a factory in Maryland."

"What's the difference between them and silk trunks?"

"Silk ones look better under the lights."

"I'm just gettin' started, and I don't think it's worth a buck and a half just to look better."

"How many fights you have?"

"One."

"Didja win or lose?"

"Lost a decision."

"Stick with the celanese. Any money you spend on looking better isn't gonna help you fight."

With the decision about his boxing trunks out of the way, he asked about boxing shoes. The store carried only one brand, and he found a pair in size nine that fit him. When he tried them on, he was pleased to find the smooth leather soles ideal for his evasive fighting style. He could easily glide back and forth and side to side.

He also selected a Wilson jockstrap cup. Dwaine accidentally dropped the protective device, and it made a metallic clunk. He asked the man waiting on him, "Does it make that sound if I get hit in the nuts?'

"Depends on how much you have to protect. The less in it, the louder the clunk." Dwaine nodded as if he understood, but had a blank look on his face. The sales clerk thought, "What a fool! Hope I don't have to draw him picture."

Simpson asked about a robe. The salesman said, "We carry Everlast, and there are several styles. A terry cloth lined silk robe is forty two dollars, a terry lined celanese is thirty five bucks and… "

"Never mind that," interrupted Dwaine. "What's the cheapest?"

"We have terry cloth robes for fifteen dollars."

"Think I'll get by without one."

When Simpson paid for his purchases, he was warned, "You can't return any of these things for a refund. You understand that, don't you?"

Dwaine nodded and said, "Yeah." As he left the store, the salesman said to a co worker, "I wonder how long it'll take that guy to get a busted nose, cuts over his eyes and a cauliflower ear."

"Not long. He's too good looking to be a fighter, and he won't be in it long enough to need a robe."

FIGHT NIGHTS AT THE MOOSE LODGE

Dwaine had the mistaken idea he could show up at the Moose Lodge and be matched in a fight whenever he wanted, so he didn't bother to contact Dick Lee beforehand. Lee recognized him when he walked in and said, "Hey there, college boy! Lookin' for more excitement?" He chuckled as he added, "Ya got a nice smile, let's get rid of it."

Simpson answered, "I'm ready. Got anybody for me?"

"Sure, college boy, I got someone perfect for you." The wavy haired promoter thought, "Let's see if Mr. Blue Eyes takes home a black eye."

Dwaine spotted Jack McKiernan and walked up to say hello. They shook hands and Jack asked, "Back for more?"

"Yeah, and this time I have the right equipment." He opened his canvas bag to show McKiernan his recent purchases. Jack asked, "Need somebody to work your corner?"

"Yeah, but I don't have any money."

"That's okay. Dick's payin' me to hang around here. It'll give me somethin' to do, otherwise I'd just be sittin' around once the fights start."

When McKiernan asked Dick Lee if it was all right to work in Dwaine's corner, the promoter said, "That's up to you."

Jack had one question. "Who's Dwaine gonna fight?"

"Wait and see. It's a surprise." Amateur fighters were usually matched according to weight and experience, but Dick Lee had his own way of doing things. He didn't bother to conduct weigh-ins for amateur bouts, so Dwaine didn't see his opponent until it was time to enter the ring. Jack McKiernan took one look at who Simpson had been matched with and said, "Oh brother! You're gonna be in against the Florida amateur lightweight champion."

Dwaine asked, "What do I do?"

"Either get outta the ring or run."

"I had a feelin' you'd say that again."

A sellout crowd packed the Moose Lodge and when the opening bell rang, the clean cut, blue eyed blonde used the same "keep movin' and avoid all contact style" as he had in Opa-Locka. This drew lots of noise from the crowd. They seemed evenly split. Half the paying customers rooted for Dwaine, and the other half had an instant dislike for him. A fat guy at ringside holding a can of beer shouted, "KNOCK THE YELLAH DOG OUT! PUT 'IM ON HIS ASS!"

Simpson learned a great deal from his first fight and figured out he could keep his opponent's fists away from his head by jabbing effectively with his left hand. The bout lasted the entire three rounds, and Dwaine landed enough ramrod jabs to be awarded the decision. Dick Lee should have had dollar signs for eyes because of his new gate attraction, but he wasn't pleased. As far as he was concerned, his new star was a smart ass college boy not macho enough to be a real fighter. Still, he couldn't deny the eyes of the crowd were on the lanky boxer with the close cropped blonde hair, and they either loved or hated him. Lee paid him his three dollar honorarium and scheduled the newcomer for another bout the following week.

For Simpson's second fight at the Moose Lodge, he was matched with the Florida Golden Gloves welterweight champion. Once again, Dick Lee withheld the information from Dwaine until the very last moment. All the while, he was thinking, "It's time for college boy to go down. Hope he don't start cryin' while gettin' his beatin', 'cuz I hate to see a grown man cry." The blue eyed, blonde pugilist surprised everyone. He made dodging punches look easy, danced his way out of trouble and used his left jab to fill his opponent's face with leather. He went the distance, won a decision and again picked up three dollars. His method of boxing stirred up the predominantly male beer drinking crowd, several of whom came into the arena carrying large paper bags stuffed with cans of their favorite brew. Some fans thought he was the funniest fighter they'd ever seen. Others disliked him intensely and formed an impromptu cheering section. They chanted "WHIP HIS ASS! DAMN STRAIGHT! WHIP HIS ASS! DAMN STRAIGHT!" throughout the entire fight. Simpson further incited those who despised him by blowing kisses to them at the conclusion of each round. When the referee raised Dwaine's hand in victory, a hater threw a full box of popcorn at him. He missed, but the contents were scattered all over the canvas. The lanky blonde looked at the referee and said, "Least it wasn't a full can of beer."

Dwaine was good for business, but the promoter could never get past his deep loathing of everything the quick, slick, crafty West Virginia native represented. They were from two different worlds. Simpson had been to college, while Lee barely made it out of high school. Lee had served in the U.S. Navy during World War II, while Simpson had always been a civilian. Dick repeatedly hurled insults at Dwaine, but the fighter wouldn't back down and came back with humorous retorts.

When the promoter and Jack McKiernan watched Simpson enter the Moose Lodge for his third appearance there, Dick Lee spoke to McKiernan in a loud enough voice for the lanky blonde fighter to hear. "Hey, Jack, maybe you better write inside Dwaine's boxing shoes 'TGIF'... 'Toes go in first.'"

Simpson responded with, "Dick, I can tell ya got a nice lookin' nose 'cuz it's handpicked. If I punch ya there, I might break your finger."

Lee retorted, "Know what a college boy and a bottle of beer have in common? They're both empty from the neck up."

Simpson wasn't about to let the promoter have the last word. Before heading to the dressing room, he said, "Just remember, Dick, a match can't box, but a tin can."

Lee asked McKiernan, "What the hell's he mean by that?"

"Dunno. Guess you'd have to go to college to get the joke."

Dwaine used his fancy stepping, bounce, shuffle and jab method to win his third fight in a row. The victory reassured him he was using the right strategy. He relaxed in the dressing room and thought, "I've got it all figured out. If a guy takes a step toward me, I take three or four steps to get away from him. I'm a 'stick and move guy,' just like Gentleman Jim Corbett."

Dick Lee walked in and immediately became enraged by the look of contentment on a man he regarded as cowardly. He walked up to Simpson, positioned his mouth within inches of the boxer's nose and said, "You're a chicken shit fighter who needs to get their mind right!"

Dwaine had a sour expression on his face as he responded, "Wooh! Dick, ya oughta try some breath mints."

"Nevah mind if I stank! I've found just the man to beat ya ass, and I've matched ya with him."

"Who is he?"

"Don't worry 'bout it. You'll find out soon enough. Just be here next week. If ya don't show up, I'll tell ever'body you're yellah." Lee tossed three singles at Simpson's feet and said with a contemptuous tone, "Here's your money, college boy." After the promoter walked out, Dwaine bent over and picked the bills up. Every dollar counted.

Simpson showed up at the lodge the following week, immediately sought out the promoter and said, "All right, Dick, I'm here and I'm ready. Tell me who I'm gonna fight."

Lee pointed in the direction of a white man without a neck. He was the same height as Simpson, but much stockier and with bulging muscles. Dwaine asked, "How much that guy weigh?"

"One fifty two."

It was obvious Dick Lee was not telling the truth. The other fighter weighed one sixty five, while Simpson weighed one forty one. A weight difference of twenty four pounds was not a fair match.

Simpson asked, "Who the hell's he?"

"That, my chicken shit friend, is the Floreeda Golden Gloves middleweight champeen. He came down from Canada. His name is Larry Portress."

Simpson thought, "How can a Canadian win the Florida Golden Gloves?" Then he remembered Jack McKiernan mentioning Dick Lee controlled amateur boxing in the Sunshine State.

Dwaine said, "I'm a lightweight and he's a middleweight. Jeez, he's way too big for me!"

"Well, if you're SCARED..."

"Hell, you'd be scared too if you were fightin' somebody bigger'n you."

"Well then, I'll just have to tell everybody you're a chicken shit." Lee had pushed Dwaine's button. He knew Simpson longed to be accepted by the other boxers and was willing to go an extra mile in order to prove himself. Dick was a master at provoking fighters by challenging their manhood and knew just how far to push them before they might retaliate. He purposely tried to make boxers feel uncomfortable whenever he was around them because it helped him maintain the upper hand.

Dwaine gave in to Lee's goading. "Aw, hell! I'll do it. They can kill me, but they can't eat me."

From the opening bell of the bout between the mismatched opponents, Dwaine was bobbing and weaving, bouncing, shuffling, reeling and rocking. He used every evasive move he could think of, cleverly pulling his head back to avoid punches, and kept it up for the entire fight. Whenever the much bigger man from north of the border threw a power shot, Simpson managed to get out of the way at the last instant and felt a slight breeze as the fist went past. It was more suspenseful to watch than a mystery movie. With each near miss, he heard some of the spectators give out a loud "OOOOH!" while others were yelling, "BOOOO!" The Simpson haters yearned to see the boxer who shied away from contact flattened on the canvas, but the judges disappointed them by scoring the fight as a win for Simpson. Dick Lee muttered "Chickenshit!" as he handed Dwaine his three dollars. Dwaine thought, "He didn't throw the money on the floor this time. Maybe he's startin' to like me a little."

FINE DINING AND FAMILY HISTORY

Dwaine arrived home from work to find Ramona preparing one of his favorite meals. She was listening to WQAM's top 40 as she dipped pieces of bacon in milk, dredged them in flour, sprinkled salt and pepper, placed them in a cold skillet and then placed the skillet on a hot stove. She turned the pieces of bacon once, removed them when they were brown and managed to do the cooking while moving in rhythm to Perez Prado's Cherry Pink and Apple Blossom White. All the while, she was puffing on her cigarette holder and enjoying a Chesterfield.

After giving her a kiss on the cheek, he sat down at the kitchen table. Ramona had placed a tablecloth, salt and pepper shakers, a toothpick dispenser and napkins on it. He took a toothpick from the dispenser and put it in his mouth without taking his eyes off his wife. She said to him, "Do you like what you see?"

"Oh yeah... ya can observe a lot by watchin'."

"That's one of the most intelligent things you've ever said, honey."

"Whatever brains I got, I inherited from an aunt on Ma's side. Did I ever tell ya about Aunt Aggie?"

"I don't think so."

"She did the crossword puzzle in the local paper each and every night. She wasn't very bright, but always finished it in an hour."

"That's pretty fast for someone who's not very bright."

"Well, she had a system. She didn't worry 'bout any of the words makin' sense as long as every block had a letter in it. Sometimes she'd put two letters in a square."

"Did she share any of her knowledge with you?"

The toothpick dangled from his lips as he spoke. "Yeah, she was really good 'bout readin' comic books to me whenever she had time. She said it was the best way for a person to get educated."

"I agree with her," said Ramona. "Everybody knows what they put in comic books is true. There's a comic book code they have to obey, or they get in trouble with the government."

"Aunt Aggie was the one who taught me there are all different kinds of animals," added Dwaine. "Before that, I thought dogs and cats were the same, just like hats and caps are both things ya put on your head. She also straightened me out about the sun and the moon. For the longest, I thought the sun turned into the moon at night 'cuz I didn't see 'em at the same time. What I learned from her helped make third grade the most enjoyable four years of my life."

"Are you puttin' me on, husband?' Ramona asked in a laughing way. "You didn't spend four years in third grade, didja?"

"Not really, but it sure felt like it. I was always gettin' in trouble and spendin' time after school writin' 'I will not misbehave' on the blackboard. I'd have to do it day after day 'cuz I didn't spell the words right all the time. Aunt Aggie saved me sometimes by tellin' the teacher, 'He has to help me at my business.'"

"What business was that?"

"Deliverin' her moonshine."

"You never told me about this. Why was she in moonshining?"

"She took over after Uncle Vernon died. He was known all over the county for his powerful 'shine. One time, Aunt Aggie's canary got a sip of it. He threw open the birdcage door and chased the cat around the room."

"How did your uncle die?"

"He fell into a whiskey vat. Some men tried to pull 'im out, but he fought 'em off and drowned. Aunt Aggie had 'im cremated and he burned for three days."

"All you mention about West Virginia is coal mining and moonshine. Is that all they have up there?"

"It was coal mine, moonshine or move on down the line."

"So that's why you came to Florida."

"Yeah, by way of North Carolina, but that's another story. I'm too hungry to keep talkin'. Let's eat."

Dwaine had already wolfed down two Bisquick biscuits before Ramona placed a large plate of food with a crispy brown crunchy coating in front of him. She said, "You won't leave much room for the bacon."

"I'll always have room for it. Ya really caught on about how to make it, didn't ya?"

"It takes a little more time than your other favorites, but it's worth it."

"Does it take longer'n baked beans with hot dogs and onions?"

"Yep, and it takes longer than ketchup spaghetti, fried okra or that sorghum molasses and hot cakes you like for breakfast. The fastest thing to prepare you like is canned corn." She then said, "I'm gonna check on Sheree before I sit down and eat."

After returning to the table, she said, "Darling, can you leave a little more grocery money tomorrow. Publix has a sale on pork loin for thirty nine cents a pound."

"When are those crazy food prices gonna come down? A nickel ain't worth a dime no more. Coupla years ago, pork and chicken were nineteen cents a pound and I thought that was high. Trouble is there's too much tainted money."

"What do you mean by that?"

"Money that tain't yours and tain't mine."

"Well, we can't do anything about the prices. We've gotta eat."

"You're right, honey. The future ain't what it used to be. You're so smart. You can add, subtract, multiply and divide... all those things I could never do. I still can't understand how two PLUS two could be four and two TIMES two can also be four. You're a walkin' addin' machine. I don't know why you put up with me."

She replied with an encouraging smile, "You've been doin' better since we've been married. You've gone from way below normal to less than normal. Someday you may be normal or even average, but I think it's gonna be tough for you to get up to mediocre." He nodded in agreement because he knew she was right about everything.

HE HATES ME, BUT ITS NOTHIN PERSONAL

Dwaine won nine straight fights and in the process, acquired a reputation as "the punchless wonder with feather fists and dancing feet." He was accepted by the other boxers, and Jack McKiernan became his best buddy. The tall, slim built McKiernan worked as a fireman and spent some of his spare time at the gym used by Dwaine and the other boxers. Jack wasn't a fighter. He was an expert at cowboy fast draw and spear fishing, but enjoyed being part of boxing. His father had been a legendary fight manager and promoter who did business under the name "Jack 'Doc' Kearns."

Doc Kearns was a beguiling man with a reputation as a master of the con. He was a free spending, swashbuckling, carefree leprechaun type with twinkling blue eyes and an ever present smile. No other manager had the capability of doing as much for their fighters. He was not only an expert at training prize fighters and judging boxing styles, he was also an extremely shrewd businessman who could hoodwink promoters into his way of thinking, particularly when it came to the actual amount of money taken in at the gate and how it would be split up. He was an amiable rogue.

Kearns' real name was John Leo McKiernan, and he was born in Waterloo, Michigan in 1882. He received international fame when he guided Jack Dempsey from rags to riches and talked Tex Rickard into promoting the first million dollar gate with Dempsey matched against French war hero Georges Carpentier.

Early in their friendship, Jack McKiernan brought Dwaine to his house to meet his father. Jack's dad wasn't what Simpson expected. He thought he'd be a thick muscled bruiser with a full head of hair. The father turned out to be a slender man with big ears, a knobby, bald dome and a slouch that gave his chest a concave appearance. Jack pointed to a framed photo on a table. It showed his dad standing next to Dempsey, the famous heavyweight champion. He said, "When Pop was young, he had a full head of hair, but that's what happens when ya get old."

Doc Kearns said to Dwaine, "Speaking of hair, I'm gonna tell you a story about my days up in Alaska. I was weighing gold dust for a Chinese laundryman in the Yukon, where I met Jack London, Robert W. Service, Rex Beach, Tex Rickard and Herbert Hoover. In comes a friend, Wilson Mizner. I complained of making only a few bucks a day weighing gold dust. Mizner took me aside and poured some molasses on my hair. 'Now, kid,' he said, 'every time you handle that gold, wipe your hands through your hair, get it?' I got it, and I earned a lot of gold over the years using my head."

"Wow, that's really inspirin', Mr. Kearns," responded Simpson. "I'm gonna try usin' my head more. I'm also gonna do more to keep what few brains I've got from bein' scrambled by hard punches."

"The best way to do that," said the legendary manager and promoter, "is to stay out of range and never stand still for a second."

"That's just what Dwaine's been doin'," said Jack McKiernan.

"Well, keep up the good work," said Doc.

"Thanks," replied Dwaine. He thought, "Doc Kearns is such a friendly guy. Why can't Dick Lee be friendly? Maybe it's 'cuz of somethin' I did wrong."

Shortly after visiting the legendary manager and promoter, Dwaine was in a luncheonette with his friend, drinking ice tea. Simpson asked the firefighter, "What's Dick Lee got against me?"

Jack poured sugar into his drink as he said, "Not any more than anybody else. He treats all fighters the same; like dogs. He has a good side, though. He's never run off with ALL the money and left the fighters with nothin'."

"That'd be crazy. Where I come from, we'd give 'im the 'West Virginia High Low.'"

"What's that?"

"One of us would crouch down on all fours behind 'im and another of us would push 'im over the guy in a crouch. Then we'd all start kickin' hell out of 'im."

"Is that what they call 'Mountain Justice?'"

"Damn straight."

"Dad says there's many people in the fight game bent on plottin', plannin' and schemin' fighters outta things. Gettin' caught doesn't scare 'em. At least Dick always pays up. It may not be much, but it's somethin'."

"I still think he treats me worse'n anyone else," said Dwaine. "He acts like he hates me."

"Well, ya got several things against ya. Ya went to college, you're a civilian and he don't like the way ya fight. Lemme tell you somethin' about Lee."

"I'm listenin'," said Dwaine while chewing on a toothpick.

"He was a pro for five or six years and says he was a main event welter-weight, but I've never bothered to look up his record. I remember him tellin' my dad he fought all the way out in California and they called 'im 'The Florida Tornado Who Puts 'Em All on the Floor.'"

"I thought they had hurricanes in Florida, not tornadoes," said Dwaine.

"Well, they do, so you just learned something new. Anyhow, Dick said he won twenty four in a row before he lost a fight at the Olympic Auditorium in L. A." McKiernan took a sip of his tea before continuing. "The way he told it, he got his jaw broke and had to ride back to Florida with a big bandage on his head and his teeth wired together. He couldn't fight for four months and ended up in the orchards, pickin' fruit so he and his family would have money to eat."

"What does all that mean," asked Dwaine as he tossed his toothpick on the floor. "I never had much use for history 'cuz I never thought I'd see it again."

"Well, what it all boils down to is Dick thinks he's pretty tough. He thinks any fighter should be willin' to go through what he did. In his mind, he's not askin' 'em to do anything he wouldn't do. He just doesn't think you're up to that."

"He was in the Navy, right?" asked Simpson.

"Yeah, he was."

"I wouldn't want him to be captain of any ship I was on."

"Oh, he was far from a captain," said McKiernan. "Only time he came near one was when he was swabbin' out their quarters. He claims he was captain of the U.S. Navy boxing team at Mayport Naval Station near Jacksonville, but I doubt it. I don't think he was any more'n a seaman. He often mentioned how much he hated officers, especially ones who went to college. That's why he hates college boys so much. Aren't you lucky to have so many strikes against ya? You've set an all time record."

"Well, it's a relief knowin' there's nothin' personal between him and me. He just hates my guts on general principles."

Not long after Dwaine's conversation with Jack McKiernan, Dick Lee matched the crew cut blonde with a one hundred thirty five pound black fighter who had unusually long arms and skinny legs. His name was "Spider" Dubois, and had recently arrived in South Florida from Paris, France.

Just before the fight, a fan hollered, "HEY BLACK BOY, GIVE THAT COWARD A WHITE EYE!" When the opening bell rang, the Frenchman's arms seemed ten feet long to the blonde fighter. He tried to stay beyond his opponent's reach, but Simpson took a punch to the head and went to the canvas for the first time in his amateur career. Dwaine thought, "I just got hit by a guy with a tennis racket."

He got up before he was counted out, but was knocked off his feet twice more. In desperation, he tried running at the French boxer while throwing a flurry of punches. It didn't change anything because he had foolishly abandoned the style of fighting that had worked so well for him. The bout went the distance and Spider was awarded the decision. Simpson thought, "Once is bad enough, but three times on the floor in three rounds is too much."

Watching the college boy being repeatedly knocked to the canvas put Dick Lee into such a joyous mood he crowed, "AT LAST!" when the fight was over. Other Simpson haters pelted the blonde fighter with empty paper cups and other litter. Dick smiled as he handed him the usual three dollars for his night's work. Dwaine thought, "I've had enough." It had given him satisfaction to see Lee cringe whenever he won, but enduring physical punishment and abuse from fight fans for so little money was too much to bear. Dwaine went back to occupying his spare moments with basketball and part time jobs.

DWAINE BECOMES A WHITE COLLAR WORKER

Simpson's retirement from amateur boxing coincided with his getting a better job. He was hired by a finance company at one hundred fifty dollars a week; three times what he made at Parks and Recreation. He was also provided with a brand new air conditioned 1955 Buick, and performed his duties wearing a white shirt and tie. He was the first white collar worker in his family.

Simpson soon learned white shirts sometimes have dirty rings around the collar. The finance company was not the most wholesome place. His employer was making $600 loans to customers of used car lots who really couldn't afford to own an automobile. The payments were $35 to $40 a month, but the cars were pieces of junk that sometimes broke down after a month or two.

Dwaine was hired to be the "adjuster." He was assigned accounts behind in payments by two months or more. Most had lost their jobs and the only option for the company holding the notes was to repossess their cars. His company car came with a tow bar so he could either drive or pull the cars back to the finance company.

On the day he was hired, Dwaine walked in the door of his home to find his wife at the stove preparing baked beans, hot dogs and onions for dinner. He approached her from behind, put his arms around her waist and kissed her on the cheek. He said, "Mmm, mmm, my favorite meal and it smells good! Everything has been perfect today. Guess what happened."

"What?"

"I got a new job that pays a lot more. They gave me a company car with air conditioning and even a radio. Now you can use the Ford whenever you want. Only trouble is I hafta work nights."

"Why's that?"

"I hafta take cars from people who can't pay for 'em, and gotta do it when it's dark out so nobody'll see me."

"You think the darkness makes you invisible?"

A look of amazement came to Dwaine's face. He snapped his fingers and said, "Honey, how come you're so smart? Ya always come up with the answers. I knew they wouldn't be able to see me at night, but I didn't know why. Now you've explained everything. The dark makes me invisible."

"What if I'm wrong?" asked Ramona.

"You're never wrong. After we eat, I'm gonna write my brother Harmon and tell 'im I got a white collar job. I'm also gonna tell 'im I married a genius."

"Well, give him my best."

When they were finished with dinner, Dwaine sat at the kitchen table to write a one page letter to his brother. A half hour went by and he still hadn't finished. Ramona asked, "Why are you writing so slow?"

"'Cuz Harmon's not a fast reader."

LIFE AS A REPO MAN

Dwaine began his first night at his new job searching for a 1947 Chevrolet Fleet Master coupe. The address he had been given turned out to be an apartment building. He drove around the neighborhood trying to spot the eight year old car and was pleased to find the Chevrolet parked on the street, two blocks away from where the customer lived. No one bothered him while he hooked up the Chevy to the company Buick. After he was finished, he went to the customer's apartment and knocked on the door. No one opened it, but a male voice responded with, "Whaddya want?"

Dwaine replied in a loud voice, "Finance company. I'm here to pick up your car."

The door suddenly opened and a white male appeared. He was wearing a t-shirt and boxer shorts, hadn't shaved for a couple of days and reeked of liquor. He peered at Dwaine through bloodshot eyes and said, "Go ahead and take the piece a shit. It runs like crap."

Simpson replied, "Fine. Do ya have the keys?"

"I could say no, but what the hell." The customer went to another room of the apartment, came back with the car keys and tossed them to Dwaine.

Simpson caught them in midair and said, "Well, hope things get better for ya."

"Don't worry 'bout me. I got enough dough for the rest of my life, 'long as I die before mornin'."

A week later, Dwaine drove to an address at the end of a dark, dusty graveled road. Lights were on in the customer's house, but the 1948 Ford Super Deluxe coupe on his repo list was nowhere in sight. He carefully walked through high weeds in the front yard, hoping he wouldn't encounter any snakes, and saw a man sitting on the front porch with a shotgun in his lap. Dwaine thought, "He's lookin' right at me. He must have amazin' eyes to be able to see somebody invisible."

The man with the shotgun growled, "What ya'll want, boy?"

"Mason Blanchard live here?"

"Who wants to know?"

During Dwaine's training, his boss, Herman Slaker, had suggested lying to family members and friends of delinquent customers in order to obtain needed information. Simpson thought, "When you're talkin' to a man with a shotgun, honesty is the best policy." He said to the man on the porch, "I'm with the finance company. We're lookin' for his '48 Ford."

"Well why didn't ya say so? That piece of shit made my sister miserable. He hid the car in back uh the house."

"Show me where it is, and I'll tow it outta there."

"No sir, we don't want ya goin' ta no trouble. I'll wake her up, get the keys and drive it up to the front road for ya."

"Well, thanks a lot."

"You're welcome, anythin' to make trouble for that bastard."

Not all of Dwaine's repos were as easy as the '47 Chevy and the '48 Ford. He was told to bring in a dark blue 1950 Ford four door, and spent three days driving around the customer's Miami neighborhood without any luck. The man's name was still on the mailbox, but never seemed to be at his apartment. Dwaine drove back to the finance company and told Herman Slaker, "Can't find that blue Ford."

Slaker parked his cigar in an ashtray, pounded on his desk and blurted, "Dammit, bastard's hidin' it somewhere!" He handed Dwaine a new repossession order and said, "Here's a '52 Buick to pull. Customer lives in the same neighborhood as the guy with the Ford."

Dwaine drove back to the neighborhood he had become so familiar with over the past few days. Three blocks away, he passed a pizza place and noticed a dark blue 1950 four door Ford in the parking lot. He parked the Buick around the corner from the restaurant, walked back to the parking lot and went up to the Ford. It was the car he was looking for. Keys were in the ignition and the engine was running. Dwaine hopped in, took off and headed straight to the finance company. When he arrived, he parked the Ford in the company lot and took the keys into his boss.

Slaker was overjoyed. Dwaine asked, "Can I get a ride back to where I parked?"

"Sure." The boss walked to the garage area next to the office and called out to a mechanic dressed in coveralls, "Hey Floyd, inspect the Ford Dwaine just brought in and then give 'im a lift."

The mechanic tried to start the repossessed vehicle, but it wouldn't turn over because the battery was dead. Dwaine said, "When I found it, the engine was runnin', so I got in and came straight here."

Floyd replied, "The guy prolly got the car goin' by gettin' a push and poppin' the clutch. Once he had it runnin', he couldn't shut it off." He looked at Dwaine for a moment before saying, "You're lucky he didn't report the car stolen."

"Man, you're right. I took it in broad daylight when I wasn't invisible."

The man in the coveralls looked at Dwaine oddly, then chuckled and shook his head. He asked the repo man, "Were you born here in Florida?"

"Naw, I was born in West by God Virginia."

"Well, that explains everything."

GRUDGE MATCH

Late one afternoon while searching for cars on his repo list, Dwaine passed by the Wynnwood Park recreation building at 3400 NW First Avenue. Out of curiosity, he parked his company car and entered the structure. He discovered the building housed a boxing gym and was surprised to find Dick Lee in charge. Dick was talking in a loud voice to a lad in his teens. "Joe Louis was a cotton picker, Jack Dempsey was a hobo. Gene Tunney was a shippin' clerk. They all made it big. So can you if ya do what I tell ya."

The wide eyed youngster paid close attention as Lee continued. "Fighters come here to wage war and if ya don't earn your scars, I kick ya outta here. If you're good 'nuff to make it through the sparring ya get here, you'll have no problem gettin' through a real fight. I don't want ya wearin' headgear. Only keeps your skin tender and makes it easier to get cut up when you're fightin' for real. Don't use no Vaseline or other greases. Ya gotta make your skin tough and be tough all the way through. Life is a tough game for tough people. When ya prove you're tough enough, I'll let ya get in the ring with other tough fighters." Out of the corner of his eye, Lee caught a glimpse of Simpson, and instantly turned away from the teenage boxer. Dwaine walked up to Lee and asked, "How's it goin'?"

All the promoter had to say was, "We missed ya at the Moose Lodge." It was the truth. Many of the paying customers at Lee's shows wanted to know when Dwaine was going to fight again. One had said, "I'll give ya ten times the price of admission if you find someone who'll give that candy ass another beatin'."

Dwaine told the promoter, "Been busy."

Dick Lee said with a smirk on his face, "Ya look like ya been keepin' yaself in shape. How 'bout gettin' in the ring with me... or maybe you're chicken."

Lee was 5'7", had a big beer belly, very short arms and outweighed Dwaine by thirty pounds. He was wearing shorts, a t-shirt, boxing shoes and gloves, while Simpson was dressed in a short sleeve white shirt, blue tie, navy blue slacks with cuffs and brand new black wing tips that set him back nine bucks. The repo man replied, "I don't have any boxing gear."

"Don't worry, college boy. Nuthin' serious, we jes gonna spar a little." He grinned as he asked, "You scared of me?"

Dwaine thought, "This is my own damn fault. Shouldna come in this place and start talkin' to him. If I walk out now, I'll never live it down. Don't wanna give the bastard the satisfaction of seein' me afraid." He looked Lee in the eye, nodded his head and said, "Okay, where are the gloves?"

He removed his tie and someone offered to wrap his hands, but he pushed them away. He was handed a pair of boxing gloves. He slipped the gloves on, had them laced up and then stepped into the ring to face the promoter. Everyone in the gym stopped to watch the two men spar without headgear. They sensed the bad blood between them. When the sparring began, Dwaine was ducking, moving backwards and bouncing from side to side. He wasn't landing any punches, but neither was Lee. Dwaine hadn't worked out in months, but his shorter opponent couldn't lay a glove on him. The longer they sparred, the angrier Dick Lee became. He verbally challenged the taller man in street clothes. "LET'S SEE WHAT YA GOT! CROWD ME! FORCE ME TO THE ROPES! YA GOTTA LEARN TA FIGHT INSIDE! YA GOTTA STAY INSIDE!"

Simpson replied, "Ain't gonna hit ME with your alligator arms."

As Lee chased Dwaine all over the ring, he thought, "Bastard won't fight like a man." There was no point to what they were doing, but Dwaine wasn't about to give his taunter the satisfaction of seeing him give up. The sparring session in the hot, stuffy gym lasted three rounds and left Simpson's clothes drenched, but he had shown Dick Lee he wouldn't be broken. They shook hands afterward, but Dick sneered and said, "Not bad for a college boy… but you'll never be a pro 'less ya fight inside. All that runnin' around ain't gonna cut it. Ya can use a pan ta fry a fish, but whadya do when ya got a shark to deal with, huh?"

Dwaine replied, "I got nothin' to prove in the gym. I show it when it counts, and I'm not one of your boys who like runnin' their faces into other guys' gloves."

"Somebody's gonna rearrange your face, pretty boy."

"Not if I can help it."

As a parting shot, Lee said, "When you die, I'll dance on your grave."

Simpson replied, "Good, I'll make sure I'm buried at sea," He turned and walked away. Dwaine couldn't imagine having anything more to do with Dick Lee.

DWAINE RETURNS TO THE RING

After the Wynnwood Park sparring session, Dwaine put aside all thoughts of boxing and settled for getting exercise from basketball and part time work. Physical activity helped take his mind off his full time job. The finance company paid well, but he found the work more and more depressing as time went on. Simpson spent a Saturday morning picking up extra cash by mowing neighbors' lawns. Ramona had her eye on a blue halter dress with pockets in the front, and he planned on buying it for her. Some of his customers were so pleased he didn't miss any sections of their lawns they gave him tips in addition to his pay. He finished his work in time to cool off during the hottest part of the day. Just as he was about to open the front door of his home, Billy Hall and Boots Burkhalter pulled up in Boot's tan 1953 four door Chevy. Billy and Boots were professional boxers, and Simpson had beaten both in amateur fights.

The wins meant something. Billy Hall had been a state amateur welter-weight champion. He was originally from Georgia and was a slender, but very tough man. Tampa born Boots Burkhalter lived in Opa-Locka and was known as "Kid Boots." He was two years younger than Dwaine and won the Florida amateur lightweight title, but had not done nearly as well after turning pro. His professional record was one win, eleven losses and four draws, but only one of his losses was by knockout. Boots' lone victory came in his very first professional bout. Ironically, it was a four round decision on points over his good friend Billy Hall.

Boots said to Dwaine, "Ya haven't been fightin', have ya?"

"Naw, busy with jobs and keepin' up the house. You two still fightin'?"

Boots was the more talkative one. He grinned as he replied, "We got more pro fights'n we can handle. We was scheduled to fight four rounds 'gainst each other tonight in Fort Lauderdale and we're also supposed ta fight each other three days later in Miami Beach. So, we gotta problem. If we fight each other tonight for Dick Lee, Chris Dundee'll take us off the card at the Beach, and it pays more'n Lauderdale."

"Why would he do that?" asked Dwaine.

"In case ya didn't know, Chris and Dick hate each other's guts." He momentarily paused before asking Dwaine, "How 'bout you substitutin' for one of us tonight?"

Simpson wasn't sure it was a good idea to cross paths with Dick Lee again, but asked, "How much is in it for me?"

"Forty bucks."

Dwaine rubbed his right hand along his jaw as he thought, "Forty dollars would buy a month's worth of groceries. Why not?" He responded with enthusiasm, "Well, hell, I'll do it. Which one of ya am I gonna fight."

"We'll flip for it. Winner gets to fight and get paid," replied Boots. He asked his friend, "You gotta quarter?"

Billy pulled a handful of change from his khaki trousers, fished out a twenty five cent piece, put the rest of his money back in his pocket and said to his buddy, "Call it in the air."

As the coin tumbled in mid air, Boots said, "Tails."

The quarter landed face up on the ground. Boots picked it up, looked it over and said with a grin, "Just makin' sure it ain't a two headed coin." Simpson would fight in place of Boots Burkhalter.

Since Boots wasn't going to be paid, he took the night off and didn't bother to show up in Fort Lauderdale. Billy and Dwaine drove there in Simpson's Ford. Along the way, Dwaine said to Hall, "I thought Dick Lee was strictly with amateur boxing."

"Naw, Dick's like horseshit, he's all over the place."

"He might not let me fight. We didn't part on good terms last time I saw 'im."

"Don't worry. Lemme do the talkin'."

The sight of Simpson and Hall walking into the arena was a hopeful sign to Dick Lee. He thought, "Maybe I can talk the college boy into fightin'." He didn't like anything about Dwaine, but knew he could use him to make money.

Billy went up to the wavy haired promoter dressed in a gray Robert Hall suit that concealed any ashes dropping from his cigarettes or cigars. He said, "Dick, Boots, can't make it tonight. How 'bout if Dwaine fights me instead?"

Dick Lee looked at Simpson, put on a mock look of exasperation and replied, "Oh, it's you again." He gave a loud sigh before saying, "Well, I suppose so." Inside, he was happy at the thought of the candy ass college boy getting hammered. He thought, "Mr. Boolah Boolah's gonna learn his chicken shit act won't cut it in the pros."

The Hall versus Simpson four rounder went the distance and the judges awarded the fight to Billy. There were no knockdowns and no blood was spilled. The promoter thought, "What's a fight without blood? That's what people pay for." The fans thought differently. Even though neither fighter landed any blows, they were captivated by Dwaine's dancing feet and connected him to the cartoon character Bugs Bunny who always avoided getting clobbered at the last instant. Since he had not been training and had been mowing lawns all morning, it was all Simpson could do to avoid taking any solid punches and last the four rounds. He was exhausted at the end and needed ice water poured over him before he could get up from his stool and stand in the center of the ring to await the decision.

When it came time to pay the two fighters, Dick Lee came up with a new wrinkle. He said, "Boots was s'posed ta have a fight, but didn't get paid. How 'bout ya'll chippin' in some money for 'im?" Billy and Dwaine looked at each other, shrugged and nodded their heads. Dick took ten bucks from both purses, reducing each one to thirty dollars. Then he took out two dollars and fifty cents for tape and gauze, and that wasn't the end of the deductions. Lee took $13.34 from each fighter, saying, "You guys cain't fight as pros without a manager, so I acted as your manager tonight. Managers get a third." They couldn't argue with him because they had already fought and of course, he was running the show.

Instead of forty dollars apiece, Billy and Dwaine each ended up with $14.16. Dwaine said, "Ya know, Boots got twenny bucks. He got more'n we did, and didn't hafta fight, lucky bastard."

There was more to the story. Boots Burkhalter realized professional boxing was not for him and left town. He returned twenty years later and found work as a heavy equipment operator. Dwaine happened to run into him and they began talking about old times.

Simpson said, "Remember when we had the fight in Fort Lauderdale and Dick Lee took ten bucks from me and ten bucks from Billy Hall to give to you? You made more money than us, and we had to fight." Dwaine was smiling as he told the story.

Boots was surprised at what he was told and replied, "He didn't give me any money."

Dwaine's expression became dead serious. "Are you kiddin' me?"

"Naw, he didn't give me any damn money. What you talkin' about?"

Simpson exclaimed, "That son of a bitch!"

Dick Lee had goosed his fighters once again.

BIRTH OF THE BISCAYNE BOXING CLUB

Long time fight promoter Major W.H. Peeples, Jr. established the Biscayne Arena, opening the facility in 1931. It had a seating capacity of two thousand and in the course of the first twenty five years of its existence, amenities such as air conditioning were added. The promoter was interested in staging weekly boxing shows, but unable to find enough local pros. He needed someone with a pipeline to amateur boxing, and Richard Duane Lee could fill the bill. He phoned Lee and set up a meeting at his office in the arena.

Peeples began their conversation by saying, "I got a call from Jim Norris of the IBC. They need twelve hundred fighters for their televised shows. They'll pay $10,000 for the contract of any fighter we refer to them and they accept." IBC stood for International Boxing Club, an organization headed by Norris that staged nationally televised bouts on Monday, Wednesday and Friday nights.

Dick Lee replied, "Ten grand! Ya could buy a nice house with that."

"It's time I start holding weekly shows," said the major. "Are there enough fighters around here that could be promoted and possibly sold to the IBC?"

"Absolutely! I got a list of fifty who've fought in my amateur shows at the Moose Lodge."

Peeples took out a pack of cigarettes from a side drawer in his desk and offered one to Lee. After they both lit up and took puffs, the long established promoter dressed in a navy blue Brooks Brothers suit, white shirt and light blue tie said, "I'm thinking of forming a Biscayne Boxing Club that would be a stable of young fighters with potential. What if I make you president and matchmaker of this new club, and we sign as many amateurs as we can? We should be able to find somebody good enough for the IBC."

"What's the job pay?"

"A hundred a week, plus we'll split any manager fees deducted from their purses and any money from selling their contracts."

"That'll be great," said Lee as he removed a strand of tobacco from his tongue, "but I wanna be able to book fighters into other places when they's no fights at your place."

"Might be a good idea," replied the major. "The possibility of getting many fights would encourage boxers to sign with us. But Biscayne Arena shows must come first."

"I'll make sure they's no conflicts.

"How long do you think it'll take to sign enough fighters?"

"Umm… 'bout a month."

"Outstanding!" replied Peeples. Both men rose from their seats. The major offered Lee his hand, and they pumped arms briefly. Peeples said, "I'll have a contract drawn up for us, as well as blank contracts for the fighters to sign. You should have all the paper work in a few days."

As Dick Lee left the promoter's office, he thought, "This is the break I been lookin' for! Major Peeples has the arena, the reputation and the connection with the IBC. We can tie up the local boxers and let those Dundee's down in Miami Beach bring in all the out of town guys they want. It's cheaper to deal with local boys. Ya don't hafta get 'em a place to stay and they'll fight for less."

DWAINE SIGNS A PRO CONTRACT

Dwaine Simpson was making the most he ever had, but was very unhappy working for the finance company. He heard some of the world's saddest stories on a daily basis, and the depressing environment he found himself in ate away at him. He saw too many disturbing sights worse than what he experienced growing up in coal mining towns. He walked into the house of one of his delinquent customers and found wooden slats in the kitchen instead of a floor. A recent leak had flooded the room with two inches of dirty water attracting swarms of mosquitoes. After seeing that, Dwaine asked himself, "Why am I botherin' this poor soul?"

His customers would try to hide cars from him, but none threatened him with violence or pulled guns. The most resistance he encountered was from those who chased after him as he towed their cars away, shouting, "STOP! STOP! I JUST NEED IS A LITTLE MORE TIME!" When he mentioned this to his boss, Herman Slaker replied with a grin, "Tell 'em they'll get tired if they run alongside the car but if they run behind it, they'll be exhausted." Slaker laughed uproariously at his own joke. Dwaine chuckled politely, but didn't think the remark very funny.

One night while hauling away a 1951 Oldsmobile, Dwaine was startled when someone sat up in the back seat of the vehicle he was towing. Simpson pulled over, got out of his Buick and walked back to the Olds. He discovered the person in the back seat was a man and asked, "Who're you?"

"Beau Stevens. I'm the owner of this car."

"Ya were the owner, now the finance company has it."

"Aw shit, shoulda known I couldn't sit in the car all night and keep 'em from takin' it."

"Well," replied Dwaine, "I'm headed to the finance company. What do ya wanna do?"

"Could ya'll drop me back at my place?"

"Guess I could manage that."

Dwaine dropped Beau off at his apartment, and the former owner of the Olds handed Simpson the keys. The repo man said, "Hope things get better for ya."

"They will. Least I won't hafta stay up all night worryin' about that damn car."

As Simpson drove away, he thought, "Am I gonna spend the rest of my life takin' cars from down and outers?" He had been with the finance company over a year and he and his wife had a second child, but he was feeling such deepanxiety he decided the money wasn't worth it. He went in to see his boss and said, "I can't do this anymore. I can't keep makin' things harder for poor people." Slaker tried to talk him out of quitting, but Simpson's mind was made up.

He returned to the Opa-Locka Parks and Recreation Department and was placed in charge of tennis courts, a swimming pool and an officers' club converted to a recreation building. He no longer went to work wearing a white shirt and tie, but performed his duties in a seventy nine cent work shirt and matching work pants costing ninety nine cents. It meant a big reduction in income but he was able to look at himself in the mirror again and not feel guilty. Unfortunately, peace of mind didn't put food on the table. He said to his wife, "Honey, if I could get ahead as fast as I get behind, I'd be rich. They say money talks, but all mine says is 'Bye Bye.'" Dwaine took on any part time job he could find and even sold a pint of blood for ten dollars. He needed money.

Word reached him through his boxing pals about Dick Lee assembling a stable of fighters for professional boxing shows to be held at many venues: Biscayne Arena, the Dade County Armory, the nightclub in the Sir John Hotel, Overtown's Harlem Square Club and the Palace Arena in the middle income black community of Liberty City. Dwaine thought, "I came home with fourteen bucks for twelve minutes work first time I fought as a pro. I don't know how much an hour that is, but it's gotta be more than house paintin', mowin' lawns or even my regular job."

He drove to the Wynnwood Park recreation building, found Dick Lee in the gym and said to him, "I hear ya puttin' together a stable of fighters."

"Think ya can cut the mustard, college boy?"

"How many blue eyed, blonde fighters do ya have?"

"Ya gotta a point, Boolah Boolah. Ya do sell tickets. Step over ta my office."

Simpson and Lee went into a cluttered, closet like room with a small desk and two chairs. Lee said, "Have a seat."

Dwaine had to remove a couple of boxes from a chair before he could sit down. The fight manager took a blank contract from a drawer and laid it on the desk for Simpson to read. Lee said, "Okay, here's the deal. Ya sign this and ya guaranteed five hunnert dollars a year, whether ya fight or not. That's nearly ten bucks a week for doin' nothin'. Ya'll can buy groceries with that."

"Lemme look at this."

"I know, I know, you college boys love to show off how smart ya are 'bout readin' small print. Are ya a real Boolah Boolah boy? Did they sing that stupid song where ya went?"

Dwaine thought, "He's just tryin' to distract me and get my mind off my readin'." He said to the promoter, "Well, they did teach us big print gives ya things and small print takes 'em away." The first words that caught Simpson's eye were "exclusive rights for ten years." He exclaimed, "Hey Dick, this is a ten year contract!"

"It certainly is. Jes' think of the job security I'm givin' ya."

"What if ya don't get me any fights and someone else offers me some?"

Lee responded with a look of disbelief. He asked Simpson, "How would that ever happen?"

"Just the way I said. Ya don't get me any fights and somebody else offers me some."

"Never happen. All the other managers want hitters, and that's somethin' you ain't. Nobody else is gonna give ya nearly ten dollars a week for doin' nothin'." A smile came to Lee's face before he said, "Don't worry, feather fist. I'm gonna get ya more fights than ya can handle. I'm just lovin' the thought of ya gettin' ya ass kicked."

"And they better be fair fights. No more puttin' me in 'gainst guys twenty pounds bigger'n me."

"Absolutely, this is the pros, not the amateurs. We hold weigh-ins."

Dwaine let out a loud sigh and said, "Oh, alright, gimme a pen and I'll sign."

Dick Lee had been filling out a printed form with his only pen while they were talking. He said, "Before ya sign, I gotta finish fillin' out this form. I got everythin' but your date of birth. What is it?"

"Ya mean my birthday?"

"Right."

"January twenty sixth."

"What year?"

"Every year."

"I meant the year you were born, dumb ass."

"1934."

The fight manager wrote down the year on a document to be turned into the Miami Beach Boxing Commission. When he was finished, he handed his pen to Dwaine so he could sign the contract. Once Lee had his signature, he said, "Okay, be here every day for trainin'."

Simpson angrily responded, "Oh no, this is thirty five miles from my house. Gas is twenty five cents a gallon. Costs too damn much to come out here every day. I'll do it every three days."

"Why should I treat you special?"

"'Cuz people pay to see me!"

Dick Lee thought for a moment, then said, "Okay, we'll do it your way 'long as ya stay in shape. There's somethin' else I gotta talk to ya about. Don't have sex for a month before any fight I get ya. If ya have sex before ya fight, it puts ya a week behind."

Dwaine blurted out, "Hell, I can't do that!"

"Why?"

"If sex puts ya a week behind, I'm already four years behind and I'll never catch up."

Lee couldn't keep from smiling. All he could say in response was, "Wise ass college boy."

SIMPSONS NEW TOY

Dwaine's mother in law came to Florida for a visit. It was the first time Lola Carter had seen her daughter and son in law's home. The house was clean but sparsely furnished, with no thought given to its décor. There were no headboards for the beds, no vases, no coffee table and the white walls were unadorned. Lola asked, "Why isn't there a chandelier?"

Dwaine replied, "'Cuz Ramona and me don't know how to play one. I can play the ukulele, though." His mother in law rolled her eyes.

Lola turned to her daughter and said, "I was hoping to take you and my grandchildren on a weeklong trip."

Ramona looked at Dwaine and asked, "Is that alright with you, honey?"

"If ya really wanna do it, it's alright with me."

She turned to her mother and asked, "Are you sure you can afford it?"

"Money's no problem. I've done well in the stock market."

Dwaine said to Mrs. Carter, "Never woulda guessed ya knew anythin' about steers and hogs."

"Why would I know about them?"

"'Ya said you're in the stock market. Isn't that the place with fences 'round it where ya go to buy 'em?"

Ramona said, "No, dear, that's the stockYARDS."

Her mother's response was, "I can see who has the brains in the family. Will it be safe to leave Dwaine alone for a week?"

"He'll be fine, Mom. He doesn't play with matches and won't let strangers in."

Dwaine's mother in law added, "Your husband's unique. I never thought I'd meet a man whose family tree had no branches. Are you sure he wasn't hatched?"

"He's different, Mom, but he's a good man."

Lola sighed and said, "Oh, maybe you're right. Perhaps his talent has been dormant."

Dwaine chimed in, "Oh no! I'm not doin' that kinda work. I was doorman at a hotel one summer, and didn't like it at all."

His mother in law rolled her eyes again and said, "I think we should get the car packed and try to be on the road before dark."

Within minutes after his wife, kids and mother in law pulled away, Dwaine realized he had forgotten something important when he told his wife she could go on the trip. He knew nothing about preparing meals. Making coffee was the extent of his cooking skills. Dealing with pots, pans and cooking utensils was too complicated for him, and he spent his week of "batching it" with nothing to eat but cold pork and beans straight out of cans, baloney sandwiches and Moon Pies. Time went by very slowly, and he appreciated his wife more than ever when she finally returned.

When Ramona walked in, she complimented him on how well he kept the house in order. He replied, "I did the best I could, but I'll never be as good a housekeeper as you."

She smiled and said, "Honey, I know you do the best you can, considering where you came from. Remember what I said the first time you told me you were born in West Virginia?"

"Yeah, 'Congratulations on bein' able to read.'" He chuckled, and then gave her a hug and a kiss.

He suddenly remembered something and said, "Guess what I did while you were away?"

"I give up."

"I bought a unicycle."

"Why in heaven would you do that?"

"I got a good deal on it, and it's somethin' I can use. Wait here and I'll show it to ya." While he went into their utility room to retrieve his new one wheeled vehicle, she thought, "There he goes again!" He took her by the hand and said, "Come on outside. Wait'll ya see how it works."

Ramona stood on the front lawn and watched Dwaine ride his new toy up and down the street. They made quite a contrast. The husband was in shorts and a t-shirt, while the wife was wearing flats and a blue halter dress with white polka dots her mother had bought her. After he was done, he said, "It's great for my balance."

She replied, "I hope you don't fall off but if you do, make sure you land on your head 'cuz that won't hurt anything."

"I'll remember that. I like how you're always lookin' out for me."

"Now all you have to do is learn how to juggle and you'd be a great clown."

"That's a TERRIFIC idea!" His eyes lit up, and he made excited gestures as if he were juggling balls in the air. "I'm gonna put a clown on the back of my boxing robe. Just imagine me ridin' in on my unicycle wearin' that robe."

The thought made Ramona laugh so hard she had tears. She said, "I don't think boxing is ready for a clown like you."

"Aw, honey, only reason I clown about fightin' is 'cuz I don't think I'm ready for IT. I'll never be a knockout artist. Maybe if I get'em laughin' at me, I might catch 'em off guard."

"Is that how you caught me?"

"Thought it was the other way 'round. You're the one with the brains in the family."

With a laugh, she replied, "I might have caught you, but I'm still trying to figure out what to do with you."

PART TWO:

BOXINGS CLOWN PRINCE

DWAINE LAUNCHES HIS CAREER AS A BOXING CLOWN

Simpson's first bout under his ten year contract took place on a Monday night after Thanksgiving at the Biscayne Arena. When he entered the two thousand seat facility at 850 NW 23rd Street, Dick Lee greeted him. "Didja hear the news, Boolah Boolah? They upped the drinkin' age in West Virginia to thirty two ta keep booze outta the high schools. That's your home state, ain't it?" The promoter was laughing so hard at his own joke he failed to notice Dwaine was carrying a unicycle along with his equipment bag bearing the message "Have Gloves Will Travel, Have Sense Will Run." .

Simpson replied, "I still don't know who I'm fightin' tonight. When I signed that contract, you promised to tell me who I'm gonna fight ahead of time."

"Tried to, but the guy I was gonna match ya with didn't show up. I've got ya down for four rounds with Jack Canada. He's standin' over there." Lee pointed out a somber looking fighter with large brown eyes and a deep cleft in his chin. He appeared to be the same size as Simpson.

"Oh no," replied Dwaine, "you're not gonna stick me with another Canadian like Larry Portress."

"His NAME is Canada, but he's not FROM Canada, shit for brains. He's from Miami and he weighs 'bout the same as you, so ya got nothin' ta bitch about."

Simpson carried his bag and unicycle to the dressing room. He was determined not to let Dick Lee spoil the evening for him. No matter how things turned out, he was going to have fun.

Jack McKiernan had agreed to be Dwaine's corner man. The blonde fighter found it relaxing to engage in light conversation with his friend while waiting to be called to the ring.

Dwaine asked Jack, "Do ya think Jack Canada's ever been to Canada?"

"I don't know."

"Have ya ever been up there?"

"No."

Simpson then said, "I've always wondered how people overseas in Canada hook up electric power in their igloos. Guess they drill a hole and run a cord."

"They don't have igloos in Canada, Dwaine. That's further up north where there's Eskimos, like Alaska or the North Pole."

McKiernan's remark surprised the fighter. He replied, "Wow! Boy, you really know your stuff. Bet ya know all about the moose hatcheries up in Canada, huh?"

McKiernan rolled his eyes, then said, "Naw, but I'll find out and let ya know. Ya better forget about that and think about the fight."

"Don't worry, Jack. I'm gonna have fun tonight. Doesn't matter if I win or lose, I'm gonna have a ball."

By the time Dwaine was called to the ring, the large crowd had settled into their seats under a cloud of tobacco smoke. They expected to see him walk into the arena like every other fighter, but he surprised them by making his entrance on his unicycle. Someone shouted, "WHAT IS THIS, A CIRCUS?" Another fan hollered, "LOOK, HE'S GOT A CLOWN ON THE BACK OF HIS ROBE!"

Simpson's stunt upset Dick Lee, and he blurted out, "Sonuvabitch didn't clear his showboatin' with me, and he ain't pullin' that crap no more! He's under contract and hasta follow orders." He bit down on his cigar and was about to confront Dwaine when Jack McKiernan intervened. Jack said to the promoter, "Wait a minute, Dick, listen to the fans. Everybody likes it. Even the ones hopin' he gets knocked out are smilin'. Remember Billy Kilgore?"

"Ya mean that southpaw middleweight from Alabama who brings his dog inta the ring with him?"

"That's him." Kilgore had a female boxer named Lady, and the dog would accompany him into the ring so announcers could introduce both Lady and Billy. Once the introductions were over, the canine was led away. McKiernan added, "If Billy Kilgore can have his dog, then Dwaine should have his unicycle."

Dick Lee sighed loudly before replying. "Yeah, I guess it's good for the box office and brings money. Ah, I don't care how stupid he acts as long as he gets put on the canvas tonight."

Lee didn't get his wish. It was a perfect night for Dwaine. He worked up the crowd, was showered with an equal amount of cheers and boos and won a decision. His purse was fifty dollars but after Dick made deductions for tape, gauze, a license and one third share as manager, Simpson ended up with twenty six bucks.

The blonde lightweight followed up on his success by fighting to a draw a week later, and then was matched with a lanky southern white with mean looking eyes named Paxton Ward. McKiernan mentioned to Dwaine, "Ward's a proud rebel from Alabama and both his great granddaddies fought for the South." Hearing this, Simpson decided to try something different when he walked to the middle of the ring for final instructions from the referee. He thought, "If I move my hips and legs like Elvis Presley, I might get 'im upset." When Dwaine started wiggling his legs and shaking his hips, Ward angrily shouted, "AH TAKE OFFENSE TO THAT, SUH! I'LL CHEW YO' HEAD OFF AND SWALLOW YA WHOLE!"

Simpson retorted, "Then you'll have more brains in your stomach than in your head."

At the opening bell, Ward's temper got the better of him, and he charged at Simpson like a wild bull assaulting a red cape. One of Dwaine's haters bellowed, "TEAR 'IM UP, BAMA BOY! PUT THE RAMMER JAMMER ON 'IM!" Paxton put full force behind an overhand right, but Dwaine skillfully stepped out of the way at the last instant. This frustrated the Alabama fighter. He kept trying to force Simpson into the ropes, but the lanky blonde boxer kept eluding him. After two rounds, Ward became so drained of energy he could barely keep his hands up. Dwaine, the "hitless wonder," landed a left jab on his opponent's nose. Blood leaked from Ward's nostril and he briefly dropped to the canvas before getting back on his feet. The referee stopped the fight, ruled Paxton Ward had been outclassed and awarded Dwaine a TKO; the first knockout of Simpson's boxing career. There was jubilation among Dwaine's supporters, but fire in Dick Lee's eyes.

When Lee entered the dressing room to pay Simpson his share of a forty dollar purse, he held an envelope containing $23.67. Placing it in the fighter's hand, he asked, "What the hell was ya doin' out there, tryin' to be Elvis?"

"I got a new idea. When I walk out for final instructions, man, I'm gonna move my feet accordin' to who I'm fightin'. If I fight a black man, I'll give 'im some rhythm and blues. If I fight a Latin, I do a rhumba or cha cha cha. Tonight, I was in against a hillbilly, so I moved like Elvis. He got really pissed at me and I stopped 'im, didn't I?"

"Real men don't do things like that."

"Dick, ya just don't understand ya gotta keep your center."

"What center ya talkin' 'bout?"

"Person's gotta stay centered on what they're doin'. I got the other guy upset with me and he wanted to tear my head off. He lost his center, ran outta gas, let his guard down, stuck his head up and I stopped his ass."

"Where'd ya learn all that?"

"Health and phys ed class in college."

The answer so infuriated Lee a vein began popping out of the promoter's forehead. He blurted, "I don't wanna hear no more college crap or Boolah Boolah bullshit!" He waved his fist under Dwaine's nose and growled, "I'm gonna find someone who's gonna destroy your face!"

"Well, Dick, guess the glow in our relationship is over."

Lee turned his back to Simpson and walked away, muttering "Smart ass college boy!"

Dwaine got in the last word. "My ignorance is just as good as your knowledge and prolly better."

As angry as the promoter was with his drawing card, Dwaine's fans were elated. They never imagined him knocking anyone out and talked about his technical knockout for days, as if they had witnessed a reenactment of David and Goliath.

Simpson expected retaliation, but felt ready for anything. Two weeks after Dwaine's TKO, the tight fisted promoter matched him with Kenny "Cooter" Parker in a six rounder. Simpson could see trouble on the horizon when told what he'd be paid. Dick spoke with an unlit cigarette dangling from his mouth. "I'm givin' ya eighty bucks and since it's your first six rounder, I won't make no deductions." After saying that, Dick Lee thought, "I hope to hell ya get the beatin' of your life."

Dwaine knew the promoter didn't do things out of kindness and suspected he was walking into an ambush. He'd never heard of Cooter Parker and none of the other fighters knew anything about him. The first time he saw Cooter was during weigh-in on fight night, and his opponent was a disturbing sight. Parker was bald, had so much scar tissue on his face it looked like a crossword puzzle and had the dark eyes and cold stare of a man who killed and enjoyed it.

He went to Dick Lee and said, "This guy Parker ya matched me with looks like an axe murderer."

Lee replied, "Well, if you're scared of him..."

Keeping up a brave front, Dwaine quickly replied, "Naw, I don't give a shit." He thought, "Eighty bucks buys a lotta groceries. The ref'll keep Cooter in line."

Simpson kept his distance from Parker while in the dressing room and avoided making direct eye contact. Dwaine began shadow boxing to work up a sweat and noticed something in his peripheral vision. He turned to see Cooter knocking back a shot of bourbon from an Old Charter pocket flask. Dwaine thought, "Hope he isn't a mean drunk."

In the first round, Cooter opened with a flurry of punches, but swung wildly, as if in a barroom brawl, and none of them connected. He tried to chase Simpson down, cut him off and limit the space he could maneuver in, but that didn't work. Cooter decided on something drastic. The two fighters went into a clinch and when the referee said "Break," Parker used the laces of his gloves to rake Dwaine over both eyes, causing a torrent of blood to flow. Simpson glared at Cooter, and many of the fans let out a resounding "BOOO!" Even ones who normally rooted against Dwaine didn't approve of what had been done. Using laces to inflict cuts was unthinkable and none of the boxers bothered to tape over laces on their gloves. This made no difference to Cooter. He was an angry, defiant man capable of violence.

Dwaine wondered why the referee did nothing about it until he smelled liquor on the official's breath. He thought, "Damn! He's prolly Cooter's drinkin' buddy." When the round ended, the men in his corner couldn't stop the blood drizzling down his cheekbones, but he was allowed to continue because it didn't hamper his vision. He spent the rest of the fight staying away from Parker and managed to go the distance, but the judges scoring the bout awarded the decision to Cooter. On his way back to the dressing room, he passed Dick Lee, smiling like a kid on Christmas morning. Dwaine thought, "He sure loves to see me in misery." Lee followed him into the dressing room, handed him four twenty dollar bills and then walked over to the man who inflicted the cuts. Simpson thought, "I made the bastard happy. I wonder how much blood money he's givin' Cooter."

The downcast lightweight saw rhe promoter count out five twenties and hand them to Parker. The menacing fighter accepted them without a word. He had nothing to say to anyone and offered no apologies. After taking a swig of 86 proof whiskey, he dressed without showering and left. Simpson thought, "I've heard of high brows and low brows, but Cooter's the first no brow I've seen. Maybe he's goin' home where he lives with the Creature from the Black Lagoon."

It took a month for the injured blonde fighter's cuts to heal. Once he was good as new, Simpson was matched with a Korean named Yank-Sang Hoak at the Legion Arena in Lake Worth. Jack McKiernan warned Dwaine, "Dick Lee says the Korean's hands are fast as the speed of light."

Simpson's brow furrowed as he replied, "Ya know, Jack, I always wondered why nobody talks 'bout the speed of dark."

"I don't know, but you'll do better worryin' about the Korean's quick hands."

Dwaine found the Legion Arena a strange place for holding boxing matches. The fighters' dressing room was located under the floor of the building, and they reached it through a trap door in the floor connected to a stairway. When he walked into the changing room, he was shocked at what he saw. The ceiling was only seven feet high, and there were no windows or ventilation. The cement floors felt slightly sticky, as if mopped with a mixture of sugar and water.

Instead of lockers or hooks to hang things on, wooden dresser drawers were stacked up to the ceiling without being secured to the wall. All drawers closest to the floor were taken and a fighter precariously balanced himself on a stool while trying to use one at the very top. The entire building's bathroom piping went through the dressing room and every time a toilet was flushed, the wooden drawers wobbled and boxers could hear the sound of rushing water above and around them. Dwaine chose to keep his things in his canvas bag and not bother with the drawers.

There were four toilets with nothing between them. When Dwaine went to use one, he discovered it was two inches lower than standard, with a bowl much smaller in diameter than usual. He thought, "Hope I don't fall off this thing in the middle of takin' a crap."

When he went up the stairs leading to the trap door, Simpson tripped on a step a quarter of the way up. He caught himself in time and thought, "That one's higher'n the rest of 'em." He was very careful, but nearly tripped on another raised step three fourths of the way to the top. Once in the ring, the blonde lightweight noticed the seating rose from the floor at an angle. He said to himself, "First I gotta go through a sewer to get into the ring, so I can fight at the bottom of a pit."

Neither Dwaine nor his Korean opponent landed any solid blows and were booed throughout their fight by bloodthirsty fans. The loudest and nastiest insults came from a morbidly obese woman with a misshapen mouth and a red faced man sitting next to her with little pieces of toilet paper stuck on razor nicks. He had three chins and the buttons on his shirt were about to pop as it tried to cover his protruding gut. Between rounds, Dwaine shouted at the fat lady, "LAST TIME I SAW A MOUTH LIKE YOURS WAS ON A FISH AT THE END OF A HOOK!" The four round preliminary ended in a draw, which incited the crowd even more. Someone yelled, "WE WANT HITTERS, NOT DANCERS!" Another shouted, "I DIDN'T COME TO SEE NO TRACK MEET!" The two fighters were pelted with cigar butts, hot dog wrappers and cardboard cups as they left through the trap door and headed to the hot, stuffy dressing room.

Simpson hoped a refreshing shower would invigorate him, but was disappointed to find the water slow to heat up and once it became hot, instantly turned cold. The small threadbare towels supplied made it difficult to completely dry off. Jack McKiernan could tell his friend was feeling low, and tried to brighten his mood by saying, "You've come a long way since ya fought Robert Morale in Opa-Locka. I can't believe ya never boxed before that."

"I boxed with my brother, cousins and kids in the neighborhood, and could hold my own with most of 'em."

"Who taught ya?"

"Wasn't any real teachin' or trainin'; just trial, error and survival of the fittest. For a while, I thought I was one of the unfit, 'specially after my older brother 'n his friends took me along on a campin' trip. I was lookin' forward to playin' my ukulele and singin' 'round the campfire."

"What happened?"

"Well, we didn't bring any campin' equipment or any food. They said, 'Dig a trap, cover it with leaves and then we'll hide in the bushes 'til some animal comes along.' After I finished, I forgot where I dug the trap. I fell in and had to be pulled out. Next day, I climbed up a tree and fell out of it. Lucky for me, I wasn't hurt. My brother asked me, 'What happened?' I said, 'I got up just fine, but forgot how to climb down.' After that, no more campin' trips."

McKiernan was laughing so hard his eyes were tearing up. When he could talk again, he said, "You earned a Coke for that. Want one?"

"Okay."

Jack went out in the hall, bought two bottles of Coca Cola from a vending machine, came back in the dressing room, handed one to Dwaine and asked, "Was basketball the first sport ya became good at?"

Simpson took a sip of his soft drink and then replied, "Yeah. Startin' when I was eight years old, I played basketball four hours a day, seven days a week, 'til I was twenty." Jack seemed interested in hearing about it, so Dwaine told him more. "I was 5'2" my freshman year in high school, but grew to 5'11" by my junior year. We won the North Carolina Class B Championship my last two years playin' for the Camp Lejeune High School Devil Pups. I made All State two years, All Tournament two years, Senior East/West All Star and got a full basketball scholarship to Western Carolina."

"Where's that?" asked McKiernan, opening his Coke.

"Cullowhee, North Carolina. They had eight hundred in the school when I went there. It was a teachers college, and they call those places 'normal schools.' Guess they liked the challenge of bringin' in a way below normal student."

"Why ya say that?"

"I had sixteen courses in high school and got fourteen D's and two C minuses. After I was offered the scholarship, I flunked English. I went to the teacher and said, 'Me fail English, that's unpossible!' I tol' her 'bout my scholarship, and she figured if she didn't pass me, she'd have me again. She was sick of lookin' at me, so she let me through with a D."

"Whadja study in college?"

Dwaine replied with a grin, "I didn't study nothin'. They studied me."

Jack laughed and said, "Don't put me on. Whadja really do there."

"I allus went to class 'cuz the chairs were comfortable 'nough to sleep in and the sound of the professors' voices could cure insomnia. I learned it was better to sleep than try to take part 'cuz every time I said anythin', I screwed up. One time, a professor asked me, 'Mr. Simpson, name a European country.' I said, 'Africa.' He shook his head at me and laughed, so I tried again by sayin' the first country to pop in my head. I said, 'Sorry, I meant to say Japan. I never want to go there 'cuz I don't like eatin' fish, and I know that's what people eat out there in Europe.' That made it worse. He said, 'You're more than stupid. Talkin' to you is like talkin' to somebody with amnesia.' 'Nother professor got just as upset when I asked, 'Is eye color a behavior?' He ignored my question, but said to the class, 'I want all your eyes forward and lookin' at the blackboard.' I piped up and said, 'My eyes are always forward, otherwise I'd be lookin' into my own head.' He gave me a dirty look and said, 'I can't believe you're that ignorant. When are you gonna open up your mind?' I tol' him, 'I'm scared to do that 'cuz my brain might fall out.' That really made him mad. Guess that's why teachers didn't mind if I slept in class."

McKiernan was cracking up. He laughed so hard his sides began to ache. He then asked, "What happened when they gave exams?"

"No big deal. All tests were multiple choice and four answers ta each question... 'A,' 'B,' 'C' or 'D,' so I'd just circle 'B' all the way down the page."

"Didja ever try to cheat?"

"Naw, I tried that once in high school and got caught. There were ten questions, and ya wrote the answer in a space under the question. I was peekin' at the paper of the guy next to me. We both got nine outta ten right, but for the one he missed he wrote 'I don't know the answer' and I wrote 'Me neither.' When the teacher saw that, he gave me an F and said, 'You're too dumb to cheat. Never thought I'd meet a mushroom with eyes 'til you showed up.' I had to take the course over again with the same teacher and didn't do any better. When it came time for the final exam, he said, "If I give ya the same test as everyone else all it'll prove is how empty your head is. I don't wanna see ya again. So fill in the blanks, put down any kinda answer and don't cheat, and I'll give ya a hundred percent... five percent for answerin', ten percent for honesty and eighty five percent for neatness."

"He musta been desperate to keep from lookin' at ya."

"Mosta my high school teachers were."

"Whydja come to Florida?"

"I was a startin' guard on the basketball team, but was still takin' freshman courses my junior year. They put me in a remedial course called Mathematics 100, and we spent the whole semester learnin' how to count to a hundred. My grades were so bad I set a record as the first Western Carolina athlete to get all F's and lost my scholarship. After that, I decided to go to Miami 'cuz somebody tol' me, 'Hot rolls in the sand cost nothin' down there.' I didn't know they were jokin' 'til I got here and couldn't find fresh bakery goods layin' on the beach for the takin'. By then, my stepdad was stationed at Opa-Locka Marine Air Station. I figured I'd have a good time 'til I was drafted in the Army but when the draft board finally called, I was married with a kid and another on the way. Needless to say, they didn't want me. See what happens when ya go out to have a good time?"

McKiernan finished his Coke and asked his friend, "Feel better now?"

"Yeah, least I didn't lose and Dick didn't match me with another man eater like Cooter."

A DOUBLE KNOCKOUT

Dick Lee decided Dwaine had been sufficiently humbled after his matches with Cooter Parker and Yank-Sang Hoak. He thought, "College boy's been taken down a peg and needs money. Let's see if his mind's right and he'll obey orders." He approached Dwaine while he was punching a heavy bag at the Wynnwood Park gym and said, "I can getcha a four round prelim to a TV fight at the Miami Beach Auditorium for seventy five bucks, but ya gonna do what I say. No arguin' or smart ass remarks, unnerstan'? I give the orders and ya follow 'em."

Dwaine nodded and said, "Okay, we'll do it your way." The purses seemed to be getting bigger ever since he signed with his pot bellied manager.

"Good," replied Lee. "Fight's in two weeks. Ya better show up each and every day for sparrin' 'til the day before the fight."

"Who'm I fightin'?"

"Kid Pie Jordan."

"He's a bantamweight."

"That's right, but this time he can weigh one thirty nine, and ya gotta make the same weight."

"That won't be any problem for me."

Lee's eyes turned cold. "Don't gimme that 'no problem' crap. I'll make damn sure ya weigh one thirty nine."

Dick Lee viewed the upcoming fight as a chance to indoctrinate Dwaine into how a real pro gets ready for a match. This meant as much to the manager as winning the bout. He loathed Simpson and wanted more than anything to make the lanky blue eyed blonde obedient, control him and keep him under his thumb.

Dwaine managed to fit tough sparring sessions around his work schedule and felt ready to give his best against an opponent with a record of five wins and three draws. Kid Pie was being watched closely by Chris and Angelo Dundee as a possible addition to their stable. He was a slick fighter with boundless energy, throwing punches in bunches like a human piston. If Jordan proved he could crowd the elusive Simpson and batter him with body shots, he would be someone the Dundee's could sell to the IBC for ten grand.

Two days before the fight, Dick Lee gave Dwaine a strict order. "Don't eat or drink nuthin' tomorra."

"Not even water?"

"Nope, gonna dry ya out. Any top pro knows that's how ya get ready for a fight, and we gotta make sure ya make one thirty nine."

After being without food or water an entire day, Dwaine wondered what affect his fasting had on his weight. He stepped on an official scale in the Opa-Locka Parks and Recreation building. The bar settled at precisely one hundred thirty nine pounds.

Next morning, Dick Lee picked Dwaine up, drove to a YMCA and put him on the Y's regulation scale. The manager became angry when he saw his fighter weighed one forty two. Lee ordered him into the steam room and had him shadow box in the heat until he almost passed out. They went from there to the weigh-in, where Dwaine's weight was recorded at one thirty seven. He was two pounds under the limit and feeling very weak.

He had six and a half hours to regain his strength, and told his manager, "I gotta eat and I'm dry as a bone."

"Don't worry. I'll getcha a steak, baked potata and green beans."

Lee took him to a restaurant near the Miami Beach Auditorium. He ordered a grilled cheese for himself and a steak dinner for his fighter. When the waitress brought their food, Dwaine was unable to force any of his meal down. He ended up having a bowl of chicken broth and several glasses of water, while his manager devoured the sandwich plus the steak with all the trimmings. After gorging himself, Dick Lee lit a cigarette and took a puff. He said, "Can't let good food go ta waste. Think I'll have a beer for dessert." Dwaine felt too weak to respond.

Simpson spent the rest of the afternoon and early evening in one of the auditorium's dressing rooms. He sat on a bench and tried to quench his enormous thirst. He couldn't hold down any solid food, but was able to drink three quarts of water.

When it was time to fight, Kid Pie jumped all over Simpson at the opening bell, but landed nothing solid. Dwaine held his own through the first two rounds, but the lanky blonde with close cropped hair had almost completely expended his energy. He had to go for a knockout before there was nothing left in his tank. Dwaine saw an opening and connected with a right hand to the chin. He delivered his punch at a downward angle in the same direction Kid Pie's jaw opened. The resulting shock to Jordan's nervous system immediately buckled his knees. He was mentally in a thick fog, feeling nauseous pain and appeared ready to go down when Dwaine fell flat on his face from exhaustion. He slowly staggered to his feet but by then, the referee had stopped the fight and declared Jordan the winner. That was the last thing Dwaine remembered. He was later told he left the ring before Kid Pie's TKO victory had been announced, walked three hundred yards to his dressing room, entered it and collapsed.

Kid Pie Jordan won, but had been knocked out and didn't know he was the winner until emerging from his mental fog hours later. He lost out on his hopes of having his career advanced. Chris Dundee said to his brother Angelo, "The guy was unconscious when the ref held his hand up as the winner. Simpson can't crack an eggshell and if he can knock Jordan out, he's got no chin. What the hell good is he?" Angelo nodded in agreement.

Jordan was unbeaten, but word of Dundee's opinion quickly circulated and Cinderella's glass slipper turned into a glass jaw. He was unable to get more fights and drifted into obscurity.

When Simpson awakened in the dressing room, Dick Lee handed him an envelope with his share of the purse and said, "Damnedest thing I ever saw. Ya knock a guy out then ya lose the fight by fallin' on your face. How come ya couldn't go four rounds? Ya never had that problem before."

Dwaine was still weak, but gathered enough strength to shout, "'CUZ YA DAMNED NEAR KILLED ME WITH YOUR DRYIN' OUT CRAP! YOU'RE DUMBER'N A HORSE TURD!"

Lee had nothing to say. He decided not to argue and thought, "College boy ain't no old time hardass fighter, but I'll put up with his bullshit 'long as I make money off 'im."

ANYTHING TO PUT FOOD ON THE TABLE

Brutality suffered at the hands of Cooter Parker, combined with abuse from Lake Worth fight fans and Dick Lee's sadistic training methods took a toll on Dwaine. He finally made up his mind to tell his manager he was through. He thought, "This is it. I'm not goin' to the gym after work. I'm goin' home and tell Ramona I'm finished with boxing."

She heard the Ford pull up in the carport and came out to greet her husband with a smile before he could open the driver side door. She said, "What a surprise! I didn't expect you home so soon. Why aren't you going to the gym?"

"There's somethin' I wanna talk about."

"And I've got something to talk to you about."

"Ya go first," said Dwaine.

"You always want me go first."

"That's 'cuz you're the woman."

"Well... I was late this month. You know what that means."

"We're gonna have a baby?"

"You're absolutely right, my love."

"Wow, been a long time since I got an answer right."

"Well, this is our third child. You're learning from experience."

He went to her, held her close to his heart and began gently rubbing her tummy. He said, "I'm so excited we're gonna have another kid," and then he kissed her.

Pride of fatherhood brought a broad smile to his face before reality set in. He thought, "One more mouth to feed." Ramona interrupted his self reflection by asking, "What was it you wanted to tell me?"

"Oh, I was just wonderin' if you minded me boxing so much."

"I don't mind. It's something you like to do, and we can use the money... especially now."

Dwaine hugged her and whispered softly in her ear, "I'll always do my best for you and our kids." He thought, "I'll do it even if I hafta put up with that miserable bastard Dick Lee."

Another thought suddenly occurred to him. "Dick's got a boxing show scheduled tonight. I'm not on the card, but maybe somebody won't show up and they'll put me in at the last minute." He said, "Ramona honey, I just remembered I'm fightin' tonight. I better get goin' or I'll be late."

"Go ahead, we'll be rooting for you… all four of us."

He gave her a sensuous but brief kiss, and then said, "Let's have a better one." He held her and kissed her once more before departing, and this time it was long and lingering.

Dwaine walked into the arena with his equipment bag, but not his unicycle. Dick Lee rushed up to him, saying, "I need a fight to fill out the card. I'll give ya twenny bucks and won't deduct nothin'."

Simpson thought, "I must be psycho, like those mind readers." He asked the promoter, "I get to pick who I fight, okay?"

Lee grimaced as he replied, "Ooh, all right. What 'bout Herman 'Scatterhawk' Dixon?"

"No way, he's a middleweight. He's way bigger'n me. He's got a knockout punch that can open up everthin' that's closed and close up everthin' that's open."

"Well, who WOULD you fight, college boy?"

"How 'bout Jack McClain standin' over there?"

"Him," Lee replied indignantly. "He ain't won a fight. He hauls guys in from bars at the last minute just so's he can go four rounds for twenny bucks."

"Look, you tol' me to pick someone to fight. I'll fight HIM."

"Oooh, all right," grumbled the promoter. "Ya both get twenny bucks for four rounds."

McClain agreed to fight Simpson, and they hurried to the dressing room to change. While putting on his boxing gear, Jack said, "Thanks for gettin' me the fight, Dwaine. I know you're better'n me…"

"I've beaten you twice," interrupted Simpson, "but anythin' can happen in four rounds." He was thinking of his new responsibilities and wasn't in the mood for light conversation with his opponent.

McClain added, "What I'm tryin' to say is do ya think ya could lemme go the distance?"

Dwaine thought, "I've knocked him out twice and haven't knocked many guys out. What the hell, I'll carry him." He said to his opponent, "Okay, I'll see that ya go four rounds."

"Oh, one other thing."

"Yeah, Jack."

"Don't hit me in the nose if ya can avoid it."

Simpson looked at McClain with an expression of disbelief and thought, "Is this guy for real? Now he wants me to protect his beak." With a loud sigh, he replied, "Okay, Jack, I won't hit ya in the nose… if I can avoid it."

Within moments after their four round preliminary began, McClain and Simpson went into a clinch. The referee ordered them to break it up, but Jack wouldn't move away and continued throwing body blows and uppercuts. Dwaine thought, "Guess Jack forgot about our deal. He's actin' stupid, so I'll knock some sense into 'im." After the two fighters were pulled apart, McClain dropped his guard long enough for Simpson to deliver a knockout blow to the chin. Dwaine had won and said to his fallen opponent, "I kept away from the nose, Jack."

The two fighters had returned to the dressing room when McClain asked, "Whydja do that? Ya was supposed ta lemme finish the fight."

Dwaine replied, "We were s'posed to work together and then ya suddenly decide to take me out. That's dirty fightin', and ya gotta pay for that." McClain had nothing more to say because he knew he was in the wrong.

Dick Lee was smiling as he came into the room. He always beamed whenever a fight ended in a knockout. He handed each fighter twenty dollars and said, "Ya guys put on a good show, so I'm not deductin' nothin'."

"Thanks," said Dwaine. "I really appreciate that."

"You're welcome," replied Lee. He thought, "He's never been that respectful before. Maybe there's somethin' wrong with him. Hope it's nothin' I could catch."

There was nothing wrong with Simpson. He was simply determined to do whatever it took to feed his growing family. He would have gone into the ring every night if possible.

In the month following his knockout win over Jack McClain, Dwaine fought five bouts in ten days; winning them all and grossing a total of one hundred twenty dollars. The one paying the most was a four rounder at Miami Beach for forty bucks. After all the deductions, he netted less than sixty.

There was finally a break in the grinding schedule, and Dwaine had a rare night off to spend with his family. Driving home from work, he thought, "How long can I keep this up? We need the money, but I don't see how I can keep fightin' every other night."

He opened the front door and saw his wife at the kitchen table. He said, "Hey, are ya home?"

She didn't answer, but got up from her chair, went to him and gave him a kiss. Her pregnant condition still hadn't become noticeable. Suddenly, there was a look of terror on her face. "DWAINE!" she shouted, "THERE'S A WASP!"

He swatted at the insect and missed, but it flew out the front door. Dwaine said, "Shoulda come in the back way. Woulda been farther from the wasp."

"I don't think that would've made any difference. At least it flew out of the house." She handed him an envelope and said, "Here's a letter for you. It looks important."

Dwaine checked the return address and saw the letter was from the Miami Beach Boxing Commission. He sat down at the kitchen table and read the official correspondence. It was a notice he had been suspended for ten days. The commission cited his "fighting too many times within a short period."

"Anything important, honey?" asked Ramona.

"Not really. Boxing commission gave me a ten day vacation. They're doin' me a favor. I can spend more time around the house, help ya with the kids and maybe mow a few more lawns."

"I'm glad you're getting some time off," she said. "You know, honey, I've been thinking about what you were like when you were a little boy."

"Why's that?"

"I don't know. Maybe it's a sign we're gonna have another son. Anyway, when you were little, what did you want to be when you grew up?"

Dwaine thought for a moment before he replied. "First, I wanted to be a police dog."

"That's different."

"When I got a little older, I wanted to grow up to be a polar bear 'til I found out they lived in real cold places."

"Why do you think you wanted to be one of those animals?"

"Prolly 'cuz nobody picked on 'em and they never had to worry about gettin' somethin' ta eat."

"Was that one of your worries?"

"We always had somethin' ta eat, but it was the same thing alla time. I liked tryin' new things when I was little."

"You're not that way now."

"I stopped doin' it after I ate a yellow crayon and didn't feel too good afterwards."

She laughed and said, "I hope you didn't eat any more crayons, did you?"

"It took me a while to figure things out. I thought 'Maybe I tried the wrong flavor,' so I ate a red crayon the next day. I felt even worse after that, so I stopped tryin' new things. Besides, you know a lot more about food and are much better'n me in the kitchen."

Ramona chuckled and said, "We learned that when I asked you to get a pot ready to put spaghetti in and you put the pot in the stove without any water."

"That's 'cuz nobody tol' me the difference between broilin' and boilin' 'til you came along."

"Remember the time you left the wooden cutting board on the gas burner and started a fire?"

"I put it out quick, didn't I?"

She placed her arms around his neck, gave him a peck on his cheek and said, "You always come through when you have to, but it might be best if none of our kids take after you. One of you is enough."

He replied, "Funny ya mention that. I remember Ma sayin' the same thing."

DICK LEE WELCOMES TWO SERVICEMEN BACK TO BOXING

John Tombley was a welterweight who came to Miami from Valdosta, Georgia. He was a skillful boxer with a knockout punch, and his pro career got off to a blazing start in 1956. He won nine of his first eleven fights and the other two ended in draws. Major Peeples and Dick Lee were about to sell the unbeaten fighter's contract to the IBC for ten grand, when their plans were waylaid by John receiving his draft notice.

Tombley fought as an amateur while in the Army and when discharged, joined the Miami police force and resumed his boxing career under Dick Lee's guidance. Dick knew the welterweight had a big following and his return to the ring would sell a lot of tickets. The fight manager wanted to match Tombley with the right opponent for a "welcome home fight," so he chose Dwaine Simpson, a fighter in Lee's stable with little chance of beating the former G.I.

Dwaine didn't like the idea of being overmatched with John Tombley in a six rounder. He told Lee, "He's in a higher weight class and could knock me out. Forget it."

The manager thought, "I gotta get the college boy to fight Tombley. It'll be good box office. Lotta people love seein' Boolah Boolah get knocked on his ass." He said to Dwaine, "What if I pay ya eighty bucks and not take my third?"

Simpson rubbed his hand over his hair and pursed his lips while mulling over the offer. After a moment, he replied, "Tell ya what, I'll do it if we fight two-minute rounds." Lee agreed to that condition, and the match was set.

Dwaine was very worried about taking on a far superior opponent. Since he and John were good friends, he talked things over with him a few days before their bout. Simpson said, "I know I'm not in your class and ya could knock me out any time ya want. Why don't we treat the fight like an exhibition or sparring session? Nobody tries for a knockout. How 'bout it?"

Tombley replied, "Fine with me, makes no difference one way or the other."

When fight night arrived, Tombley pulled a surprise. He chose not to follow the script and knocked Simpson down twice in the first round. Dick Lee bounced up and down with glee in his ringside seat and exclaimed, "College boy's gonna get an ass whuppin'!'

Simpson spent the last five rounds running for his life, and Tombley couldn't catch the lanky blonde or force him against the ropes. John won the decision, but his forehead looked like chopped liver after being hit by Dwaine's torrent of rapid fire left jabs. Dick Lee was disappointed the fighter he loathed wasn't knocked out. When Simpson and Tombley were back in the dressing room, John said, "Sorry I knocked you down after sayin' I wouldn't."

Dwaine replied, "Don't worry 'bout it, but if I'd known what ya were gonna do before the fight, they woulda had to call Miami Crane Service to drag me into the ring."

Dick Lee's hopes for Tombley contending for the world welterweight crown didn't pan out. In his next nineteen fights, he won eight, lost six and five of the bouts ended in draws. John Tombley saw the handwriting on the wall, retired from boxing and enjoyed a rewarding career in law enforcement.

Eddie Ludlow was another boxing friend of Dwaine's drafted into the Army. While serving his hitch, Eddie won the All-Army Lightweight Championship and acquired the nickname "Fast Eddie." Hearing of Ludlow's success, Dick Lee thought, "Didn't think the guy was gonna make it after I signed him to a contract." Eddie fought fifteen times before entering the military; winning only once, losing twelve and fighting two draws. Lee wrote Ludlow and expressed how much he was looking forward to arranging fights for him when he returned from the Army.

To the fight manager's dismay, Fast Eddie came back to Miami badly out of shape. He admitted he hadn't fought or trained in six months. Lee was still willing to take a chance on the lightweight because he was a slick boxer with a rock for a right hand. He wanted to start Ludlow out by matching him with Dwaine Simpson in a six rounder, since there would be little chance of a man ridiculed for having fists of putty posing a danger to the military veteran. Dwaine agreed to fight six two-minute rounds for sixty dollars, with Lee getting his one third manager's fee. Simpson took the fight only because Eddie Ludlow wasn't likely to go the distance.

Dwaine weighed in at one hundred forty one pounds, while Eddie weighed one thirty five and was two inches shorter. The recently discharged soldier came out like a ravenous tiger, trying to take his opponent out before running out of gas. Dwaine connected with every left jab he delivered and inadvertently hit Eddie with the top of his head when he brought it back up after ducking a punch. In the third round, Ludlow charged at his taller opponent, and his mouth hit Dwaine on the forehead. Simpson suffered a small cut, but Ludlow's lower front teeth went all the way through his lower lip. Eddie bled profusely from a two inch cut requiring four metal clamps to close it. The fight was stopped and Simpson was awarded a TKO.

Ludlow's injury satisfied the bloodthirsty fans, but Dick Lee's plan of matching out of condition Fast Eddie in a "safe" fight was foiled. The fight manager had forgotten there is no such thing as a "risk free" professional bout. Eddie Ludlow went on to a long pro career, but never achieved the level of boxing success he enjoyed in the Army. His record was eighteen wins, thirty losses and four draws. After retiring from fighting, his life spiraled downward, and he served ten years in prison after being convicted of manslaughter for the death of his wife. He paid his debt to society, and then became a trainer, working with future heavyweight contender and Florida Boxing Hall of Fame inductee Jose Ribalta. Dwaine often saw Fast Eddie at various boxing shows and would always say to him, "Hey, remember the time YOU knocked YOURSELF out on MY head?" It never failed to get a laugh from Ludlow.

THE BISCAYNE BOXING CLUB ROAD SHOW

Dick Lee was convinced there was an untapped market of fight fans in small Florida towns and came up with the idea of selling boxing shows to social clubs, charitable groups and fraternal organizations. On nights there was no boxing at Biscayne Arena, he would put on shows for four hundred dollars and let those who hired him worry about selling enough tickets to make a profit. Out of the four hundred bucks, he was able to put nearly two hundred in his pocket. Lee amassed a tidy sum holding two or three fundraiser shows a week.

The letter Lee sent to potential customers stated, "Many of the boys fighting in our shows are appearing at the Miami Beach Auditorium. The complete cost of the show to your club or organization is only four hundred dollars. That is very low, considering it includes all officials needed to run the event, including judges, referees, handlers, etc." Lee never mentioned ring physicians or ambulances since he didn't bother arranging for doctors or emergency vehicles to be present at any of his boxing shows. The fighters or their corner men could handle any cuts or bruises and if there was anything more serious, Dick would holler, "IS THERE A DOCTOR IN THE HOUSE?"

He painted a glowing picture for his prospective clients. "If you sell tickets to five hundred of your members, their guests or the general public at two dollars apiece, your profit will be six hundred dollars. If you sell a thousand tickets at a dollar apiece, you will have the same return. When you see your dances and other promotional efforts have been in vain as far as profits are concerned, let us help your activities become moneymakers."

Dick exaggerated how large his organization was by claiming twenty five men were needed to stage a boxing show, when in reality he was doing it with far fewer than that. Several boxers appeared on the Biscayne Boxing Club's letterhead as holding executive positions, and Dwaine Simpson was listed as "Sales Manager." None of the boxers knew about it, let alone received compensation.

Most fundraisers were within easy driving distance of Miami but on weekends, Dick Lee's road show traveled to such places as Tallahassee, Gainesville, Tampa or Jacksonville. It was a grueling experience to drive long distances at night along Highway 27, the two lane road serving as the main route through the state. The entire crew traveled in three cars plus the truck carrying the boxing ring. Their caravan operated on a tight schedule, stopping only for gas and using rest rooms. No matter how far they had to drive, Lee's weary band returned home the same night. While riding back from Jacksonville, Dwaine found it difficult to sleep in a crowded car. The fighter next to him was dead to the world with his mouth open and using Dwaine's shoulder as a pillow. Simpson thought,

"Dick is really burnin' our candles at both ends." He and his fellow travelers didn't arrive back in Miami until mid-morning the next day. Simpson went through the ordeals because he needed the money.

Each fundraiser offered twenty eight rounds of boxing, consisting of four four-round bouts and two six rounders. Dick Lee tried to keep the shows from lasting more than an hour and a half by reducing the rounds to two minutes instead of the usual three. The boxers not only fought but also unloaded the ring, set it up, took it down after the show and packed it back into the truck. Lee kept a third of each of his fighters' purses because he had contracts with all of them to act as their manager and by doing this, was able to supply twelve fighters at a net cost of less than one hundred seventy dollars.

Every fundraising show was topped off with a Battle Royal. Six blindfolded boys between the ages of eight and ten were put in the ring and told, "Go at it!" They tried to fight for a full three minutes, but usually ended up tripping over each other, swinging away at thin air, going into a clinch or grappling on the canvas. It was always a big hit, and audiences would throw quarters and half dollars into the ring in appreciation of the boys' efforts. After Dwaine saw how much the kids were divvying up, he said to Dick Lee, "It ain't right. They made more tonight than I did."

Lee replied, "I'll getcha more money. Ya can fight the last four rounder."

The last four rounder often matched one of Lee's boxers against local men willing to try their hand at fighting. At the third fundraiser Simpson participated in, a hometown tough guy named Jeff Olney, who outweighed Simpson by over forty pounds, wanted a chance to get in the ring. Lee said to Dwaine, "Ya fight this guy Olney and there's an extra purse in it for ya."

Simpson had already fought and won the first four rounder. He looked at the overweight man with a shrewd eye and said, "He looks like a runaway beer truck. I'll take the fight." Dwaine's assessment proved correct. Jeff had never been taught how to box and repeatedly ran into Simpson's left jabs. He lasted less than two rounds before Dwaine was awarded a technical knockout. Simpson's two purses amounted to forty dollars but after Lee deducted for tape, gauze, a corner man and his manager's fee, the crew cut blonde family man ended up with $23.46. He did far better than Olney, who was paid nothing for taking a beating.

From that point on, Dwaine usually fought twice during each fundraiser, but had to be careful of which local fighters he took on. At a fundraiser held outdoors at a park in Hollywood by a railroad track, Dick Lee asked Dwaine to box a local boy who was 6'4" and weighed 165 pounds. Simpson said, "No, he's too big."

Lee replied, "Come on, you're twenny six, and he's only seventeen. Ya know the ropes, he don't."

"That's the problem. If I lose, people'll make fun of me. If I win, they'll hate me for beatin' up a kid."

The seventeen year old turned out to be Tony Alongi; a brash, gangly teenager with a long neck, long pointy chin and Tony Curtis spit curl. He was a heavyweight prospect backed by Chuck Serianni. Serianni had forty dollars to his name when he started Di-Mar Paving Company and in less than fifteen years became a millionaire with controlling interest in the Rolling Hills Golf and Country Club. The wealthy fight fan eventually hired Rocky Marciano and Rocky's legendary trainer Charley Goldman to guide his protégé. Under the guidance of Marciano and Goldman, Alongi developed into a heavyweight contender when he was in his early twenties. Even at seventeen, he would have been far too much for Dwaine to handle.

Dwaine ended up fighting nineteen year old Travis Weldon in the last four rounder of the Hollywood fundraiser. Weldon had been a star running back in high school and was home on leave from the Army. He had never been in a ring before and approached boxing as though playing linebacker. He unsuccessfully tried to run over Dwaine three times, suffered a cut in the second round and became very tired. Dwaine didn't try to take advantage of the wound, inflict a beating or knock the clean cut kid out. His corner threw in the towel in the third round, and Simpson was awarded a TKO.

Dick Lee's fundraising road shows continued until 1960, when the IBC was broken up due to violation of anti-trust laws. Attendance at Biscayne Arena went into a decline and Major W.H. Peeples chose to discontinue his weekly boxing shows. This brought an end to the Biscayne Boxing Club and Lee's traveling attraction. Many years later, Dwaine would talk about those times and say, "They did a movie about Dick's fundraisers called Dumb and Dumber."

A SMALL TIME PROMOTER GETS ANOTHER SHOT AT BECOMING BIG

Dick Lee was sitting in his bathrobe and striped pajamas with his morning coffee. He was reading the paper and almost wished he hadn't bothered. The sports page had a big write up about the latest Chris Dundee promotion at the Miami Beach Auditorium. Lee had no interest in the story because good news about the promoter who hailed from Philadelphia always upset him. It was because of jealousy. Dundee was an "A level" promoter, while Lee was strictly "Class C." He thought, "If it wasn't for the dago's connections with managers up north, he'd be nothin'. My day is comin'. Miami ain't like New York where there's no small clubs 'cuz of TV fights and closed circuit. People down here are starved for entertainment. I got forty pro fighters under contract, and can give 'em what they want... blood and knockouts."

He lit a cigarette, took a long drag, blew a smoke ring and thought, "Major Peeples and me made it work at Biscayne Arena. All I need's another place that'll let me run things my way. They's gotta be one out there and I'm gonna find it." The phone rang, and the voice on the other end said, "Dick, my name is Neil Composto. I don't know if you remember me... "

"Sure do. Ain't ya the guy who promotes stock car races?"

"You got it, Fridays at Hialeah Speedway and Saturdays at Palmetto Speedway. Look, Dick, I need your help. I'm working with some Masons who put up an air conditioned building on 2nd Avenue in Little River. They want attractions that sell tickets. They have wrestling on Tuesday nights and want boxing every Thursday. How many fighters do you have in your stable?"

"I got forty under contract."

"Well, that should do the job. Would you be interested in being my matchmaker?"

"How much the job pay?"

"A hundred and fifty each week there's a show. You'll have to pay for your phone calls, stationary and postage out of that."

"The money's okay. You know anythin' about boxing?"

"Nope."

"Ya let me handle things without buttin' in and we'll get along fine."

They agreed to meet the next day and after Lee hung up, he exclaimed, "Now's my chance!"

Composto had a full time job as executive director of both the Miami Showmen's Association and the organization's cemetery. Dick met with Neil at his office. After greeting each other, Composto spoke first. "Receipts from the first show, after expenses, have to go to the Masons' Crippled Children's Fund. How much will it cost to put it on?"

Lee replied, "When I was president of the Biscayne Boxing Club, I put on fundraisers with twenty eight rounds of boxing... four four rounders and two six rounders. Cost 'bout a hundred and seventy bucks for the fighters. The shows closed with a Battle Royal."

"What's that?"

"Ya put six liitle boys in a ring and blindfold 'em. Those kids would do some of the craziest stuff. The crowd loved it, and they'd throw money at 'em."

"That might be interesting."

"AND we can have the fighters set the ring up and take it down. That'll save a few bucks."

"How much does each fighter get for being in a show?"

"Twenny bucks for four rounds, thirty for six and fifty for a main event,"

"Will they fight for such small amounts?"

"If they don't follow orders, they don't get any fights. Also, I got jobs for some of 'em and if they don't go along, they lose their jobs. I also cut the amount of time for each round from three minutes to two minutes. With less time to work with, that'll make 'em more aggressive and we'll get more knockouts... and knockouts sell tickets."

Composto nodded his head. After taking a moment to process the information Lee had given him, he said, "Would you say that the entire cost... boxers, officials, everything... would be five hundred dollars?"

Lee chuckled and replied, "Not nearly that much. Since we wouldn't hafta go on the road, we could do it for three hundred."

Neil did some quick calculations on a note pad and then said, "Let's say we charge the Mason's five hundred. Figuring in all the expenses outside of the boxing, you and I should still be able to split nearly two hundred dollars. And that's in addition to your salary." This brought smiles to both their faces. Composto added, "Dick, there's charitable organizations who'd buy the boxing shows for five hundred bucks, as long as they get to keep all the receipts. I can think of the Jewish War Veterans for one."

"Sounds good to me. By the way, how many seats in the place?"

"Eight hundred twenty five."

"Well, if they charge a buck for general admission and two bucks for ringside, they oughta do all right."

"They should. After all, the place is air conditioned. Not every boxing arena can say that."

WEIGHINS ARENT ALWAYS WHAT THEY SEEM

Billy Hall showed up unexpectedly at Dwaine's job. After greeting each other, Hall said, "You're fightin' regularly at Little River, aren't ya?"

"Yeah, I can always use a few extra bucks."

Hall replied, "I need some dough too. Let's ask Dick Lee to put us on the card this week as middleweights."

"Fine with me, but there's one problem."

"What's that?" asked Hall. He had started as a welterweight, grown into a middleweight and had eaten his way out of the one hundred sixty pound weight class. His stomach lopped over his belt.

"Ya put on too much weight," said Dwaine.

"Whadya talkin' about?"

"I know where there's a scale. Let's see how much we weigh."

They went to a room in the recreation center with a regulation scale and weighed themselves. Dwaine was one forty and Billy tipped the bar at one seventy eight. Both would have to be within the one hundred sixty pound range in order to be permitted to fight as middleweights. Dwaine said, "We won't get past the weigh-in."

Billy replied, "Don't worry. I know what to do."

They went to the phone in Dwaine's office and Billy called Dick Lee. When he got the matchmaker on the line, he said, "Hey Dick, this is Billy Hall. I'm here with Dwaine Simpson. He says he's ready to fight me Thursday."

Prior to receiving the call, Lee was short one bout for that week's show. He thought, "Great! Now I have a full card," but didn't want to appear eager. He replied, "Wait a minute. I might hafta juggle a few things 'round." Lee set the receiver down and had his caller wait for over a minute before coming back on the line. "Coupla guys who never fought before wanna go four rounds to settle a grudge. Ah, I can put 'em on any time. Okay, I'll put ya and college boy down for four rounds. Ya get twenny bucks each and since it's only twenny, there'll be no deductions. Weigh in before noon Thursday."

"We'll be there," said Hall with a smile before hanging up. He turned to Dwaine and said, "It's all set. We weigh in Thursday morning."

"How we gonna get past that?"

"No problem, I have a plan."

Billy and Dwaine showed up at Little River Auditorium late Thursday morning. Before leaving their car, Hall handed Simpson two five-pound weights and said, "Put these in your pockets."

"You're crazy. This ain't gonna work."

"We'll see," replied Billy.

The two fighters headed straight to the room for weigh-ins. They walked in to find a man holding a clipboard who had been assigned to mark down fighters' weights on a form to be turned into the Miami Beach Boxing Commission. No one else was around.

The man with the clipboard asked, "You guys got any I.D.?"

"About what?" replied Dwaine.

Billy impatiently said, "He wants to see your driver's license."

"Oh," replied Simpson. The two fighters slipped their licenses out of their wallets and showed them to the inspector. He asked them, "What class you guys fightin' in?"

"Middleweight," answered Billy.

"Uh huh, that means you gotta make one sixty."

Simpson looked at his friend for a hint of what to do next.

Billy Hall scratched the back of his neck and said, "Uh… Dwaine, you go first."

Neither fighter removed their street clothes. Simpson stepped on the scale wearing his shoes, and his heart was beating so fast he was sure the inspector standing close to him on his right could hear it. The inspector didn't say a word until he announced Dwaine's weight as, "One hundred sixty pounds."

Simpson stepped off the scale and allowed Hall his turn on the device. The inspector once again stood very close to the right side of the man being weighed. Dwaine saw his friend stiffen his left arm as he stepped on the scale and knew what to do. He immediately placed a hand under the arm and then pulled up on it. The inspector announced Billy's weight as, "One hundred fifty eight pounds." The deception worked.

That night, Billy and Dwaine's fight went the distance and the judges scored it as a victory for Hall. Simpson was very unhappy with the result because he landed several jabs and was more aggressive than his opponent, but those scoring the fight didn't see it that way. The two friends sat in the dressing room after being paid twenty apiece. Billy could see Dwaine was unhappy, so he smiled, lit up a cigar, blew a lazy floating smoke ring and said, "Hey pal, forget how the judges voted. We both won tonight. We fooled the inspector, and we both got paid."

Simpson ran his right hand through his hair, sighed and tried to calm down before replying. "It ain't right. I was the one who held up your left arm and got ya through. I landed more punches and was more aggressive. By rights, I shoulda won. It ain't fair." Dwaine got up, grabbed his equipment bag and turned to leave. He said, "Buddy, I learned a lesson, 'Never help your opponent get through a weigh-in. It'll bite ya in the ass. Well, goodnight, Billy."

It was late when Dwaine got home, and he unlocked the front door as quietly as he could. He looked in on his children, who were sleeping soundly, before putting on his pajamas. After joining his beautiful wife in bed, he lay next to her and counted his blessings. The disappointment over losing the decision left him as he thought, "Billy's right, we both won. We had to get by the inspector to get paid, and we did it. I came home with money for Ramona and the kids, and nothin's more important than that."

He didn't want to awaken Ramona because he knew she needed her rest, but he gently put an arm around her so he would be holding and protecting her when she woke up.

ROAD TRIP TO HOMESTEAD

The phone rang in Dwaine's home. He picked it up and heard Dick Lee's voice on the other end of the line. "Hey college boy, got a fight for ya."

By now, Dwaine had become used to Lee's taunts and no longer responded with wisecracks. He felt it was better to keep everything businesslike. Simpson replied, "Fantastic! How much? How many rounds? Where?"

"Forty bucks for four rounds in Homestead. And I won't take none of the forty. It's all yours."

"I never fought in Homestead. Didn't know there were any arenas there."

"It ain't gonna be in an arena. It's in a nightclub. Meet me at Little River next Saturday at three. Gonna drive you and the other guys there."

"Fantastic! See ya then." Lee couldn't get over the absence of smart aleck remarks from the fighter he so despised.

When Simpson arrived at the Little River Auditorium, he found four other fighters waiting for Dick Lee. Lee pulled up a few minutes later in a dark blue six passenger Plymouth station wagon. Dwaine thought, "Lucky there's no heavyweights, or there wouldn't be 'nuff room."

After all the boxers were in the wagon, the promoter chuckled and said, "Anyone loses gets dumped on the side of the road with their clothes soaked in rum. That way, no one'll pick ya up." He cackled uproariously at his own joke, but the carload of fighters groaned in unison.

As Lee drove, he talked to the fighters about the show they'd be part of. "Rocky Marciano's gonna be the referee. There's gonna be five four-rounders." He told each fighter who their opponents would be. When he got to Dwaine, he said, "College boy, you're gettin' Charlie Allen."

"Charlie Allen... isn't he the middleweight who's a little crazy?"

"That's him, Boolah Boolah."

Simpson knew something about the man Lee matched him with. He weighed at least twenty pounds more than Dwaine, but the lanky blonde wasn't going to make an issue about it as he would have in the past. His top priorities were bringing forty bucks home to his family and leaving the ring uninjured. He thought, "I think I can handle Charlie. They say he don't train hard."

Dick Lee enjoyed talking so much he wouldn't turn his car radio on. The sound of his voice irritated Dwaine, and he had to do something to relax. He took out a copy of the Miami Herald he had brought along and placed it on his lap. He was sitting next to a window and rolled it down. He began tearing off pieces of the newspaper and tossing them out. The fighter next to him asked, "Whadya doin', Dwaine?"

"Whazzit look like I'm doin'?"

"Throwin' paper out the window."

"Wrong, I'm keepin' the elephants away."

"There ain't any elephants around here."

"See, it's workin'."

The other four fighters laughed so hard they nearly ran out of breath, and even Dick Lee was smiling. The humorous mood changed when they arrived at Harry Nedlow's Club Fantasia. Lee surprised his fighters by telling them, "Ya guys are gonna set up the ring." Dwaine thought, "No wonder he's not gonna deduct nothin' from my purse. He's gettin' extra work outta us, just like those damn fundraisers."

All ten fighters on the night's card tried to relax while waiting in the dressing room. This was done as a means of self preservation because tense fighters were more likely to be knocked out. Dwaine became so relaxed he was able to fall asleep on a rubbing table. Charlie Allen walked up to the table while Simpson dozed and said, "Dwaine, I don't know if I can go four rounds. It's been six months since I trained every day."

Simpson raised himself on an elbow and asked, "Whydja take the fight?"

"Got into a jam and had to come up with some dough or go ta jail. Harry Nedlow paid off what I owed, and I pay him back by doin' different jobs... like fightin' tonight."

"Who's Nedlow?"

"A friend of Marciano's. They was partners in a potato farm in Perrine. Some guy named Tucci up in New York put 'em onto the deal, but the weather went against 'em and they lost millions."

"I wonder if all that worryin' 'bout money is why Rocky put on so much weight," said Simpson. "He must weigh 'bout 250 or 260."

"Yeah, he's a lot bigger'n when he was fightin'. I put on a few pounds too."

Dwaine took a good look at his flabby opponent. Charlie was hardly in top condition. He seemed like a nice guy, so Simpson said, "Ya outweigh me, and it's gonna be my job to keep away from ya. But if ya run outta gas, I'm gonna knock ya out."

"Fair 'nuff."

Dwaine went back to sleep until it was time to go to the ring. Simpson didn't bring along his unicycle for his usual entrance, so he walked along a path cleared through the noisy fight fans packed into the nightclub. The first round of his bout was uneventful until Allen got close enough to attempt a hard punch with his right hand. Simpson ducked low, causing his opponent to miss, but inadvertently caught Charlie with a head butt when he straightened up. Rocky Marciano saw it happen, realized it was unintentional and didn't deduct any points. The out of condition middleweight suffered a cut because of the blow from Dwaine's noggin, but courageously fought on until the end of the bout. After it was announced Dwaine had been awarded the decision, he went to his opponent, shook his hand and said, "I'm sorry I hurt ya the way I did."

"That's all right, Dwaine, I know ya didn't mean it."

The two fighters were unaware of the frantic gambling going on. In addition to wagers on who would win each fight, bets were made on who would score the first knockdown, which boxer would hit the deck first, which round would end the fight and which corner of the ring would have the most winners. A great deal of money changed hands. The boxers also did not know Nedlow had paid Dick Lee eight hundred dollars to supply five fighters; $160 for each man he sent into the ring. This was why Lee was willing to pay his boxers forty dollars and not make any deductions.

For Dwaine, the evening was as enjoyable a time as any spent in the company of overbearing and controlling Dick Lee could possibly be. As Lee's station wagon rolled along through the Florida night, Dwaine felt drowsy but found it impossible to sleep with the middle passenger in the back seat leaning against him and having to listen to Lee's monologue about his childhood. He felt at peace and thought, "I met a nice guy, won a decision and have forty bucks to give to Ramona. It doesn't bug me to hear Dick go on and on. Maybe he's just tryin' to stay awake."

He heard Dick say, "When I was a kid, I put on fights in a boat shed next ta where we lived. I got all the other kids in the neighborhood ta go along. The boys fought and the girls were the corner men. The boys wore their bathrobes into the ring. We charged ten cents to watch the fights, and get forty or fifty grownups to pay. One time, we had nearly a hunnert grownups watchin' and... "

Dwaine thought, "A hunnert grownups givin' him ten cents each must come to somewhere between seven and ten bucks. He prolly paid each fighter a nickel and deducted two cents for some sort of fee. He's always been the same and nothin' will ever change, but I feel too good tonight to let him bother me."

Lee stopped his monologue long enough to ask Dwaine, "Hey college boy, how come we been gettin' along so well lately?"

"I learned a magic word."

"What's the word?"

"Fantastic."

"Come to think of it, ya been sayin' that a lot. Every time I tell ya to do somethin', ya always say 'Fantastic.' Why's that?"

"I'd really like to say 'bullshit,' but say 'fantastic' instead. It seems to keep me outta trouble."

"Whatever works is fine with me," replied the manager. "Glad to see you're finally gettin' your mind right. I hafta admit you're startin' ta grow on me. Jes' hope you're not like a fungus."

SIMPSONS FIRST SOUTHPAW OPPONENT

Dwaine became so eager for fights Neil Composto and Dick Lee began calling him "The Little River Houseboy." He was always at their boxing shows and if not scheduled on the card, was ready to pick up cash as a last minute replacement. He stored his equipment in his car and kept himself in good enough shape to go four, six or even eight rounds at the drop of a hat. One night before a boxing show began, Simpson had just eaten a twenty five cent hot dog and washed it down with a fifteen cent Coca Cola when Dick Lee came to him and said, "I need a four round fight. Can ya do me a favor?"

"What kinda favor?" Dwaine knew Dick didn't really believe in favors because he would never reciprocate.

"A roofer named Charlie Spears has been comin' to the fights with his friends and guys he works with. He's been askin' me to put him in the ring, so I matched him with a roofer who worked for a different company. Fifty of his buddies paid for ringside seats and wouldn't ya know it, the other guy never showed up." Lee puffed on his cigar before continuing. "Charlie asked about fightin' ya." There was a glint in Lee's eye as he added, "He says he's never boxed before, but claims he's a good street fighter. He's also left handed." This was an oddity. There were very few left handed fighters because any of those naturally left handed had to switch to an orthodox right handed style or no one would box them.

"Don't know if I wanna fight him," said Dwaine.

"His buddies wanna see him fight."

"For how much?"

"Thirty bucks for four rounds... and I won't deduct nothin'."

Dwaine nodded and said, "Sold American." Thirty dollars would easily cover the cost of new shoes for his four kids.

He went to his car, picked up the bag containing his fancy red robe with the clown on the back, red boxing trunks and red boxing shoes. He returned to the arena and asked Lee, "Where's this guy I'm s'posed to fight?"

Dick pointed out Charlie Spears, who had already weighed in. Spears had bright red hair and tattoos all over his body, including one around his neck consisting of a series of dots and the words "Cut on Dotted Line."

The roofer was 5'6", had weighed in at a hundred fifty and was built like a tree stump. Spears watched Dwaine weigh in. As Simpson stepped on the scale, he asked his much shorter opponent, "Whadya really weigh?"

"You'll think I weigh two tons when I'm on your ass!"

Dwaine thought, "Where'd he come from? Maybe prison or the service?"

Spears was beginning to frighten the lanky blonde fighter, and he thought, "What's the best way of handlin' this guy?" An idea suddenly came to him. He went up to the roofer and asked, "Are ya left handed?"

"Yeah, what's it to ya?"

"Ya know, society thinks havin' red hair and bein' left handed is a curse but if ya only have one or the other, ya gotta chance at life."

The remark infuriated Charlie Spears. He started to take a swing at Dwaine, but his friends grabbed him in time to hold him back. Simpson thought, "Just what I wanted. He's mad at me."

The roofer entered the ring in a rage and foolishly began the fight by rushing Simpson like a wild eyed bull. Spears ran into every punch Dwaine threw. Sometimes, the lanky blonde would step out of the way, let the tattooed man run into the ropes and pop him in the head as he went by. Dwaine was far from a hard puncher, but the roofer sustained serious cuts by causing damage to himself. Still, he never gave up and was determined to beat the hell out of a man he couldn't lay a hand on. By the third round, Spears was exhausted and Dwaine asked the referee to stop the fight. The ref agreed there was no need to continue and awarded a TKO to the fighter with the nifty feet and feather fists.

A few minutes later, Dick Lee paid Dwaine his thirty dollars. Simpson was in no mood to hang around for compliments or admiration from other fighters or any fans. He simply wanted to head home to his wife and kids, safe and sound. He had almost reached the doorway of the dressing room when Lee said, "Ya never fought a southpaw before, didja?"

"Ya mean a left hander?"

"'Course I mean a left handed fighter," Lee replied in an exasperated tone. "Don't ya know what a southpaw is, dumb shit?"

Simpson said, "Yeah, I guess it was the first time I fought a left handed guy." Dwaine was about to turn and leave, but stopped to ask the matchmaker, "Say Dick, if they call left handed people southpaws, why don't they call right handed people 'northpaws'?"

"'Cuz only dumb ass college boys like YOU get such crazy ideas."

SUGARFOOT ATTRACTS RATS

Dwaine noticed a group of twenty young men, ranging in age from late teens to mid twenties, who always sat together whenever he fought. Some were accompanied by girls in poodle skirts, penny loafers and bobby sox.

They were a boisterous group who cheered for Dwaine at the top of their lungs. One night, he heard them shout, "COME ON, SUGARFOOT! YOU CAN TAKE 'IM!" His first thought was, "They like the way I move my feet." Dwaine remembered when he danced the Sugarfoot to the Bill Doggett instrumental Honky Tonk.

Simpson won his fight that night and smiled when his group of admirers hooted and hollered over his victory, acting as though he won a world title. He was heading to the dressing room when he was approached by one of the group, a tall young man dressed in white rubber soled oxfords, gray slacks without cuffs or belt loops and a blue sport coat. He said, "I'm Bobby Bann, president of the Little River Rats."

"What's that?"

"Some people call it a 'social gang.'"

Dwaine thought, "When they handed out looks, they didn't do this guy or his family any favors. His momma prolly looks like the wicked witch in the Wizard of Oz and his dad like Popeye the Sailor Man, but he's a sharp dresser." He asked Bobby, "What's a social gang?"

"We have a lotta activities and allow girls to be part of 'em." Simpson thought, "It sounds harmless."

Another boy shorter than Bobby walked up, and Bann introduced him. "This is Ronnie Nemo. He's also in the gang." Ronnie nodded at Dwaine. He had hooded eyes, a curled lip and didn't seem as friendly as the gang's leader. Dwaine thought, "He reminds me of the guy who sat behind me in eighth grade and poked me with a pencil, then gave me a dirty look when I asked him to stop."

"We've been comin' to a lot of your fights," said Bobby. "You were great tonight. It's always fun watchin' you. We never know what's gonna happen next."

"I guess ya guys like the way I move my feet, 'cuz I heard ya callin' me 'Sugarfoot.' Ya know, I used to do a dance called the Sugarfoot."

"I don't know anything about that dance. We called you that because of Sugarfoot on TV."

Dwaine had never seen the show, so he wasn't sure what the kid meant. He said to his young admirer, "Well, Bobby, I gotta get inta the shower before this place runs outta hot water."

"Don't lemme keep ya," replied the young man. "Ya gonna fight next week?"

"I'll be here."

"Maybe we can talk some more."

"Okay."

During his drive home, Dwaine kept trying to remember anything he might have heard about the TV show the kid mentioned. He thought, "Ramona would know. She keeps up with all that television stuff."

After he walked in the house, greeted his wife with a hug and a kiss and handed her the money he'd been paid, he asked her how the kids were. "They're all fine for a change," she replied, "Nobody's sick and they're all asleep."

Dwaine went to check on them and when he returned to his wife, asked, "Honey?"

"Yes, dear."

"Do ya ever watch Sugarfoot on TV?

"Once in a while."

"What kinda show is it?"

"Well, it's a western about this cute blonde guy played by Will Hutchins who's not a rough, tough cowboy. They make jokes about him because he orders soda pop instead of whiskey when he's in a bar."

"Why would anybody watch that? Doesn't sound like he can shoot or fight."

"Oh, he can shoot and fight a little, but he's not like John Wayne or James Arness on Gunsmoke. Why do you wanna know?"

"Somebody said I looked like the guy in the show."

"Oh, you're better looking than he is. I always thought you looked like Paul Newman."

Dwaine replied, "Ya need eyeglasses. Everyone's sayin' I look like Alfred E. Neuman in Mad Magazine."

YOU NEVER KNOW WHO YOULL MEET IN THE RING

Dwaine often sparred with a black middleweight named Willie "Cadillac" James who was also part of Dick Lee's stable. The middleweight's face was easily noticed due to puffiness around his eyes from taking too many punches before his wounds had sufficient time to heal. Willie acquired his nickname because he constantly said, "Jes' wanna make enough for a Cadillac. I likes Cadillacs 'cuz they're nice year 'round cars." When Dwaine asked what he meant by a "year 'round car," the middleweight replied, "They got a heater AND air conditionin'."

Simpson said, "It'd be great to drive with the windows up and not be sittin' in a pool of sweat. If ya get a Caddy, lemme know and ya can take me for a ride."

"I will," promised Cadillac.

In pursuit of his dream of making enough to buy a Caddy, the 5'8" middleweight traveled to Massachusetts, Maine, Canada and even Italy to fight. He lost many times in many places and often to truly distinguished opponents. He never did get his Cadillac, but still kept his same pleasant smile.

Cadillac weighed eighteen pounds more than Dwaine, but there was mutual respect between them and neither tried to hurt the other whenever they sparred. One day in the Wynnwood Park gym, Dick Lee ordered James and Simpson to spar. Dwaine was surprised when the workout became unusually heated. Cadillac James was forcing him to the ropes and trying to knock him out. Simpson asked, "What the hell's goin' on, Willie?" There was silence from the middleweight.

James avoided eye contact with Dwaine and just nodded his head at someone standing behind the blonde fighter. Dwaine turned around in time to see Dick Lee punch the palm of his left hand with his right fist. It was a signal for Willie to go after his opponent and knock him out. Simpson shouted, "HOLD IT! THAT'S IT!"

Dick said, "What ya doin'?"

"I'm not sparrin' anymore."

"Why?"

"Hell, Willie's too tough for me. He's bigger'n me and you're tellin' him to beat me up."

A cigar clenched in Lee's teeth bobbed up and down as he hissed, "Ya can't quit in the middle of a round!"

Dwaine responded, "Ya get your little fat ass up here in the ring and spar him yourself if ya don't want the round interrupted. I'm under contract with ya. You're s'posed to be my damn manager and lookin' out for me and ya pull that crap."

Lee's response was, "Grow up. It's time ya learned friends, relatives and fighters ain't any damn good unless ya can use 'em to your advantage. If I can ever turn ya into an inside fighter, it'll be an advantage for both of us."

Simpson quickly removed his gloves, angrily stomped off to the dressing room, changed without showering and left the building with Dick Lee's cries of, "YA HAVEN'T GOT THE GUTS TO BE A MAIN EVENT FIGHTER!" ringing in his ears.

Jack McKiernan was entering the gym as Dwaine stormed out. He could see his friend was very upset and asked, "What's the problem, buddy?"

"Jack, loan me your double holster and Colt 45's so I can murder a sonuvabitch in the first degree."

"Who ya talkin' about?'

"Dick Lee. Bastard ordered Cadillac James ta beat the shit outta me. He should be cultivatin' me, but he's plowin' me under. I swear he graduated from a course in sneakiness magna cum loudmouth."

"Ya mean magna cum laude."

"That's what I said."

"Cool off, pal. He's not worth killin'. Ya got a wife and kids ta worry about."

"You're right. I'll just stay away from him for awhile."

Dwaine stopped going to gyms for workouts with heavy bags and speed bags. He developed his own method of conditioning and stayed in shape by playing basketball and riding his unicycle. He would sometimes go to the beach on weekends and spar outdoors with men in their late teens and early twenties interested in learning how to box.

After their blowup, Dick treated Dwaine like a red headed stepchild for a couple of weeks before they declared a truce and resumed their arrangement. Lee would continue to act as the lanky blonde's manager, but Simpson steered clear of any gyms associated with him and was allowed to use his own methods of staying in shape.

Simpson's first fight after the two let bygones be bygones, was against "Irish Gene" Robinson in the Miami Beach Auditorium. It was a preliminary to a sold out bout between light heavyweights Gregorio Peralta from Argentina and Willie Pastrano, a native of New Orleans fighting out of Miami. Robinson was given the fight moniker "Irish Gene" to make sure the paying customers knew he was white. This helped sell tickets.

The boxing show took place while Ramona and the children were visiting her mother in Washington, D.C. It had been awhile since Dwaine was left alone for a week and didn't know how to prepare any meals. After that, he learned how to fry eggs and fix other simple dishes. On the morning of his fight with Irish Gene, he went to the refrigerator and found only one egg left, which happened to have a brown shell. When he cracked it open, he saw the egg was filled with blood. He said out loud, "Man, some rooster musta had a lotta fun with a hen!"

Dwaine wondered if he should throw the egg out, but it was the only one he had. He thought, "Long as I cook it and make sure it's done all the way through, it should be all right." After his egg, toast and coffee were ready, he sat down to breakfast. As he put the first forkful of the bloody egg in his mouth, he thought, "Ummm, not too bad."

That night while Simpson was going through final preparations in a dressing room at the Miami Beach Auditorium, Angelo Dundee, Willie Pastrano's trainer, walked in. He was accompanied by a slender man in his sixties with eyes like blue green ice cubes, stooped shoulders and a shuffling gait. Dundee said, "Dwaine, I'd like you to meet Evil Eye Finkle... greatest hexer in the world."

Simpson shook hands with Finkle and asked, "What does a hexer do?"

"I'm paid to put the evil eye on people. Angelo's asked me to put the whammy on Peralta."

"Is that like a curse or voodoo?"

"Pretty much. I've got dybbuk blood in me. That's Jewish voodoo."

Dwaine turned to Dundee and asked, "Is he on the level?"

"Absolutely," replied Angelo. "During the war, he was assigned to put a hex on Hitler. Tell'im what happened, Evil Eye."

"A general had me stationed on the top floor of the tallest hotel in Paris. He pointed in the direction of Germany and said, 'See what you can do.' Every day, I'd go through all my hexes. Two weeks after I started, word came back Hitler killed himself."

Dwaine looked at Evil Eye Finkle in amazement and said, "I'd never want ya ta get mad at ME." The hexer beamed proudly.

Angelo Dundee spoke up. "I came by to tell you something about this Irish Gene guy you're going to box. He outweighs you by a little bit and was one of Willie's sparring partners. Willie says he's a tough sonuvabitch. He doesn't smoke, drink or use profanity and has never fought as a pro before, but he can really hit."

"What the hell ya tellin' me this for? You're scarin' me to death!"

"Just thought you'd like to know."

Simpson turned to Evil Eye Finkle and asked, "Can ya put a hex on Irish Gene for me?"

The man renowned for his supernaturally powerful right eye replied, "There's a slight fee involved."

"How much?"

"A hundred dollars."

"A hunnert bucks! Ya might as well ask for a million. I'll just hafta keep runnin' and try ta stay away from the guy."

Dundee and Finkle's visit had upset the lanky blonde. Dwaine was more worried than he had ever been before a fight. Butterflies swirled in his stomach, and his mind was racing a hundred miles an hour. He became more frightened when he first saw Gene Robinson. The fighter had no neck and muscle layered upon muscle.

All his concern was for nothing, because his bout with Robinson turned out to be his greatest night in the ring. He could do nothing wrong. His hands were magically transformed from fists of putty to deadly weapons. He didn't miss any openings and every time he saw one, he delivered punches that connected. His left jabs were like pistons operating at the speed of a bullet. He threw punches in bunches and all were on target. Irish Gene displayed how tough he was by standing up to the assault. His legs wobbled, but he stayed on his feet the entire four rounds. Simpson landed so many blows he won the decision on points. As the lanky crew cut blonde's hand was raised in victory, he thought, "The bloody egg had the power of male sperm in it! That's what did it for me." Later that night, Willie Pastrano lost a unanimous decision to Gregorio Peralta, despite Evil Eye Finkle's hex on the tall Argentinian with slender arms and legs. After seeing that, Dwaine knew he was onto something. He thought, "I don't need hexes or voodoo. All I gotta do is eat eggs with blood in 'em."

He became even more convinced of his secret weapon when Gordon Van Loo, one of the other boxers, called him the next day to say, "That Robinson guy you fought asked several people for your address. They told 'im I knew it. When he asked me, I said, 'Why ya wanna know?' He got really pissed and said, 'I'm gonna go to his house and beat his brains in.'"

"Didja give him my address?"

"I thought about it, but then remembered ya owe me ten bucks. If I tol' him where ya lived, I might never see the money. So, I tol' 'im, 'They're wrong. I useta know, but he moved.' Ya better watch your butt, 'cuz he might still be lookin' for ya. By the way, when ya gonna have my ten?" Dwaine promised to pay up later that week.

There was no doubt in Dwaine's mind he was onto something. He had beaten the most dangerous man he'd ever faced because of an egg filled with blood. They were worth their weight in gold, and he had to get as many as he could. He called Ronnie Pierson, his friend who had a dairy business. When Pierson was on the line, Dwaine said, "Ronnie, I just fought my greatest fight!"

"I know, I was there, remember? I was gonna ask if ya did anything different in the way ya trained."

"That's what I'm gettin' at. Do ya know anythin' 'bout chickens and eggs?"

"Sure, I grew up on a farm."

"Where can I get eggs with blood in 'em?"

"Well, ya never know until ya crack 'em open. You can't just find 'em. They happen. Why ya askin'?"

"'Cuz I ate a bloody egg before the fight that put the power of male sperm in me, and that's how I won. I gotta get all the bloody eggs I can. If I eat enough of 'em, I might get a killer knockout punch and if I had that, I'd be world champion. Man, if I ever won a title, I'd never take my championship belt off. I'd even wear it to bed. Come to think of it, I don't know if Ramona would put up with that. What do ya think? "

Ronnie chuckled and replied, "I don't know what she'd say about wearin' that belt to bed and as far as the bloody eggs go, well, I hate to tell ya, Dwaine, but I've never heard about bloody yolks havin' rooster sperm in 'em. I was always told it's caused by a tear in the hen's egg makin' system. If there's a tear, blood can get trapped in an egg as it forms."

"I say it came from a rooster, and that makes it male sperm."

"Maybe you've got somethin' there," said Ronnie. "I know it's okay to eat bloody eggs. My dad used to say, 'The blood is just a little extra drop of protein.'"

"Ya sure there's no way ya can tell if an egg has blood in it?"

"Well, brown eggs are more likely to have blood than white ones. Ya might find more bloody ones at small farms."

"Thanks, Ronnie. Ya been a big help."

For the next few months, Dwaine tried to buy nothing but brown eggs. He was thrilled whenever he found ones with blood in their yolks and savored them, thinking they were making him stronger. Ramona didn't agree, was nauseated at the thought and made Dwaine cook his own eggs. She also worried the blood filled eggs would cause problems for her husband but after a while, there didn't seem to be any negative effects. After a year went by and Dwaine's punches were no more powerful than before, he decided to stop trying to eat so many bloody eggs. He concluded, "They're so hard to find I'll never be able to eat enough of 'em. Maybe I was just lucky to get sperm from a super powerful rooster when I fought Gene Robinson."

He forgot about Robinson until twenty two years later when he happened to see his former opponent's picture in a front page newspaper story. Simpson was sitting in his office as he read every word of the lengthy article. One of his co workers walked in and asked, "What's so interesting?"

"I'm readin' about this guy I fought a long time ago. It says he turned himself in to the FBI here in Miami. They been huntin' him for four days."

"What'd he do?"

Dwaine looked up from his paper and said, "Shot two FBI men."

"Wow! And you fought that guy?"

"Yeah." Dwaine's eyes were suddenly attracted to a paragraph in the newspaper story. He said to his co worker, "Listen to this," and began reading the article aloud. "Robinson had been a fugitive for six years at the time he shot the FBI agents. Lawmen marveled at his coolness under fire, his skill in planning, his flair for disguising himself with masks, wigs and dyed hair. He could aim and suddenly release a blow hard enough to tear patches of hair from another person's scalp." Dwaine shook his head and added, "Ya know, I won a decision over this guy, and he was so upset he tried to find out where I lived so he could beat me up."

"That's crazy."

"Lucky for me I caught him on an off day. It goes to show you never know who you'll meet in the ring."

BOXING ON THE HIGH SEAS

His growing family kept Dwaine in a financial bind and made him willing to take as many fights as he could. He was sitting on a bench in the Little River Auditorium's dressing quarters when Buddy Pack approached him and said, "Howdja like to fight a ten round main event for a hunnert dollars?"

A hundred bucks was a sizeable sum. Dwaine had received a raise by transferring from Opa-Locka's parks and recreation to the water department but was making only seventy five a week. He also liked working with Buddy Pack more than Dick Lee. Buddy was all about money while with Dick it was about both money and control. "Just tell me when and where," he replied.

"In three weeks. It's gonna be on a cruise ship."

"A cruise ship! Never been on one. I didn't know they boxed on boats."

"Don't let the captain hear ya call it a boat. It's a big ship with hundreds of passengers. We'll be makin' history! I'm callin' it 'The First Boxing Show Held at Sea.'" Pack moved his hands as he spoke, as if placing letters on a marquee. "Boxing Illustrated said they'll do a big story on it."

"Who ya want me to fight?"

"Bobby Marie."

Simpson thought, "Oh brother!" He had fought Bobby Marie in a four round preliminary at the Miami Beach Auditorium. At the time, Marie was an unknown fighter. Billy Hall was present when he weighed in and told Dwaine, "You're gonna knock him out 'cuz he's the skinniest, weakest, most pitiful lookin' boxer I ever seen." This made the lanky blonde tingle with anticipation because he seldom knocked anyone out.

He didn't see his opponent until Bobby entered the ring. He was wearing a blue satin robe with "Tri State Golden Gloves Champion" on the back. Dwaine thought, "He prolly borrowed it from somebody." Marie was skinny, with no chest and pipe stems for arms and legs. He was so pale the white trunks he wore looked like a tanned part of his body. Simpson made a huge mistake by not fighting in his usual style. The thought of putting his opponent on the canvas was firmly planted in his mind. From the very start of the bout, he tried to knock out the Youngstown, Ohio native and in the process, was made to look ridiculous. Bobby gave Dwaine a boxing lesson for four rounds and won a decision.

Simpson asked Pack, "What's Bobby's record now?"

"9 and 0."

Dwaine ran his hand through his hair and pursed his lips before saying, "I'll fight for a hundred dollars, but not ten three-minute rounds. I'll go eight two-minute rounds."

He expected an argument from Buddy, but the promoter surprised him by quickly accepting his terms. Dwaine thought, "They must think I'll be easy for Bobby." Pack concluded the negotiations by saying, "Be at the pier at Biscayne Boulevard at eight thirty at night on May eighth."

When Simpson showed up at the appointed time, he was directed to a gaudily painted 240 foot cruise ship named the Orange Sun. A sign posted at the gangway read, "Tickets for Cruise $6.50." Dwaine thought, "That's more'n three times what people pay for ringside seats. Somebody's makin' money."

He made his way up the gangway, was allowed to board the vessel after his name was checked against a list and walked into a floating night club, complete with a five piece calypso band and gambling tables. A large number of passengers were gulping down free drinks as fast as six harried waitresses could serve them.

Buddy Pack noticed Dwaine and greeted him with a smile. "Glad ya made it. Lemme show ya to the dressing room. We lucked out. The sea is very calm tonight."

As they walked around the ship, the short, stout promoter proudly pointed out the ring. "They said it couldn't be done, but there it is!" Dwaine took one look and thought, "Hell no!"

The ring had been hastily assembled by tying ropes around four iron poles supporting the deck, and the ropes were only ten feet long on each side. This was less than half the regulation length of twenty to twenty four feet. Dwaine was shocked to see an absence of padding on the poles. He thought, "What if my head bounces off a pole? I could die here." It was too late to back out, so he had to go through with it. Besides, he needed the money.

When he entered a room being used for the fighters' dressing quarters, his pale, slender opponent had already changed into his boxing gear. Simpson walked up to the man he was about to fight, shook his hand and said, "How's it goin', Bobby."

"Fine, how you been?"

"Okay."

Neither fighter was interested in chit chat. Rather than hang around the dressing room, the Youngstown lightweight turned to his handler and said, "I'm gonna run a coupla laps 'round the deck. Gotta get my legs used to the rockin' and rollin' of that water." Dwaine chose to sit in the dressing room until called to fight. When the time finally arrived and he made his way to the tiny boxing ring, he overheard someone say, "Didja hear what happened to Sonny Jordan? He didn't really get knocked out. He went down 'cuz he was seasick." Dwaine thought, "Oh great, now I gotta worry about pukin' all over the ring in the middle of a round."

The start of the main event was delayed so two local boxing celebrities could be introduced by ring announcer Sammy Spear, who was moonlighting from his regular job as Jackie Gleason's bandleader. Spear, known for his flamboyant jackets, was clad in an animal print blazer which once caused Gleason to quip,

"I've heard of Tiger Rag, but this is ridiculous." Willie Pastrano, the reigning world light heavyweight champ, and 230 pound Ollie Wilson, a heavyweight who was one of Muhammad Ali's sparring partners, walked to the center of the ring, waved to the crowd and shook hands with Bobby and Dwaine. The ring was so small the fighters were able stand in their corners and shake hands with the celebrities. There was so little distance between the boxers they held a conversation without raising their voices. Simpson said to Marie, "Hell, we don't have to walk into the center to shake hands. It's like doin' the mambo in a phone booth." Bobby smiled in response.

The passengers were the same mixture of tourists, elderly couples and teenagers found on any cruise ship. While preliminary bouts were contested, more and more of them began drifting away from the fight deck to feed slot machines or play other casino games. The clicking and ringing of the one armed bandits combined with groans of frustration from losers to form a strange backdrop for the main event.

At the opening bell, Simpson tried to go into his usual routine of fast stepping, running and clowning, but when he attempted to reel like a merry go round after springing off the ropes, he found himself jaw to jaw with Bobby Marie. He tried to skip around his opponent, but discovered it was like walking uphill and couldn't get anywhere. Any attempts at bobbing and weaving were foiled by the rhythm of the waves, and he couldn't solidly plant his feet where he wanted. Between rounds, Dwaine said to his corner man, "If the sea's calm tonight, I'd hate to be here if it was rough."

Early in the second round, the fighter from the Ohio steel town took advantage of the close quarters to land a short, quick punch that rocked Dwaine. The lanky blonde thought, "He didn't hit me that hard, but my legs are wigglin' like Elvis. Hey, I just remembered. We're on a boat that's rollin' and shakin'."

The fight lasted the full eight rounds, and it took a long time and a great deal of conversation before the judges arrived at a decision. One argued, "Marie hit Simpson consistently in the early going, but Simpson cut Marie over the eye in the seventh round and won the last two." Another judge took a drag on his cigarette before saying, "Neither of 'em showed me much punching power." The impatient crowd began chanting, "DRAW! DRAW! DRAW!" Simpson said to his corner man, "What is this, an art class?"

Sammy Spear ended the suspense by intoning over his microphone, "The fight has been declared a draw." Bobby Marie angrily blurted out, "BULLSHIT!" Dwaine shook his opponent's hand and said, "Don't worry about it. I think you won, but maybe they just liked my personality."

"Ah, they're blind," Marie replied. He eyed Simpson suspiciously and said, "Ya didn't pay 'em off, didja?"

"With what? I'm poorer than you. Look at it this way. We're 'Co-Champions of the Atlantic Ocean.'"

That remark brought a smile to Bobby's face. He said, "You're right. I've never been through anything like this. I wouldn't do it again, 'less they paid me a lot more."

Dwaine replied, "If they come up with the dough, I'll go along with a rematch. But I wouldn't hold my breath."

The boxing card was over at ten forty five, but gambling and partying went on long after the ring had been taken down. The Orange Sun followed a circular course until two in the morning, which was perfectly all right with those on a winning streak. A man way ahead in blackjack took off his short brimmed felt hat and placed it next to him at the table. He was so absorbed in the game he mistakenly rested a lit cigarette butt on the hat instead of an ashtray. He forgot about the cigarette and when told it was time to go, put on his headwear, not realizing it was smoldering. Lucky for him, George Rothsiden, general manager of the ship, was there to put out the fire with a seltzer bottle.

Just as the cruise ended, a short, chunky woman named Eloise pulled a lever on a quarter slot machine and three sevens came up. The machine lit up and emitted a loud "DING, DING, DING." Three hundred silver dollars poured into its tray. After scooping her winnings into a purse, she started to walk away from the one armed bandit, but quickly turned around. She changed her mind about leaving and was about to sit down at the same machine when one of the men working in the gambling area said, "All passengers must leave the ship."

She argued, "Please let me try again. Sometimes they hit consecutively."

"No, ma'am. It's time to go. No passengers can remain onboard."

Eloise glared at the man and said, "I don't care. I'm not leaving this machine until I'm finished with it."

He called out to a co worker. "Give me a hand. This woman won't leave." The two men picked up both Eloise and the stool she was sitting on. As they carried her to the gangway, she hollered, "YOU'RE ANGRY I WON A JACKPOT AND YA DIDN'T WANT ME TO GET ANOTHER ONE! YA KNEW I WAS ON A HOT MACHINE!"

The men carrying the jackpot winner were stoically silent. As they approached a couple waiting in line to exit the ship, the husband shouted, "THEY'RE DOIN' YA A FAVOR BY KEEPIN' YA FROM GIVIN' IT BACK TO THE ONE ARMED BANDITS."

George Rothsiden and Buddy Pack watched Eloise being forcibly removed from the ship. George shook his head and said, "Some people don't know when to quit. If I'd let her, she'd sit at the slot machine 'til she gave it all back and more."

Buddy said, "Guess that's why casinos are open twenty four hours. They make sure the suckers have enough time to lose everything."

Everyone but Eloise seemed to have had a good time when the cruise vessel finally docked past three in the morning. There were losers at the gambling tables and nearly half the boxers lost their fights, but Bobby Marie and Dwaine Simpson were not among them. They came home even-steven, with money in their pockets. Buddy Pack was pleased with the feature story that appeared in Boxing Illustrated, but decided against holding more "boxing shows at sea." Pack had learned a hard lesson: Oceans will never be calm enough for prizefights on cruise ships.

THE TRAGEDY OF TONY MAMARELLI

Dick Lee needed a constant flow of boxing talent to assure enough available fighters for each weight class. To solve this problem, he took advantage of the rapid growth of Miami area businesses desiring full time employees. He acted as an unofficial labor agent by luring fighters from northern cities with promises of "sunshine, steady jobs and a chance to make even more money boxing." Marv Tragash, a fight fan who owned a fruit and vegetable packing plant in South Dade, was one of the businessmen Lee supplied with workers.

Tony Mamarelli and Tommy Schafer were two lightweight fighters from Pittsburgh who arrived in Miami on a Greyhound bus and were put on Tragash's payroll the same day they signed management contracts with Lee. Twenty one year old Mamarelli came highly touted. Dick Lee boasted, "He's a carbon copy of Willie Pep. Ya heard of guys who can catch a fly with their hands, well Tony's so quick he can snatch five at a time. He's gonna be a world champ." Schafer was not as highly regarded, but was the sort of rugged prospect Lee used to fill out boxing cards. He had served in the U.S. Marine Corps and worked as a gravedigger up north. Life in Florida was a definite improvement over digging up frozen soil for funerals held in the dead of winter.

Three weeks after Dwaine fought on the cruise ship, he was hired to work in Tony Mamarelli's corner for what would be the Pittsburgh native's biggest fight. He was matched against Henry Dominguez in a ten round main event at Miami's Dinner Key Auditorium. Dominguez was from Odessa, Texas and had a New York manager named Honest Bill Daly, who had been linked to organized crime for decades. Mamarelli came into the fight with a 19-0 record, while Dominguez was 16-2-1, with eleven of his wins coming by way of knockout. It would be the first time he fought outside the state of Texas.

The Texan went after Tony in an all-enveloping rush and transformed into a wrathful tornado of flying leather. He hooked, jolted and beat on Mamarelli savagely. Tony's nose was smashed and bleeding, his mouth was crushed in the second round and he suffered a gash under his left eye that bled from the fourth round on. The game lightweight from "Smokey City" was knocked down twice, but amazingly was still standing at the end of the fight. Henry Dominguez was awarded a unanimous decision and left the ring with his face unmarked.

Thirty minutes later in a cramped, stuffy dressing room without air conditioning, Mamarelli lay on a rubbing table. Dwaine Simpson held an ice pack to the beaten lightweight's forehead while Dr. James J. McCormick stitched the gash below the fighter's left eye. Lighting was so dim Simpson had to multitask at one corner of the rubbing table by holding Tony's head and telling the physician where to insert his needle. Just as the sixty year old practitioner pulled the fifth and final stitch through the flesh, Dwaine fainted while standing in front of a trash barrel. He lost consciousness, fell backwards and landed in the barrel folded up with arms and legs hanging out. The doctor called two men into the room to assist Simpson. His eyes opened as they lifted him from the container and carried him to a chair. Once he was seated, he asked, "Whassamatter? What's goin' on here?"

One of the men said, "Ya passed out. Are ya all right?"

Simpson tried to explain by saying, "It's SO hot in here." After he was fully revived, he asked Dr. McCormick, "Where's Dick Lee?"

"Dunno. Haven't seen him."

Dick Lee never went to Tony's dressing room after the fight or spoke to the boxer again. Dwaine later learned Lee went into a state of shock because he couldn't imagine anyone beating his fighter as badly as Henry Dominguez had. Dick failed as a fight manager by not carefully choosing opponents. He dealt with the Tony Mamarelli situation in a cold way. Lee quickly disassociated himself from the Pittsburgh native by selling his contract to Chris Dundee, a man he despised. This did not work out well for Mamarelli. Dundee threw the true lightweight in against welterweights. The game little fighter from a steel town fought seven more years and compiled a record of thirty three wins, three losses and two draws, but sustained brain damage, dooming him for the rest of his days.

A CLOWN CHAMPIONSHIP FOR BOXERS

Two months after fighting Dwaine to a draw on a cruise ship, Bobby Marie was knocked out in the first round by a black welterweight named Moses Shaw. It was an amazing performance because Marie had never been knocked out or even knocked down during a fight and Shaw had never been taught how to box. He was a street fighter who hung out in bars, seldom trained, was never in any kind of shape, but was born with a devastating knockout punch. He became a crowd favorite not only for his lethal overhand right, but his innate ability to duck his head, dodge punches, bob, weave, use evasive movements and make his opponents look ridiculous. He was a one man pugilistic version of the Harlem Globetrotters.

Shaw's quick knockout of Bobbie Marie gave Buddy Pack a brainstorm. He approached the welterweight and said, "You and Dwaine Simpson oughta fight for the Clown Championship of Boxing. I'll get a special trophy made up, and we'll hold the fight as a main event at Little River. Each of ya will get a hundred dollars." The hard punching welterweight was all for it. A C note could buy a lot of booze.

Dwaine was opposed. He told Pack, "No way am I gonna fight that guy. He hits too hard."

"You won't do it for a hundred?" replied Buddy Pack.

"Nope."

The promoter was persistent and repeatedly called Dwaine, offering additional inducements. After two months, Simpson caved in. He agreed to take on Moses Shaw for two hundred dollars in an eight round main event, fighting two-minute rounds. After agreeing to the fight, Dwaine regretted doing so. He agonized over what might happen when he stepped into the ring against a man with a nuclear bomb for a right hand. He thought, "Moses is shorter'n me. When he bobs and weaves he drops lower and makes himself a smaller target. He wobbles his head a little, and that makes it hard to hit 'im. Since he don't know how ta box and doesn't train, he's gonna be on me like stink on a skunk. How'm I gonna protect myself from his right hand?" Thinking about Moses Shaw increased Dwaine's anxiety and cost him sleepless nights as the day of the fight approached.

On the morning of the bout, Dwaine nervously paced back and forth at the weigh-in. He was shocked when Moses Shaw didn't show up. He wondered, "What happened? Is this some kinda gag?"

Within a few minutes, Buddy Pack walked in with a disgusted look on his face. He said in a somber tone, "Moses isn't gonna be fightin' for a while."

"What happened?" asked Dwaine. "Is he hurt? Is he sick?"

"No, he's gonna be occupied because of a misunderstanding."

"What kinda misunderstanding?"

"He called me real late last night," replied Pack. "Way he explained it, he was out doin' some roadwork and the cops stopped 'im."

"Why would they do that?"

"They were suspicious 'cuz he was runnin' with a portable TV on his shoulder. He tol' 'em he was carryin' extra weight to get in shape, but they didn't believe 'im. He wanted me to bail 'im out so he could make the fight."

"Do ya believe 'im?"

"It's possible, but I don't believe 'im enough to bail 'im out. He's goin' up for burglary, and I don't think he'll be boxing in the free world for a few years."

"That's too bad," said Dwaine. Simpson felt like a man who received a last minute pardon while walking to the electric chair. It was difficult to keep from smiling, but he managed.

"I know you were lookin' forward to the fight," said Pack. "I got a clown trophy that needs to be used. I'll try to find someone else for ya to fight, but trouble is nobody's as big a clown as you are."

"It's nice of ya ta say that," replied Simpson. He thought, "I'm not fightin' for a clown championship unless it's somebody who can't hit hard enough to bust a paper bag. I don't wanna be a clown with tears in my eyes and mush for brains. I gotta protect what little intelligence I have."

Ronnie Pierson was also at the weigh-in, and the milk route owner asked Dwaine, "Were you really lookin' forward to fightin' Shaw? You coulda been seriously injured."

The lanky blonde lightweight pulled his friend aside and candidly said, "Moses Shaw scared me to death. I hardly slept the last two nights. Worryin' about what he might do to me got me thinkin' about the Big Hick."

"Who's he?"

"His name was Guy Pulliam, but we all called 'im Buddy. He was the best friend I had in college. Coach Gudger assigned us to be roommates. Coach tol' me, 'Buddy's got an IQ of 165 and if ya can get up to half that by spendin' time with 'im, it'll be well worth it.' It didn't work out like the coach hoped 'cuz Buddy liked to sleep. He cut his mornin' classes ninety times so he could sleep in."

"Were his grades as bad as yours?"

"Oh no, he had a photogenic memory."

"What's that?"

"He had girlfriends who'd loan 'im their notes and he'd run his finger down each page while lookin' at 'em, then close the notebook and tell ya what was in it, word for word."

"You mean Buddy had a photographic memory."

"That's what I said."

"He sounds like quite a guy."

"He was. We were on the college radio station, WWOO, ev'ry Saturday mornin'. They called it the Big Hick and Lil' Dwaine Show, 'cuz he was 6'4" and I looked like I was 'bout twelve."

"What did you do on your show?"

"I'd sing and play the ukulele and Buddy'd back me up with harmony. We'd sing Detour and Mountain Dew."

"Detour I've heard, but I can't recall Mountain Dew."

Dwaine sang a verse.

"MY UNCLE MORT IS SAWED OFF AND SHORT AND STANDS 'BOUT FOUR FOOT TWO. BUT HE THINKS HE'S A GIANT WHEN HE GETS HIM A PINT OF THAT GOOD OLE' MOUNTAIN DEW. THEY CALL IT MOUNTAIN DEW AND THEM THAT REFUSE IT ARE FEW. I'LL SHUT UP MY MUG IF YA HAND ME A JUG OF THAT GOOD OLE' MOUNTAIN DEW."

"Gotta admit it's catchy. Whatever happened to Buddy?"

Dwaine's face suddenly became somber. He replied, "Buddy went in the Air Force and became a pilot. One day, he was flyin' to a base so he could pick up his flight pay. Somethin' went wrong with the plane and it crashed. The whole crew was killed. I thought 'bout that all week and realized I could be joinin' Buddy earlier than expected if I got in the ring with Moses Shaw and his right hand."

"It's too bad you lost your friend that way," said Ronnie.

"Yeah, Guy 'Buddy' Pulliam was a helluva man. I named my son Guy after him."

TOO MANY TIMES THE HUSBAND IS LAST TO KNOW

Ramona and Dwaine struggled financially during the earliest years of their marriage. She was unable to work because of all the time spent cooking, cleaning and caring for their four children; Sheree, Guy, Paige and Dawn. They loved all their kids dearly and would do anything for them. When Dawn, their youngest, was born, Dwaine was extremely joyful. Ramona remarked, "Honey, I've never seen you so happy."

He replied, "Ya don't know how worried I was. I thought Dawn wasn't gonna look like her brother and sisters."

"What are you talking about?"

"Well, I read somewhere one out of every four babies born in the world is Chinese."

When Ramona was twenty eight, Sheree was twelve and and had become a big help to her mother. She could watch the younger children and do some of the household chores. She even learned how to take her siblings temperatures, something Dwaine had never mastered.

The first time he saw his daughter do it, he asked his wife, "Honey, what's that thing Sheree put in Guy's mouth?"

"It's called a thermometer. Haven't you ever seen one before?"

"Not that I recall. What's it do?"

She knew it would be impossible to explain an advanced concept like body temperature to her husband, so she said, "It's a death meter. Do you see that red line?"

"Yeah."

"Well, the further that line goes the worse it is for you. If the line goes all the way to the end, you'd be dead. Sheree used it to make sure Guy was fine."

"Boy, you know everything."

"I also know it's about time I go to work."

They had discussed it before, and Dwaine always refused because Ramona was needed at home. Things were different now. He chewed on a toothpick while he thought over the situation. Finally, he replied, "Well, if ya really wanna work, it's alright with me."

Ramona took a job with a Hertz Rent a Car agency at the Miami International Airport. The more he thought about it, Dwaine became convinced it was a good idea. It gave his wife a chance to get out of the house and brought in extra money.

Things didn't work out as he hoped. Ramona would come home from work dead tired. He thought it was from the stress of dealing with the public until his friend Ronnie Pierson, the successful distributor of dairy products, paid him an unexpected visit. Simpson asked his friend, "What's up? Everythin' okay with the business?"

Ronnie replied, "Dwaine, I have to tell ya somethin' that's not easy for me to say."

"What is it?"

"An old friend told me his son is doin' somethin' foolish. He's been on the Miami police force a few years and directs traffic at the airport. Anyway, he's gotten mixed up with a beautiful married woman who works for one of the rent a car companies."

Dwaine's jaw dropped and his heart sank. He thought, "I feel like a gorilla hit me with a body shot to my gut." He asked his friend, "Are ya sayin' Ramona's cheatin' on me? She's always been true blue."

"All the cop's father said was, 'My kid's been havin' lunch with that woman practically every day.'"

"Do ya know the cop?"

"I met him a coupla times," replied Ronnie. He could see his friend was becoming upset, so he said, "Tell ya what I'll do. We'll go to the airport when he's on duty and I'll point him out."

"Thanks, Ronnie. I really appreciate it."

They made a trip to Miami International and Ronnie identified the officer. They watched him direct traffic for a few minutes, but Dwaine chose to wait until a better time to confront him. Two days later, he drove to the airport when it wasn't so busy. The traffic cop was at his assigned post but momentarily unoccupied when Simpson walked up and asked, "Do you know Ramona Simpson?"

The policeman's face turned red. He swallowed hard and compressed his lips before he spoke.. "No" was all he had to say. Dwaine knew he was lying.

The betrayed husband spoke in a calm manner and tried to keep from being overheard by speaking in a low tone. "Well, my name is Dwaine Simpson. I know ya know her, and she's my wife. You're takin' her to lunch, tellin' her what she should do and fillin' her head about how she could handle her life better. You're becomin' her Jesus. Ya know what happened to Jesus, dontcha?"

The officer shook his head and said, "No." His hands were perspiring, but he was afraid to move away from Simpson.

Dwaine's eyes burned with intensity, but he didn't raise his voice. "Jesus was crucified. If ya don't watch it, that could happen to ya. That gun on your hip might be your salvation." He paused before adding, "You're messin' with the lives of five people; me and our four kids. If I ever hear about ya havin' anything more to do with my wife, I'll beat the shit out of ya." Simpson briefly glared at the policeman, then turned and walked away. The man who had been sneaking around with his wife had nothing more to say. The police officer knew he was in the wrong and had no thoughts of retaliating or making any trouble for Dwaine.

When Simpson confronted Ramona, she adamantly maintained she had not cheated on him. "All we did was have lunch together."

"But people saw ya havin' lunch with him practically every day. How come ya never told me 'bout it?"

"Oh, Dwaine, I didn't think it was a big deal. It was only lunch."

"Well, ya better remember you're a married woman with four kids. It is a big deal if other people think you're messin' with a Rudolph Vaselino and puttin' somethin' over on me."

Ramona promised she would never again keep anything from him and sealed her promise with a kiss. She had nothing more to do with the traffic cop.

Soon after that, she came home bouncing with excitement. She went up to her husband, kissed him and said, "Guess what?"

"What's goin' on? I've never seen ya like this."

"I've been offered an opportunity to sign with the most established modeling agency in Miami. What do you think, honey?" She hugged him and said, "We could really use the money."

He thought, "Guess it reminds her of when she won the beauty contests." Dwaine agreed to go along, but added, "I don't want ya doin' anything that would make me or the kids ashamed."

She hugged him once more, gave him a long, lingering kiss and said, "Yes, dear, I'll make sure that doesn't happen."

His wife was hired for numerous modeling assignments. She told Dwaine about each one beforehand, and he gave his approval in every case. The extra income made a big difference in their finances, and they were able to buy a blue 1962 Chevy six passenger station wagon with power steering, automatic transmission and air conditioning. One day, she called him from work with good news. "Honey, I've got a big chance! Playboy magazine wants me to do a centerfold." Ramona was ecstatic.

Dwaine paused for a moment to digest what she told him before responding. "We'll talk about it when ya get home from work." From the way he said it, she knew he wasn't going to go along.

That night, they sat across from each other at the kitchen table and had a long discussion. Neither raised their voice, but neither was willing to give in. She argued, "I'll get five thousand dollars to do it."

"What about the modelin' agency's cut?"

"The five thousand is my share after the agency takes their fee." From the look in her eyes, he could tell she believed doing the centerfold was the most logical course of action. She said, "We need the money."

He shook his head and replied, "I don't want men all over the world seein' ya naked. Ya got five other people to think about."

"I'm doing it for our children. Five thousand dollars can make a big difference to us, but you're too proud and stubborn to admit it."

"Aren't ya worried about what people would think of ya and what other kids'll say to ours when they find out what ya did?"

"My gosh, Dwaine, times are changing!"

"Not in this house."

He stuck to his guns, and Ramona declined the offer from Playboy. She wasn't happy about it and began to resent Dwaine's holding her back.

HIRED TO BE A HUMAN PUNCHING BAG

After Tony Mamarelli didn't pan out, Dick Lee continued searching for a contender to manage. He was driven to find the most perfect example of a punishing fighter; someone who could appear in Madison Square Garden, become a champion and make Lee as famous as his nemesis, Chris Dundee. He thought he found one when twenty three year old middleweight Gordon Lott arrived on the South Florida boxing scene from Savannah, Georgia. Outside the ring, Gordon was a pleasant, polite college student and son of a physician, but he was devoted to becoming a champion in the brutal sport of boxing.

Lott used a crushing left hook to win seven fights in a row, six by knockout. One of his victims was the tenth ranked middleweight in the world. All his matches had been at the Little River Auditorium, and Gordon became one of the biggest draws in the brief history of that venue. None of the other local middleweights wanted to take him on and acted as though he carried the sting of death in every punch. Fans clamored to see Gordon Lott fight, and Dick Lee needed an opponent for his emerging star. He turned to the fighter most in need of money.

Dick approached Dwaine and asked, "How 'bout if I match ya with Gordon Lott in an eight-round main event?"

Simpson looked at the matchmaker as if he were insane before he replied. "He's way too much for me. He can knock anybody out with one punch and outweighs me by nineteen pounds. I may be nuts, but I ain't stupid. Besides, you're only payin' forty bucks for a main event. Gotta have more'n that."

"How 'bout sixty?"

Dwaine was taking home $78.50 a week and sixty bucks could buy a lot of groceries. But it wasn't worth risking a terrible beating. He replied, "I can't agree to that."

"How 'bout a hunnert dollars… and no deductions?"

Simpson pondered for a moment before saying, "I'd fight anybody but Lott for a hundred. You gotta give me some kind of extra incentive."

Dick Lee sweetened the pot by saying, "If ya fight him for a hunnert, no matter how the fight comes out, you'll get a rematch with him in a main event at Savannah, Georgia. That's Gordon's hometown. We'll get a big crowd, and you'll get five hunnert dollahs."

Dwaine said, "I'll do it, but it's gotta be an eight round fight with two-minute rounds for a hundred dollars."

"Fine," replied Lee, "eight two-minute rounds."

Five hundred dollars was more money than Dwaine had seen at one time. After insisting his wife turn down the five grand to do the Playboy centerfold, he felt obligated to accept the offer. He told the matchmaker, "Great! Great! I'll do it."

News of Simpson being matched against Lott spread like wildfire. Jack McKiernan told him, "You're nuts. You're gonna get the crap beat out of ya. Gordon Lott's a left hook artist, and the left hook has always been your downfall. Ya always drop your right hand when ya throw your left jab."

Dwaine replied, "I got somethin' up my sleeve. Will ya work my corner if I tell ya what it is?"

"Okay, I'll do it. What's the big mystery?"

"I found a secret to winnin' in a recreation journal. Accordin' to a Midwest doctor, thirty seconds of lyin' horizontal has the recuperative powers of four minutes of sittin' upright. I tried it this week in the gym. I sparred seven rounds and stretched out between rounds. It was great. I'll be able to get on my back for thirty seconds while I'm in my corner between rounds. With all the energy I'll be gettin', I'll be shakin' and fakin' all night and wear Lott out."

Jack stared at his friend in disbelief and said, "Now I know you're insane."

On the night of the fight, Lott weighed in at one fifty eight and Dwaine weighed one forty. Ronnie Pierson visited Simpson in the dressing room and said to his friend, "You're outweighed and outgunned, but I've never seen ya so calm before a fight."

"Ronnie, it's funny how ya can relax more when ya know you're gonna get the crap beat outta ya. It can't be any worse than takin' a sleeping pill."

"Maybe, but what if ya don't wake up?"

"Then tell Ramona I was talkin' to ya just before I went in the ring and said I love her and the kids. It'll be somethin' good to remember 'bout me."

"Isn't she gonna be here?"

"Naw, she's never been to any of my fights. She hates boxing, and I wouldn't want her watchin' me get beat up."

"Well, good luck," said Pierson. "Hope ya come through in one piece. I can't believe you're not worried about what Lott could do to ya. Ya could get killed."

Dwaine smiled and replied, "I know I could get killed, and that's serious business 'cuz if ya get killed, ya lose a very important part of your life. I'm not afraid, but I'm worried and when somethin' worries me, I try to laugh about it. If ya can't have fun, it's your own damn fault."

The crew cut blonde then turned to Jack McKiernan and said, "Don't forget to spread my robe out in the corner after each round so I can lie down and put my feet up on the bottom rope."

Gordon Lott emerged from the dressing room first. He ran up the steps to the ring and climbed through the ropes to loud applause. Those in the crowd were pointing at him and shouting about his string of knockouts. A man said to the one next to him, "I heard he tried to smash a guy's nose through his skull." The other man replied, "Maybe we'll see 'im do it tonight."

After Simpson entered the ring, he went to Eddie Eckert, who was assigned to referee the contest, and said, "Eddie, I know the guy I'm fightin' is way too good for me."

"Yeah, so what the hell you doin' fightin' 'im?"

"Dick Lee talked me into it. Whatever ya do, don't let me take a damn beatin' out there."

"Okay, I'll keep my eye on you."

Dwaine was shocked when the ring announcer said into his microphone, "Tonight's main event will be ten three-minute rounds." It had been agreed there would be eight two-minute rounds. Simpson thought, "Sonuvabitch! Dick Lee double crossed me again!"

At the clang of the opening bell, Gordon Lott was all over the lanky blonde underdog like ants on sugar. Dwaine went into his usual routine of running, fast stepping, ducking and dodging. Whenever Lott tried to crowd him against the ropes, the lanky blonde went into a clinch until Eddie Eckert separated the fighters. Once they were pulled apart, Simpson would circle back around the referee and use him as a human shield. Eckert tried to separate himself, but wherever he moved, Simpson would go the same way. A fan in a ringside seat hollered up to Jack McKiernan, "WHAT'S YOUR GUY TRYIN' TO DO?"

McKiernan shouted back, "MAKE IT THROUGH THE ROUND!"

Dwaine thought, "Every time I shadow Eddie takes fifteen or twenty seconds off the clock, but I can't keep stallin' like this forever." In the closing seconds of the first round, Simpson surprised Gordon Lott by running at him, firing off four punches, none of which connected, grabbing Lott, tying him up and going into a clinch. The fans could see the lanky blonde with the crew cut was overmatched, but were riveted to their seats. He was liable to try anything and they didn't want to miss a second of it.

When the bell ended the round, Dwaine walked to his corner while Jack McKiernan hopped into the ring with the fighter's robe and laid it down just as he had been instructed. He also punched a stopwatch to time Dwaine's rest and make sure it didn't last more than forty seconds. Simpson lay on his back, placed his feet on the bottom of the three ropes surrounding the ring and revealed a surprise. He had covered the bottoms of his leather boxing shoes with white shoe polish and wrote a message in black ink on the soles. "Howdy" appeared on the bottom of his right shoe and "Folks" on the sole of his left shoe. The arena went wild with laughter and applause, and news photographers jostled each other as they tried to take pictures of the fighter's comical footwear. Dwaine wasn't able to enjoy the moment. He was laying on his back choking because McKiernan accidentally poured water into his nose.

Simpson's stunt angered Dick Lee. He bit down on his cigar and muttered, "Finish him, Gordon, finish that clown quick. Give 'em what they came for... a knockout."

The stunt actually lessened Dwaine's chances of winning. Fighters normally roughened the thin leather soles of their boxing shoes by scuffing them in resin for better traction. The shoe polish left a slick surface on his soles that made it hard for Simpson to keep his footing, and Gordon Lott kept cutting him off.

It took only thirty six seconds of the second round for the Georgia born middleweight to catch Simpson with a deadly left hook flush on his jaw. Dwaine's face was twisted into a grotesque mask, and he dropped to one knee. The lanky blonde managed to get back on his feet, but the expression on his face indicated he had been momentarily stripped of his senses. Eddie Eckert took one look at him and said, "That's it. It's over."

Simpson asked, "Do my eyes look funny?"

"Yeah, they look like they're in Chicago, and you're here in Florida."

That was the last thing Dwaine remembered. When he came to, he was standing under the dressing room shower, still dressed in his trunks, robe, shoes and gloves. As water poured over him, he wondered, "What the hell am I doin' here?"

Dick Lee suddenly appeared at the entrance to the shower. He grinned as he said to the still groggy fighter, "They shoulda carried ya inta the ring on your robe 'cause that's the way ya went out. College boy, ya ain't shit!" Dwaine was too hazy to respond.

His head had cleared by the time he dressed and Dwaine was in a good mood when he arrived home. He kissed Ramona, handed her his hundred dollar purse and said, "Honey, there's a lot more where that came from. I'm gettin' five hundred bucks to fight the same guy in Savannah, Georgia."

"Did you win or lose?"

"I lost. He knocked me out."

"And you're gonna fight him again?"

"Yeah."

"When's that going to happen?"

"In a few months."

"You've gotta get some life insurance."

The next day, people who weren't at the fight asked Dwaine what happened. He replied, "Hell, I lay down to take a rest and next thing I know, they counted me out." When asked if he was worried about permanent damage, he answered, "Naw, Ramona said I won't have any trouble 'cuz my brains were already scrambled when she met me. In fact, she hopes I get knocked out again, 'cuz a hard enough punch might unscramble 'em"

Three days later, Dick Lee drove to Dwaine's job in his Plymouth station wagon. He had something so important to tell him it had to be said in person. He found Simpson up on a ladder attaching a basketball net to a hoop. Dick didn't wait for him to finish. His jaw was tight as he looked up, pointed angrily with his cigar and said, "College boy, the crap ya pulled got worldwide publicity. Even somebody stationed in Germany saw it in the Stars and Stripes newspaper."

Dwaine was puzzled by the anger in Lee's voice. He replied, "Ya don't seem happy about becomin' known all over the world. Whassamatter, didn't they spell your name right?"

"Listen, dumb shit, this ain't good. After that crazy stunt you pulled, people in Savannah'll think any fight you're in is a setup. They wanna see the real deal, not a joke. You're out."

Dwaine thought, "He really got me this time. He screwed me twice on the same fight. No two-minute rounds and no five hunnert bucks." He said nothing to Dick Lee. He was grateful for not suffering any permanent injury after facing Gordon Lott and realized taking on the hard punching middleweight a second time would've been pushing his luck.

When he gave Ramona the bad news about losing out on the big payday, she talked to him like a stern school teacher and didn't call him "honey " or "dear." She shook her finger at him and asked, "What have you learned from this?"

"I learned Dick Lee's got no sense of humor. I'm not gonna carry a grudge, though. While I'm carryin' a grudge, the other guy's out dancin'."

"You still don't get it. You should have let me pose for Playboy. I hate being an 'I told you so,' but I'm right and you still won't admit it. You're worried about me posing naked when you should be more worried about losing what few brains you have."

Dwaine wasn't the only one who didn't have everything go his way. Gordon Lott, the knockout artist with the vicious left hook, fought for ten years. He compiled a record of thirty six wins and six losses, with sixteen knockouts, was never knocked down or knocked out, but never won a world title. He died in 2008 at the age of 67. His biggest payday was $2500, when he fought Harry Tetlow in Savannah. Gordon won a unanimous ten round decision, and Tetlow was paid the five hundred bucks originally promised Simpson.

After Harry returned to Miami, the lanky blonde lightweight went to see him and said, "You should gimme a piece of that five hundred. You wouldn't have gotten that fight if I hadn't pissed off Dick Lee." Dwaine and Harry were good friends, and he knew the remark was made in jest.

Harry was from Washington, D.C. After moving to Miami, he took a job driving a truck for Famous Food Catering Service. He was an avid record collector and excelled at swimming and ping pong. He also played an electric guitar, and Dwaine occasionally jammed with him. Harry was on guitar and Simpson played his baritone ukelele.

During their first jam session, the catering truck operator asked Dwaine, "Who taught ya how ta play?"

"Back in West by God Virginia, my Uncle Zeke played a guitar. He was a miner who picked up extra money playin' at dances. He showed me three chords I could play on the bottom four strings of the guitar. First song I learned was Five Foot Two, Eyes of Blue."

"How come ya don't play a guitar?"

"Tried to save up for one, but all I could afford was the uke."

"I gotta say you're pretty good with it. How long ya been playin'?"

"Ever since eighth grade. See, it all started with my acne."

"Acne?"

"Yeah, I had the worst case of pimples you'd ever seen. They weren't just zits, they were welts big as mountains. Instead of feelin' sorry for myself, I spent my time shootin' baskets and learnin' more songs. I learned Good Rockin' Tonight by listenin' to a record."

"I know that one," said Harry. He began picking his guitar and singing.

"MEET ME IN A HURRY BEHIND THE BARN. DON'T BE AFRAID, I WON'T DO YA NO HARM. GONNA PUT ON MY ROCKIN' SHOES, 'CUZ TONIGHT I'M GONNA ROCK AWAY ALL MY BLUES. HAVE YA HEARD THE NEWS? THERE'S GOOD ROCKIN' TONIGHT."

Dwaine said, "Ya do it almost as good as Wynonie 'Mr. Blues' Harris."

Harry smiled and said, "Ya play any other instruments?"

"Learned how to play boogie woogie on a piano. First song I learned was Caldonia."

"I know that one," said the man with the solid body guitar. Harry sang a few lines from the Louie Jordan hit.

"CALDONIA! CALDONIA! WHAT MAKES YO' BIG HEAD SO HARD? I LOVE HER, LOVE HER JUST THE SAME. CRAZY 'BOUT THAT WOMAN. CALDONIA IS HER NAME."

During their next jam session, Dwaine said enthusiastically, "I got an idea! Why don't we do an act together."

"Yeah," replied Harry. "We'll call ourselves 'The Rockin' Boxers.'"

Tetlow and Simpson approached Neil Composto and asked the promoter to let them play their music between fights at Little River Auditorium. He agreed to it, and the two fighters performed a duet of High Heeled Sneakers at two boxing shows. The crowd ate it up when they sang,

"PUT ON YO' RED DRESS BABY, 'CUZ WE'RE GOIN' OUT TONIGHT. BETTER WEAR SOME BOXIN' GLOVES, GAL, 'CASE WE GET INTO A FIGHT."

News of their performances reached the owner of Doc's Melody Bar, across the street from the auditorium. He hired the Rockiin' Boxers for a one night stand and they ended up splitting seventy five dollars, which was a little more than what they usually made for professional fights.

They were a hit and hoped for more gigs, but didn't receive any offers. Tetlow grumbled about not making it big in entertainment, but Dwaine looked at it in an upbeat way. He said, "Be happy. We were the toast of Little River. Not everybody can say that."

DWAINE S MARRIAGE GOES ON THE ROCKS

Dwaine enjoyed a boost in income by going to work for Miami-Dade County Parks and Recreation, but was making only $460 a month. With her job and modeling assignments, his wife was earning much more and wanted to be independent. By the following spring, his marriage was on the rocks. He and Ramona had separated and were in the process of reconciling, which included marriage counseling. They attended a counseling session in a large office building. On their way out, they stepped into an elevator and Dwaine suddenly had a puzzled look on his face. Ramona asked, "What's bothering you, dear?"

"Can't understand why there's a button for the floor we were just on."

"Dammit, Dwaine, are you really that stupid, or are you just trying to be funny? I thought you'd get smarter as you got older, but my mother always said you'd still be hopeless. She was right."

Ramona and Dwaine's attempts at reconciliation failed, and their divorce was finalized within two years. The house in Carol City was sold, and Dwaine relinquished his share of the profits to assure his four kids would have a nice home. He signed over the Chevy station wagon to Ramona, and she and the children moved further north to Miramar.

Child support payments of fifty dollars per week reduced his weekly take home to less than forty bucks. All Simpson had to his name were his clothes, boxing gear, ukulele and a Renault Dauphine he'd picked up cheap. The Renault was a French four cylinder car with such little horsepower Dwaine said, "Ya could time it with an hour glass." When any of his friends asked what happened, he would reply, "I had a handle on life, but it broke. I've been destitute before, but never tooted this low. My credit ratin' is down to Triple-Z."

"What's that," they would ask.

"It means don't trust 'im even if he pays cash."

His very good friend Ronnie Pierson, who owned six milk trucks and a lucrative route, came to his aid. Pierson allowed Dwaine to move into his home and stay there rent free. Ronnie also hired him to work as a deliveryman before going to his parks and recreation job. Simpson arose at four and transported three hundred fifty cases to fifteen schools and the jails in Dade County. Each case held forty four half pint containers, and Dwaine had the backbreaking work of loading them into refrigerated carts at each stop. He was paid one hundred twenty dollars a week and held the job seven years.

He also continued to box professionally. During his period of new bachelorhood, Dwaine fought Richie Smith three times. The first two matches were held at the Little River Auditorium, and Simpson won both. They were matched a third time in a six-rounder at the North Dade Sports Center in Miami.

Richie approached Dwaine in the dressing room before the fight and said, "I know you're a better boxer than me, but my family's here. All I wanna do is go the distance and look good. Whadya think?"

Simpson replied, "Fine with me. We'll just go out and box and not try for knockouts."

Smith eluded Simpson for the first five rounds, but not because of any skill on his part. Dwaine's willingness to assure his opponent would finish the fight lulled him into passivity. He failed to display effective aggression and forgot how the fight looked to the judges. Jack McKiernan was working in Dwaine's corner and after the fifth round, warned the fighter, "This is the last round. Ya gotta knock him out."

Simpson asked, "Why?"

"To win."

"I'm winnin' on all the scorers' cards."

McKiernan became exasperated. "No you're not! Ya gotta knock him out! I'm tellin' ya, you're losin' the fight. You're so far behind you'll hafta knock 'im out to get a draw."

Dwaine left his corner determined to stop Richie. As seconds melted from the clock, the lanky blonde became desperate and ran at Richie Smith while swinging both fists, something he normally wouldn't do. Nothing worked, and Smith was awarded the decision. Dwaine was fuming when the two fighters shook hands. Richie asked, "Ya mad at me 'bout somethin'?"

Simpson replied, "I'm mad at myself. That's the last time I'll go along with pullin' punches out of friendship. It turned out worse'n tryin' to reconcile with my ex."

DWAINE RECALLS HIS HIGH SCHOOL HEROICS

Ronnie Pierson and Dwaine were having dinner in Ronnie's home. Pierson came to the boxer's aid after his marriage had broken up and Simpson became a star boarder. One night, Ronnie fixed a tuna salad. After they finished eating, Dwaine asked, "Did we have chicken or fish tonight?"

"We had tuna salad. Why would ya think we had chicken?"

"'Cuz the can said Chicken of the Sea."

Their conversation turned to the upcoming football season. Dwaine said, "Ya know, I played football for three years in high school."

"I have a tough time believing that," said his host. "Aren't ya a little too light?"

"I was a hundred thirty five pounds, but played defensive end and offensive end."

Ronnie had a look of disbelief. Dwaine responded to his friend's skepticism by saying, "Ya see we had only 46 male students at Camp Lejeune High. They needed 32 guys on the football team, so if ya could walk, ya could play."

"Were ya any good?"

"I was good at catchin' passes, but defense was another story. See, every team we played used the single wing offense. Both guards and a coupla backfield men would pull out and make a wall in front of the guy carryin' the ball. It was like tryin' to stop a buncha Sherman tanks. Coach Dickson would tell me, 'Run in five steps and then retreat sideways, so ya force the guy with the ball to cut inside.' That way, Jack Barringer, who was our combination fullback 'n linebacker, could stop 'im. Jack was was six feet, two hundred five and a real hardass. Well, I tried to do what Coach Dickson tol' me but when all those guys so much bigger'n me were headed my way, I'd end up retreatin' all the way to the out of bounds line. The coach would get disgusted and say, 'Dwaine, do ya think you might POSSIBLY take just ONE blocker out?'"

While Dwaine was talking, Ronnie was puffing contentedly on his favorite pipe filled with Sir Walter Raleigh tobacco. His host asked, "Well, you were tryin' your best, weren't ya? Did ya try to avoid gettin' hit as much as ya do in boxing?"

"No, I tried to hit 'em, but just didn't have enough weight to put in their way. One time, we were playin' Jacksonville High in Jacksonville, North Carolina. A guy who weighed way over two hunnert pounds came barrelin' down the field with the ball in his hands. I clotheslined him and got my arms 'round his neck, and then got one of my legs between his legs. It didn't slow 'im up at all, and he carried me along with 'im. I hung onto his neck until some other guys on my team caught up with us and dragged 'im down. Coach Dickson said ta me, 'Ya looked like a cowboy tryin' to ride a wild stallion.'"

Pierson was laughing so hard he nearly dropped his pipe. He said, "Please, please, my sides are starting to ache."

Dwaine wasn't through. "I was much better in basketball. I could hit from way out with a two handed set shot and was middle man on the fast break. I was also mean on defense. Anytime somebody tried ta set a pick on me, I'd lower my shoulder and hit 'em in the ribs. Sometimes the referee'd call a foul, but ta me it was worth givin' up the foul 'cuz it made 'em think twice 'bout tryin' to pick me."

Ronnie got up from the table and headed to the refrigerator for a can of Blatz beer. He asked Dwaine, "You want one?"

"Don't mind if I do."

Pierson returned with the beers and asked, "What were the most memorable games you played?"

"Well, the most pleasant memory was when we won our first Class B state championship. We were playin' in the Cameron Indoor Arena at Duke University. We were tied up goin' into the last five minutes and I hit six straight set shots, a couple of 'em from near midcourt."

"Wow!"

"The most painful memory was when we were playin' Whiteville High School in Whiteville, North Carolina. They heated their gym with two old pot belly stoves, one on either side of the basketball court. The stoves divided the stands and were both at midcourt. They were actually on the court, and the out of bounds line curved around 'em. So, ya had these two red hot stoves no more'n a few inches off the basketball court. Well, I riled up the home fans 'cuz of what I did to one of their players guardin' me close. I faked passin' the ball one way and then threw it in his face and he got a bloody nose. The players on the other team started hollerin' at me, so I flipped 'em the bird. Next thing I know, somebody was tryin' to push me into one of the stoves. I put up my hands to protect myself and ended up grabbin' the top of it. Both hands ended up blistered."

Ronnie shook his head and said to his guest, "Are your hands alright now?"

"Oh, they're fine."

"Good, ya can help me carry the dishes over to the sink and then help wash and dry 'em. Do ya mind?"

"'Course not, it makes me feel right at home. My ex used to get me talkin' 'bout my high school days before askin' me to do some chores."

Thanks to Ronnie Pierson's help, Dwaine was putting his life back together. He continued boxing, and most of his bouts were at the Little River Auditorium, located in a section of Miami lacking the glamour of Miami Beach. The Masons were pleased the boxing shows staged by Neil Composto and Dick Lee attracted enough paying customers to become a weekly attraction, but there were undesired ripple effects. The promoter, matchmaker and fraternal organization went about their business unaware of the local criminal element scheming, plotting and devising ways to make money off the weekly fights. No one saw it coming and they weren't aware of it when it did happen, but it affected Composto, Lee and even Dwaine Simpson: Three men who had no idea of how corrupt and wide open Little River was. .

PART THREE:

A WIDE OPEN PLACE NAMED LITTLE RIVER

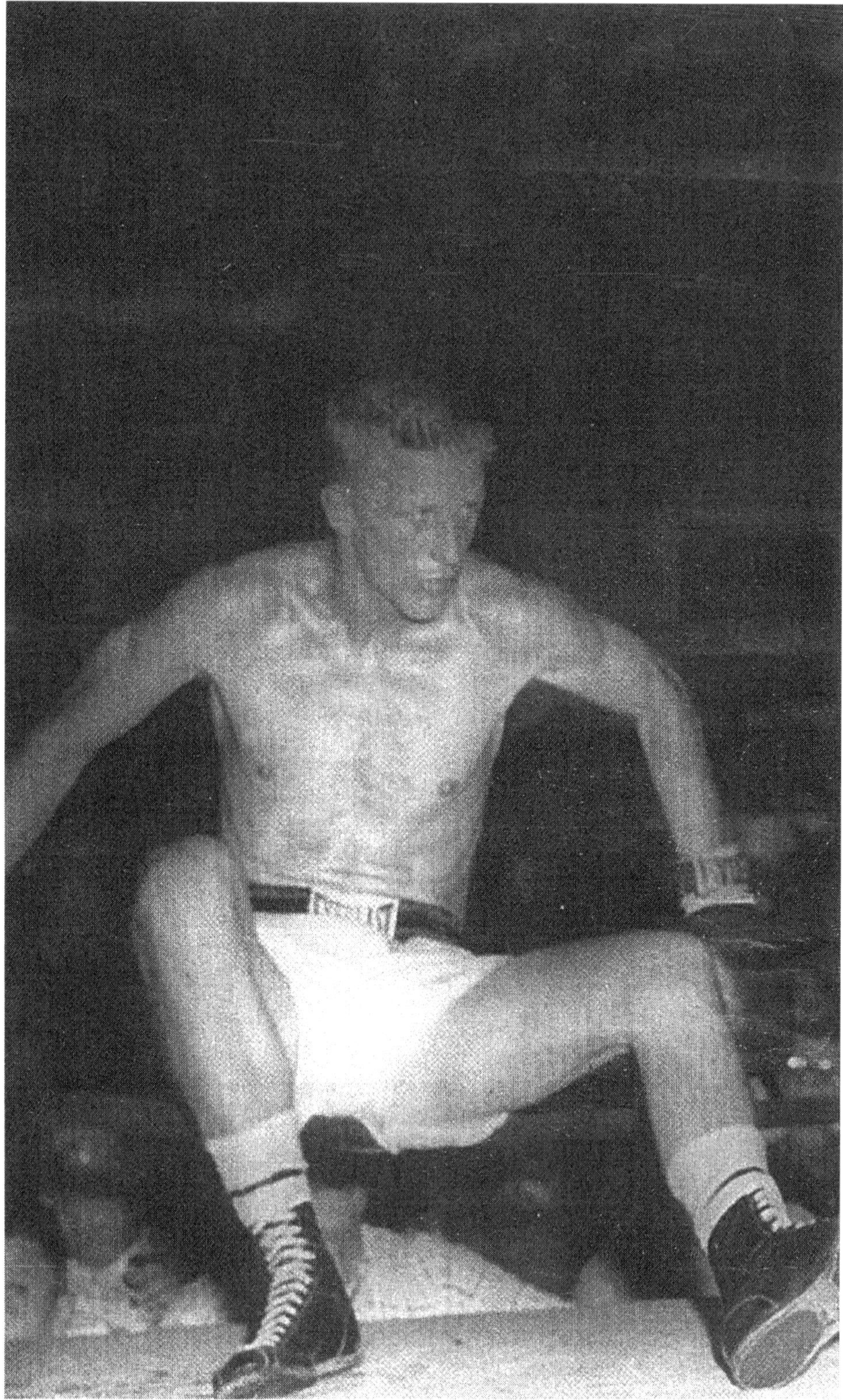

TWO JERSEY BOYS REUNITE

It was midmorning when Chappie Roberts walked into the Jersey Charlie's luncheonette on N.E. 2nd Avenue in Little River. The first thing to catch his eye was a large full color poster of a sandwich made of vanilla ice cream between two round chocolate cookies. The caption read, "Try a Flying Saucer, it's out of this world." Jersey Charlie's was owned by an old acquaintance of Chappie's named Charlie Fakish.

Chappie's real name was Carlo Campiglia. He changed his name because, "Everytime people tried to say Campiglia they made it sound woise." He was barely five feet tall, but had once been a promising lightweight. The sawed off boxer turned pro in 1928 when he was nineteen, compiled a 35-6-1 record and won the New Jersey state lightweight title, but never captured a world crown. He came to Hollywood, Florida to train Al Capone's stable of fighters. The legendary gangster trusted Chappie because his cousin, Scarface Charlie Jones, was partners with Lucky Luciano. When Capone was sent away to prison, Roberts went back up north and worked as a bartender for his cousin in a mob connected nightspot. Chappie served in the Army during World War II and after discharge, opened Chappie's Place on NW 58th Street. It was a front for a bookmaking operation. The authorities closed his club during a crackdown in the early 1950's, so he went to work for Chris Dundee as a trainer and second man in the corner. In his time, he had been associated with Carmen Basilio, Henry Armstrong, Sonny Liston, Max Baer, Joe Louis, Jack Dempsey and Primo Carnera.

Charlie and Chappie grew up in squalid surroundings near a busy intersection without a traffic signal. So many kids were hit by cars it was referred to as "the corner of Screech and Thud." The streets of their old neighborhood were full of deformed pencil sellers and midget news dealers. Few men carried wallets because of all the pickpockets, choosing instead to keep their money folded by denomination and placed in their left shirt pockets. Both Fakish and Roberts considered themselves lucky to have escaped.

Chappie was four years older than Charlie and it had been some time since they had been in contact, but his old acquaintance had called and said he wanted to discuss something important. He mentioned during their phone conversation the name of his business was "Jersey Charlie's." Roberts thought, "It's a catchy name down here, but it wouldn't go over back home."

The only other person in the luncheonette when Roberts entered was a girl in her late teens working behind the counter. He asked her, "Is Charlie here?"

"Are you Chappie? He said you'd be comin' by."

"I'm Chappie."

"Charlie's runnin' a little late today. Should be along soon. He said to give ya whatever ya wanted."

"Cuppa coffee."

The waitress served his coffee and offered him cream and sugar. Chappie smiled and said, "Thanks, but I take it black."

Roberts had taken two sips when Fakish came in. He was heavier than the last time Chappie had seen him. He was wearing a short sleeved sport shirt with loud patterns and hadn't bothered to tuck the tail in. His slacks had cuffs, and he was wearing a pair of long pointy Florsheim shoes. Roberts turned around and said to his old friend, "Ya look like a tourist."

"I know. I dress accordin' to the mood I'm in. Some days I feel like a business-man. Today, I feel like a tourist." Charlie spoke to the girl behind the counter. "Been busy, Laurie?"

"Usual breakfast crowd. It's too early for the kids from school."

Charlie nodded and said, "We'll be in the back." He turned to his visitor and asked, "Wanna take the coffee witcha?"

"Nah, I've had enough."

He led Chappie through a door to the luncheonette's back room. Most of it was used for storage, but Charlie had partitioned off a small office with a desk and a couple of chairs.

After both men sat down, Charlie said, "How long's it been, Chappie?"

"I dunno, five years at least."

"Time sure flies."

"So what's up, Charlie?"

"Well, I'm doin' pretty good for myself. Got five 'Joisy Charlie' luncheonettes and I'll be openin' a coupla more, but I can always use a little extra loot."

"Who couldn't?"

"I was thinkin' since we both had experience runnin' horse books... "

"I don't wanna get back into takin' horse bets," interrupted Chappie. "Ya gotta have a race wire and pay for protection and..."

"That's not what I had in mind. With your connections in the fight game, we could be takin' action on the fights in that auditorium up the street. You know Dick Lee, dontcha? He's the matchmaker."

"Yeah, I know 'im."

"It'll be easy... no muss, no fuss."

Chappie thought about the idea for a moment, then said, "How we gonna collect and pay off?"

"That's where my Flying Saucer Club comes in. Before I explain it, let's have a little Chivas."

"Okay with me."

Fakish pulled out a bottle of Chivas Regal and two shot glasses from a drawer in his desk. He filled both glasses, got up from his chair and served Roberts. After they toasted each other, he continued with his presentation.

"I started the Flying Saucer Club for school kids to sell Flying Saucer ice cream sandwiches. I had cards printed up and posters stapled to telephone poles near schools. If a kid joins the club, they win ice cream sandwiches or other stuff for gettin' high scores on the pinball machines. It sells Flying Saucers and gets 'em to play the machines. Why just in this store, two hunnert kids are in the club."

"What does that have to do with takin' bets on fights?"

"The place they hold the fights is run by the Masons, right?"

"Yeah."

"We'll sell cards for my Flying Saucer Club at the fights for a dollar. Anyone buys a card can turn it in for three ice cream sandwiches at any of my luncheonettes and play machines for prizes. The Masons get fifty cents for each card we sell."

"So how do we make out?"

"The cards are also betting slips for action we get from people at the fights. Each card has a number on it. We'll have a list of all numbers on the clipboard you'll use, and the list is dated. When somebody buys a card, they get to pick which fighter they wanna bet on. They hand ya the money and ya write down the information in code."

"What kinda code I use?"

"It's simple," said Charlie, as he poured himself another shot of Chivas. He asked Chappie, "Ya wanna 'nother?" Roberts waved his hand to signal "no." Fakish continued explaining the code. "Ya put down a number for which fight on the card is bein' bet on. Each boxing show has four fights, so it's either one, two, three or four. Then ya use 'A' for the favorite and 'B' for the underdog. If they wanna bet on how many rounds the fight'll last, ya write down that number. Last thing ya put down is how much they bet."

"Lemme get this straight," said Chappie. "If Joe Louis is fightin' Marciano and it's the fourth fight on the card, the first thing I write on the betting sheet is the number four, right?"

"Absolutely correct."

"Now, let's say Louis is the favorite. And the guy thinks Marciano'll last seven rounds. I write '4B7.'

"Beautiful."

"Now, how do I put down how much is bet?"

"I'm gettin' to that," said Jersey Charlie. "We work on the basis of a hundred bucks bein' the equivalent of one. Fifty bucks is .5. Ten bucks is .1. Five bucks is .05, and so on."

Roberts nodded his head and replied, "Ummhmmh," then said, "So usin' the example, let's say the guy puts down ten bucks on Marciano lastin' seven rounds against Louis, I'd write '4B7.1' on the clipboard and the back of his card."

"That's right. I think you've got it."

"Where do the winners get paid off?"

"I'm cuttin' in the owner of Doc's Melody Bar 'cross the street from the auditorium. Bill Kosofsky owns the place. He'll pay the winners and take any bets over twenny bucks. The Masons trust him and use his place to sell tickets ta the fights in advance."

"What about protection?"

"He's got a deal with the cops. A police captain hangs out there and sees nobody bothers him. Bill's also from Joisy, but I don't know if ya met him."

"Nope," replied Chappie. He pondered what Charlie told him for a moment and then asked, "What if somebody with the Masons asks why I'm keepin' a chart?"

"Tell 'em I need it to keep track of inventory. I'm dealin' with perishable moichindise what's coming in and and goin' out and need numbers in case I gotta get hold of the manufacturer about somethin'."

Chappie got up from his chair and offered Fakish his hand. As they shook hands, Roberts said, "Looks like ya got it all worked out. I'll get hold of the guys at the auditorium right away."

The day after his visit with Jersey Charlie, Chappie Roberts met with Neil Composto in his office at the Miami Showmen's Association. The barely five foot tall boxing trainer occupied a padded leather chair in front of Composto's desk. He was wearing an electric blue shirt with an open collar, while the promoter had on a white shirt and tie. Neil said, "I've heard you've been in boxing a long time. How did you get involved with a man in the luncheonette business?"

"We go way back to the days we was kids in Joisy. That's why they call Charlie Fakish 'Joisy Charlie.'"

"I see. So let me get this straight, he wants to promote his ice cream sandwiches by selling memberships in his Flying Saucer Club at the weekly boxing shows."

"That's right. See, Charlie figures if he sells lotsa ice cream sandwiches, the home office up north'll make him distributor for all of Florida, and maybe even the whole South."

"He's willing to give the Masons' Crippled Children's Fund fifty cents for each Flying Saucer Club card he sells?"

"Absolutely."

"How much does he sell the cards for?"

"A buck. For that they get three ice cream sandwiches."

"How long is he willing to keep this up?"

"Forever. He wants to become 'Mr. Flying Saucer' and nothin's gonna stop him.'"

JERSEY CHARLIES RADIO DEAL

A radio disc jockey with big teeth walked into the Jersey Charlie's on N.E. 2nd Avenue. He was dressed in a navy blue suit with gray pinstripes, a white shirt and a navy blue tie with gray designs. He was puffing on a filter tipped Kent to satisfy his three pack a day habit. The girl behind the counter was attractive, but the radio personality was recently married and faithful enough to keep his wandering eye in check. He asked the young woman, "Is Charlie Fakish here?"

"You're the guy on WFUN. I recognize your voice."

He smiled and said, "You're right."

"Charlie's in the back. Go through that door."

The door led to the storage area with an office partitioned off at the rear wall. Fakish was seated at the desk, but got up from his chair when the DJ came through the office's narrow doorway. Jersey Charlie was wearing a blue-gray summer suit, white silk shirt with brown stripes, a black bow tie and white woven belt. As they shook hands, his visitor noticed a four carat diamond ring on his right hand. Charlie said, "Glad ya could make it, Mort, have a seat."

Mort occupied the only other chair. Fakish pulled a box of Cuban cigars from a desk drawer and offered him one. After both lit up and took a couple of puffs, Charlie got down to business. He said, "You're probably wonderin' what Mort "Doc" Downey, who plays all hits all the time, can do for a guy with five luncheonettes."

"You took the words out of my mouth," replied Downey as he tapped his cigar on the rim of an ashtray.

"I want to sell all the Flying Saucer ice cream sandwiches I can... millions of 'em if possible. I got a Flying Saucer Club, and I'm sellin' membership cards at the weekly fights in Little River Auditorium. I'd like ya to talk about the fights on ya show."

"Why would I do that?"

Charlie pursed his lips and thought, "Guess I'll hafta spell it out for 'im." He asked his visitor, "How much they pay you at that station... a hunnert a week?"

"I wish... more like eighty five. They claim they can't pay more because of the all the money spent on asbestos to make sure the place was fireproof."

"Well, what if I was to give ya twenny five bucks to show up at each boxing show?"

"So let me get this straight," replied disc jockey, "I go to the boxing show and get twenty five dollars, right?"

"That's right."

"And since I'm looking forward to it, I'll talk it up every day on the air."

"Now you got the picture."

"Do I have to get in the ring and make introductions before each fight?"

"Ya can if ya wanna, otherwise ya don't hafta."

"What if I just stop in, say hi to a few people and then leave?"

"Fine, just as long as you're talkin' up the fights on your show."

Downey stood up, extended his right hand and said, "You've got a deal."

The DJ gave Jersey Charlie his money's worth and helped boost attendance at Little River Auditorium and increase gambling action. Twenty years later, the radio personality pioneered the "trash TV" format with his program, The Morton Downey, Jr. Show. His viewers feasted on anger and incivility and Downey popularized such phrases as "pablum puking liberal" and "zip it." He enjoyed goading his guests into becoming angry with each other and on a few occasions, there were physical confrontations. He became televison's *provocateur*, and his time in Miami spinning records and moonlighting for Charlie Fakish helped prepare him for that.

NEVER TRUST A UNION PRESIDENT

The phone in Dick Lee's home rang, and Chappie Roberts was on the line when Little River Auditorium's matchmaker picked up the call. The sawed off trainer excitedly said, "Dick, I got big news! Are ya sittin' down?"

"Yeah. What's up?"

"I can get ya a ten round main event at Little River between Ernie Terrell and Herb Siler."

"We can't pay the kind of money Terrell gets, and Siler might even ask for more'n we can afford."

"I got it set up so ya pay Siler a hunnert dollars and Terrell gets nothin'."

"Are we talkin' 'bout the same Ernie Terrell from Chicago who's six foot seven and twenty nine and four?"

"The very same."

"Why would he fight for nothin'?"

"I worked it out with his manager. Didja ever meet Julie Isaacson? He's based in New York."

"No, never met the guy."

"Well, Isaacson and I go way back. He's president of the International Toy and Novelty Woikers Union. Anyway, Ernie Terrell's got a big money rematch with Cleveland Williams comin' up and needs a good tune up fight. Julie told 'im fightin' Siler again in Miami would be the best way ta get ready for Williams."

"Did he actually buy that story?" asked Lee.

"Well, not completely," replied Chappie. "He put it to 'im this way... 'If ya don't fight in Florida, ya don't get the fight in Philadelphia.' Terrell WILL follow orders."

"How can ya be so sure?"

"It's always been that way. When Big Julie signed Terrell, he told 'im, 'If ya don't sign with me, ya might get a fight in Kalamazoo but even if ya do, it won't be worth nothin'.' Terrell knows how his bread is buttered."

"You're sure Siler's willin' to go for only a hunnert bucks?"

"Positive," replied Roberts. "He lost a decision on points ta Terrell and wants another chance at 'im. Plus he was in deep hock and his new manager paid off the eight grand he owed. He'll do whatever his manager tells 'im."

"What's in it for you?"

"Sellin' more Flying Saucer Club memberships. Joisy Charlie's a cinch to get his distributorship, and he's gonna gimme a piece of it."

"Okay," replied Dick Lee, "Tell Isaacson and Siler's managers they got a fight. Do I call ya once I set up the date with Neil?"

"Yeah, I'll handle everythin' else."

After Chappie got off the phone with Dick Lee, he poured himself another cup of coffee, lit a cigarette and then dialed Jersey Charlie. When the man with the string of luncheonettes picked up, Roberts said, "It's all set."

"Good. Meet me in an hour at Doc's Melody Bar."

Fakish was going to introduce Chappie to Bill Kosofsky, a bar owner who had come up the hard way. His father, Gene Kosofsky, was a disgusting man with a habit of blowing his nose on his undershirt. He rarely bathed and had bad breath. It was amazing a man with such poor hygiene could run a restaurant. Gene named his greasy spoon The Ironside, and his steaks were so tough they were nearly impossible to cut. It was a miracle none of his customers died, and all that kept him from being shut down were payoffs made to public health inspectors.

Bill's mother, Eva, was much younger than her husband. They married shortly after she arrived in America from Poland with only the clothes on her back and unable to speak or read English. He treated her like a slave. In addition to housework and taking care of their son, she did all the cooking in the restaurant while Gene drank and played cards with friends. She began to look much older than her years, and her health went into decline. With all she had to endure, she became distant from Bill and would never defend him against his father. Eva finally had enough and walked out when the boy was twelve years old.

When his mother left, his dad forced him to quit school and work in the restaurant. Gene was too cheap to hire a cook and insisted he could do it, but proved inept. He gave his son the tasks of waiting on tables and washing dishes, telling him, "Ya get nine bucks a week plus tips." The customers were dregs of society, and Bill never saw a tip in all the years he worked there. It took him until he was seventeen to save up fifty dollars, and he kept the money hidden from his father. Once he had that much, he ran away from home and never looked back.

This was during Prohibition, and Bill was befriended by Friedrich, an elderly German chemist hoping to cash in on the demand for illegal liquor. The chemist spoke little English and didn't feel comfortable conducting business in the U.S. The young man assumed that responsibility and became a trusted colleague. In return, he was taught the secrets to producing whiskey that could pass for Jack Daniels. Bill and Friedrich did very well, but the old man died shortly before Prohibition's repeal. The youngster gave his benefactor a good send off, but had been so hardened by his upbringing he never really mourned the chemist's passing. By that time, Kosofsky had invested in small clubs offering dice games, poker and roulette in back rooms. He became wealthy and relocated to Florida in the early fifties, where he opened his bar and continued engaging in shady activities.

Charlie Fakish started working even younger than Kosofsky. Charlie's mother died when he was seven and his alcoholic father abandoned him. He was taken in by an aunt and uncle who had six children of their own to raise. He was a bright kid, but unsupervised. School bored him, and the streets became his classroom.

He was hired by a bookie when he was nine years old. His job was to visit housewives who wanted to bet on horse races without their husbands knowing. He would pay out winnings and keep two and a half percent of the money collected, and always took in far more than he paid out. If any husband asked what he was doing in their house, he'd reply, "Collectin' for my paper route." As a result, Charlie earned the nickname "Paper." He continued working for bookies in New Jersey until he accumulated a sufficient nest egg to head for Florida and reinvent himself as "Jersey Charlie." Both Fakish and Kosofsky had extreme beginnings and grew into selfish men incapable of love without wives or families. When it came to women, they preferred "renting to owning." They were greedy for money and the material pleasures it could buy and weren't afraid to break rules.

Doc's Melody Bar was located on the corner of NE 2nd Ave and NE 77th Street, right across from the Little River Auditorium. When Chappie Roberts arrived, he parked his Pontiac Chieftain four door sedan along NE 77th Street and walked in the front entrance.

The walls of the establishment were decorated with winged angelic cherubs, dimly lit sconces and banquettes upholstered in naugahyde. Half the flooring was terrazzo tile and the rest polished hardwood. An impressive bar required two full time bartenders for each shift. Bill Kosofsky's place also had a small elevated stage and a huge barbeque in the backyard.

Roberts removed his sunglasses, slipped them in a shirt pocket and asked one of the bartenders, "Where's Bill?"

The bartender asked, "You Chappie?" Roberts nodded. "Go through the door marked 'Office.'"

Opening the door, the veteran trainer entered what could have been a suite. The office was originally designed as a one bedroom apartment, complete with a full bathroom and a kitchen area. Charlie Fakish occupied a wooden guest chair and a balding, heavy set man with copper colored teeth was seated behind a desk. Fakish said, "Chappie, meet Bill Kosofsky, another Joisy guy."

Bill got up from his chair, walked around in front of his desk and shook hands with Roberts. The bar owner said, "Call me Copperhead, but don't worry. I'm no snake, heh heh. Got the name years ago after a dentist gimme false choppers that look like copper." He gave Chappie a big smile to display his dentures. "I've gotten used to 'em. Still work good and fit great, so why replace 'em? Anyway, Charlie says everything's set."

Chappie nodded. Copperhead asked, "Big Julie's people know what to do?"

"Absolutely."

"Well, this calls for a celebration. We'll have some of my good stuff."

Chappie noticed a diamond pinkie ring on his host's little finger and thought, "He must be handlin' a lotta action." He asked, "Why you call your place 'Doc's Melody Bar?'"

"Goes back to Prohibition days in Joisy. I had a way of makin' moonshine that would pass for the best bourbon. They called me 'The Doctor of Home-made Booze.' The melody part is 'cuz I'm a musician."

"What do ya play?"

"The accordion over there." Bill pointed to an instrument case in the corner. "Just ask Charlie."

Fakish nodded his head and said, "He's damn good."

"Yeah," continued Kosofsky, "Been playin' since I was a kid. When I was five, I got three bucks for playin' all night at a New Year's Eve party." The bar owner took a bottle of Crown Royal from a large wooden cabinet and poured whis-key into three shot glasses. When the glasses were filled, he served his two associates and then returned to his chair. He offered a toast. "Here's ta the big fight and lotsa action."

A few days later, Doc's Melody Bar was packed with a late night crowd and Bill Kosofsky was busy helping his night bartenders keep up with the flow of customers, watching the cash register and making sure no more than ten free drinks were given out. He overheard two men at the end of the bar discuss-ing the recently announced Terrell versus Siler fight. One was wearing a skin-ny brimmed straw hat and had an unlit cigarette dangling from his lips as he spoke. "Terrell's in no shape ta handle Siler."

"Where'd ya hear that?"

"Guy at work has a brother at a toy factory near Chicago who follows the fights. Says the word on the street is Siler's ready to pay 'im back, and Terrell's overconfident. He's been doggin'it in training camp. The owner of the factory put a big bet on Siler."

"What's Siler done lately?" asked his friend, who was wearing a white short sleeved shirt and tan work pants.

"Won eleven in a row, with five knockouts."

The man in the white shirt raised his eyebrows, rubbed his chin and re-sponded with, "Ummhummh." He asked Kosofsky, "Hey, Bill, what're the odds on Terrell and Siler?"

"Terrell by 7 to 1."

"You takin' action?"

"Let's go in the back."

The bar owner led his customer to the spacious back office and asked, "Whadja have in mind, Nick?" Nick had placed bets with Kosofsky before.

Nick held out a ten dollar bill and said, "Here's a sawbuck on Siler."

"I know you're good for it, Nick, don't hafta give it to me now." Out of all the wagers Nick had made with Bill, he had picked only one winner.

"I got to. My wife goes through my pockets at night, and I might not have it tomorrow."

After Nick left the bar owner, Copperhead marked down the wager in a notebook using his special code and thought, "Isaacson's doin' his part." Terrell's manager planted the story about his fighter slacking off in training camp. In reality, the Chicago heavyweight was filled with rage about having to come to Miami and fight for nothing. He couldn't do anything to his manager, so he was training hard to make Herb Siler pay for it.

Many fight fans like Nick became convinced the pre-fight talk was true and jumped at the chance to capitalize on an upset. So many wagers poured in on Siler the odds shifted to Terrell being favored by 6 to 5.

Bobby Bann ran into Dwaine Simpson at the Jersey Charlie's luncheonette near the auditorium and asked the veteran boxer what he thought of the fight. Dwaine leaned on the counter and replied, "I don't think Siler's gonna beat him."

"Big money's goin' with Siler."

"Wheredja hear that?"

"I was at Doc's Melody Bar and I overhear Chappie Roberts talkin' to the guy who owns the place. They said some toy manufacturer down here on vacation walked in and put down a bundle on Siler. I saw the guy when he came outta the place. Just lookin' at him, ya could tell he's nobody from 'round here."

"That don't prove nothin'," said Simpson. He took a sip of coffee before adding, "I still can't figure why Terrell's fightin' at Little River. If they can pay enough to get somebody like that, they should pay us more. But that'll never happen."

"Why not," asked Bobby.

"They always find guys willin' to fight for peanuts. There's a buyer's market, a seller's market and Dick Lee believes in a 'giver's market.' He thinks fighters should give their blood, sweat and tears and don't expect to get anything. Someday he's gonna ask us ta not only fight for free, but also make a cash donation to the Masons." Dwaine had no idea how little Ernie Terrell was receiving: A plane ride to Miami, a night in a hotel, some meals, but no cash.

The Terrell versus Siler ten round main event attracted the largest crowd Little River Auditorium ever had. Fight fans were packed in so tight, many were forced to stand throughout the evening. A thick haze of tobacco smoke hung over the ring as the main event began, and the fans were yelling at the top of their lungs for Siler. Terrell was amazed at how much support his opponent had and thought, "This chump's not goin' the distance with me. I'm gonna stop his ass."

Bobby Bann and his buddy Danny Berrielt were among the lucky ones occupying seats. When the fight started, the man next to them exclaimed, "Whip 'im, Siler, whip 'im! I got fifty ridin' on ya."

Terrell went after Siler the instant the opening bell rang. Danny turned to Bobby and said, "I shoulda listened to ya and bet on Terrell. He looks like he wants to kill somebody." He had no idea how close he was to the truth. The Chicago heavyweight harbored thoughts of murdering his manager, but chose to take his anger out on his opponent. Bann munched contentedly on a hot dog as Terrell battered Siler. His money was on the favorite. Terrell's third round knockout of Siler was met with stunned silence. The vast majority attending the bout had put money on the underdog. They had bought into a myth the taller heavyweight was overconfident and ripe for an upset, but their hopes of cashing in went up in flames.

Ernie Terrell had made it look too easy, and the fans suspected something fishy. Many had questions for Julie Isaacson, but the big, loud, Brooklyn born fight manager and his boxer left the arena as quickly as possible. Isaacson told his fighter, "Don't bother to shower. Ya can do that at the hotel." Terrell thought, "The other guy got an ass whuppin', but he got a little bit of change. That's more'n I got." Following that night in Little River, he refused to speak to Isaacson and eventually got another manager, but would never know how much Big Julie won by betting on him. It was the only time bookmakers across the nation took action on a fight at Little River Auditorium, and Isaacson assigned several of his union members to make wagers for him. He cleared tens of thousands of dollars.

There were other winners besides the union president. Little River Auditorium drew its biggest crowd in history. Nearly fifteen hundred fight fans crammed into a building built to accommodate a little over half that number. Over $2500 in tickets had been sold, and the concessions ran out of hot dogs, peanuts and cokes. Even though the promotion was a financial success, the outcome of the fight troubled Neil Composto and Dick Lee. They smelled a rat and met the next day to discuss what happened. Lee blew a cloud of smoke from his cigarette and said, "Ya know Julie Isaacson prolly started the story that came outta Chicago. I wouldn't be surprised if he made a pile bettin' on his man. That's why he was willin' to take the fight for no purse."

"He treated us like a getaway town," replied Neil. "He duped us, made his money and got away as fast as possible."

Lee said, "Never trust a union president. They alluz come out way ahead of whatever they give ya."

"Ain't that the truth," replied Composto.

They laid the blame entirely on Isaacson's shoulders, never realizing Fakish, Kosofsky and Roberts took in over a hundred grand from wagers on the main event. When they carved it up, Chappie was surprised to learn twenty percent went for protection. He asked Charlie and Copperhead, "Who's gettin' that money and why so much?"

Jersey Charlie replied, "It's what the man who protects us gets for any big score, and be grateful it ain't a bigger slice. You're better off not knowin' who he is." Kosofsky nodded in agreement.

Roberts said, "Guess I'll hafta go along. Youse guys done right by me so far and what we pay the guy is still less'n what the S and G syndicate was hittin' me up for. Besides, I don't want no problems with the law. I'm gonna enjoy life."

RONNIE NEMOS CUBAN CONNECTION

Ronnie Nemo was barely out of his teens and doing well for himself. He had a sweet running 1952 Mercury coupe, a few bucks in his pocket and several hundred put aside, but wanted much more. He envied guys with Cadillacs who dressed sharp in tailored clothes, paid people to take care of their cars and had gorgeous chicks hanging on their arms. He wanted those things , but his biggest desire was to boss his own gang.

Ronnie believed he was the smartest of the Little River Rats because he was the best thief. He devoted nearly every waking hour to exploiting negligence, carelessness and the trusting natures of honest working people. He even dropped out of school so he would be ready to strike whenever an opportunity presented itself. At the age of eighteen, he assembled a homemade disc-like contraption for making duplicate keys and used the keys to break into cars. He also had a knack for locating the sweet spot of a trunk lid. If he gave it a whack at just the right place, the lid would pop open.

He felt no sympathy for any of the other Rats caught stealing. When fellow gang member Doug Murdock told him Richie Morton had been arrested for shoplifting, Nemo's response was, "The guy was stupid. He's too stupid to be a thief. All the years I been boostin', how many times I been caught?"

"None I've heard of."

"That's right, a big fat zero. And ya know why? 'Cuz I look for opportunities, but never look around to see if anyone's watchin'." Nemo spoke excitedly because he loved boasting about his skill as a thief. "Ya gotta be ready to move whenever ya see an opportunity, but gotta act like you're doin' what you're s'posed to be doin'."

As talented a mechanic as Ronnie was and as skillful as he had become at shoplifting, burglarizing stores and breaking into cars, the things he craved required far more than what he took in. He envied bookies, bolita operators and pimps who raked in large amounts of cash and yearned to be in a similar position, but was only twenty and too young to be taken seriously.

The opportunity he had been seeking arrived in an unexpected way when he befriended a Cuban refugee named Ramiro Marquez. Ramiro was a little older than Ronnie, always dressed sharp and drove a 1956 Ford convertible kept in immaculate condition. They met because the Cuban's lack of knowledge about cars made him vulnerable to an unscrupulous garage owner in Little River.

Ramiro had taken his Ford to Hayden Richards' repair shop for a tune up. He was lured by the low prices Hayden advertised but when the work was completed, wasn't happy with the way the car ran. Richards refused to do anything to solve the problem unless Marquez paid more. He felt he had the upper hand because Little River had few Cubans and the locals weren't likely to take Ramiro's side. The tall, stylishly dressed young man was in a heated argument with the garage owner when Ronnie happened to be driving by.

Nemo knew Richards, but wasn't a friend of his. Hayden recognized how talented the kid was with cars and offered him a job as a mechanic. Ronnie had seen how hot tempered and controlling the garage owner could be and declined the offer. He parked his car, walked over to where the two men were arguing and interrupted them by asking, "What's goin' on, Hayden?"

"Oh, hi, Ronnie. It's nothin' This guy don't understan' plain English. I tol' him before we worked on his car our guarantee is fifty-fifty. If he accepts the car after we work on it, then he approves of what we did. If he brings it back within thirty days and wants anythin' done over, we pay half."

Ramiro broke in by shouting, "YOU ARE A CRIMINAL!"

Richards smirked and spoke calmly. "Your Ford's nearly ten years old. I tol' ya we couldn't make a brand new car out of it. If ya want a brand new car, go to a new car dealer." He turned and walked away from the irate customer.

Ramiro's face was red with anger. He shouted, "*BASTARDO!*" and shook his fist.

Two of Hayden's workers walked up and flanked their boss. Both were over two hundred pounds and one was holding a tire iron. Richards turned away from Marquez and headed back to his office. End of conversation.

Ronnie asked the Cuban, "What's wrong with your car?"

"Are you a mechanic?"

"I'm good enough that Hayden Richards wants to hire me, but smart enough not to work for the asshole. I've got a little shop a coupla blocks from here. Let's go there and I'll see what I can do 'bout your car."

"I will pay you if you fix it right."

"You better believe it. I don't work for free." Ramiro smiled at that remark, and Ronnie smiled in return.

Nemo worked on cars in a small garage next to his dad's house. From the time he was twelve, he had to maintain his father's cars or get smacked in the face. Eight years later, Ronnie was still keeping his old man's cars going. Another reason he craved big money was to get away from his father once and for all.

Al Nemo wasn't around when the two young men pulled up in their cars. Ronnie thought, "He's prolly at the race track, as usual." Al once won three grand in a single afternoon at Hialeah Park, and that was his downfall. He became a degenerate gambler forever chasing another big day at the track. Ronnie's mother died when he was two years old, and his dad was the only parent he had ever known.

Nemo guided Ramiro's Ford into the garage. He said, "The engine's runnin' rough. Lemme check the timing." He took his timing light from his tool chest and began running a test. After a few minutes, he said, "Hayden's grease monkey didn't set the timing right." Nemo made some adjustments, and the Ford began running as smooth as when it came off the assembly line.

Ramiro was elated. "Thank you, thank you so much. What do I owe you?"

"Ten bucks'll cover it."

As Marquez handed Nemo a ten dollar bill, he said, "Oh how I would like to revenge myself against that crooked Richards!"

"I know how, but we'll hafta wait 'til tonight."

"That is perfectly all right with me. In the meantime, we will take a ride to my part of Miami."

They spent the afternoon in Little Havana. Ramiro treated Ronnie to a Cuban meal, and they killed time until it was dark and most businesses were closed.

The Cuban followed his new friend back to Little River and parked his car on a street near Al Nemo's house. They drove to Hayden Richards' shop in Ronnie's Mercury. Along the way, he told Ramiro what he had in mind. "You're gonna be the lookout. It'll be easy for me to get in Hayden's place. Half the time his flunkies leave the back door unlocked. Even if it's locked, I can jimmy it open. The big problem is makin' sure nobody's around. If ya see anybody comin' near the place, I want ya to pound on a window. Don't break it, but pound hard."

"I will do it," replied Marquez.

They parked half a block away from the repair shop. Ramiro positioned himself where he could see both front and rear entrances. Ronnie went to the back door and was pleased to find it unlocked. He entered and walked toward the section of the garage used for storing replacement parts, picking up a large empty cardboard box along the way. Nemo filled the box with spark plugs, fan belts and other repair items, then carried the box to the back door, opened the door slightly and peered outside. There was no one around. He left the box in the garage and walked briskly to his Mercury. He started his car and drove to the back entrance of Richards' garage. He carried the box from the garage to the Mercury, opened the trunk lid and dumped the contents onto the floor of the trunk. Trips between the Mercury and the garage continued without interruption until the garage owner's entire supply of replacement parts was taken.

As Ronnie drove Ramiro to his Ford, the Cuban couldn't stop raving about the daring burglary. He exclaimed, "*Dios mio*! I have never seen anyone with as much courage. You actually parked your car right next to the garage and spent all that time loading it."

Nemo replied, "Best part is the door was unlocked, so the cops'll tell Hayden it was an inside job. I don't know if he's smart enough to figure out he cheated the wrong guy, but we'll see."

Ronnie sold the haul to Copperhead, and split the take with Ramiro. The Cuban couldn't wait to introduce Nemo to his friends. They were mildly impressed when he told them how talented Ronnie was at working on cars, but their ears perked up when he mentioned what a great thief he was and he was part of the notorious Little River Rats. A meeting was quickly arranged at the home of Jose Oliva, the oldest of the group.

Arriving at Oliva's house, Ronnie was greeted by Jose at the front door and escorted to the living room. Ramiro Marquez and five other men were already there. Jose offered Nemo a seat on a couch and asked the young man if he would like some rum.

"Yeah, with Coca Cola," replied Nemo. "Don't they call that a *Cuba Libre*."

Oliva smiled and replied, "Smart young man." Nemo noticed all the men, including Jose and Ramiro, wore linen guayabera shirts. He thought, "Wonder if that's their uniform."

Jose brought Ronnie his drink and then sat next to him on the couch. As the younger man sipped his rum and Coke, Oliva asked, "Do you smoke?"

"No cigarettes, but I tried an expensive cigar once. It was alright, but it's nothin' I'd do all the time."

"Do you know what marijuana is?"

"I've heard of it. Could never understand why they call it 'reefer.'"

"Would you like to try some?"

"Not really."

"That is good. You are smart. Let me tell you something about us. We all came from Cuba. Our families lived in the hills and were marijuana farmers. They sheltered Fidel Castro while he was hiding from the dictator before the revolution. He showed his gratitude for their hospitality by promising to protect them. Our families are allowed to grow marijuana and we are here in Miami to sell it."

"How do ya get it in here?"

"Castro has spies here in Miami. They are called G2 agents, and they were trained by the KGB of the Soviet Union. They make sure our marijuana arrives without any problems. They do this because part of the money used to pay them comes from selling it. The money is good, but we could always use more. You could help us a great deal."

"How's that?"

"Marijuana is not being used very much in Little River. Would you be interested in introducing it to those in your area?"

"Where would I do it? Would I go to bars, pool halls and places men hang out?"

"Not at first. The best places to start would be where school children gather."

"You mean like luncheonettes with jukeboxes and pinball machines?".

"*Perfecto*."

Ronnie had Jersey Charlie in mind. He said to himself, "Charlie'll go along if I cut him in." He asked Jose, "How much money can I make?"

"A two pound brick will cost you six hundred dollars. If you sell all of it, you will make nearly four thousand."

All Ronnie could say was, "Wow!" He thought, "Reefer's gonna be my ticket to the good life." He had managed to put aside six hundred dollars, but it was every cent he had. He needed Jersey Charlie's help and was willing to give him a big piece of the action.

After the meeting broke up, Nemo headed back to Little River. While driving home, he thought, "Gotta talk to the other guys in the Rats about sellin' reefer, but the first thing I gotta do is get Jersey Charlie to go along."

EXQUISITE BETRAYAL

The man Bill Kosofsky kept secret from Chappie Roberts was Captain Raymond T. Tanner of the Miami Police Department detective squad. Tanner protected Kosofsky in return for a share of the bar owner's profits. The captain also took care of all payoffs, including those given to the Dade County Sheriff. He often reminded Copperhead, "I've made life simple for you."

Tanner was a fat man who could knock back amazing amounts of whiskey, and the detectives under his command knew he could usually be found at Doc's Melody Bar. He often reminded the numbers operators, bookies, pimps and prostitutes in his section of the city, "I am the law." They all paid him protection money and obeyed his code. He didn't allow any narcotics peddling or killings in Little River because those crimes brought too much heat.

The 6'0" 250 pound detective paid an early morning visit to Copperhead's spacious office in the back of the bar. Captain Tanner didn't bother to knock and sat down in an upholstered chair placed in front of Bill Kosofsky's desk. The bar owner said, "It's not even nine o'clock yet. I never see ya around here before eleven. What's up?"

The captain smiled and replied, "Just wanted to sit and talk about what's goin' on in the neighborhood. How 'bout an eye opener?"

Kosofsky rose from his desk and went to a liquor cabinet made of cherry wood. He poured a double shot of Crown Royal into an Old Fashioned glass and handed it to Tanner. The detective never put ice cubes in his whiskey. He often said, "Water is for washin', not drinkin'. Never put anything in your system that could rust a pipe." The big bellied police captain sipped his drink before bringing up what was on his mind. "Let's talk about a bright young fella you know quite well."

"Whozzat?" asked Bill.

"First name begins with an R, and last name begins with an N and ends with an O."

"Ronnie Nemo."

"Brilliant! You'd make a fine detective." Tanner got up from his chair and walked into an adjoining room. In addition to his expansive stomach, his unbuttoned suit coat revealed a .38 revolver carried in a shoulder holster. A large cardboard box had aroused the law enforcement officer's curiosity, and he opened the lid. "My my, there's lotsa cigarette cartons in here... Marlboros, Salem, Viceroys. I'm lookin' for Camels."

"Should be some in there."

"Found 'em. Gonna take a carton, okay?'

"Sure," said Kosofsky. "Surprised ya don't want no Marlboros. They got that new 'self starter' pull tab so ya don't hafta dig around for your smokes."

"Ah, I just don't like those filters," replied Tanner. "Guess ya got the cigarettes from Ronnie, huh?"

"Ya know I did."

"No tellin' where he got 'em. The kid's amazin'... a natural born thief. I don't think he's twenty one yet, and he's one of the best boosters in town. He's proud of his scores and tells people about 'em. Didja hear 'bout when he went into a Sears near closing time, hid under a bed until all the employees left and then robbed the place. He once said to me, 'I'm very selective. I only take things that begin with the letter 'A'... A box of green stamps, A coat, A set of wheel covers.'"

Bill chuckled and said, "Yeah, that's Ronnie all right."

Ray Tanner's demeanor suddenly became deadly serious. Kosofsky had known him long enough to be familiar with his volatile personality. The stout detective could go from joviality to rage in a heartbeat. Tanner's sudden change to a serious mood made the bar owner uncomfortable, but it wasn't nearly as frightening as when the captain became angry. The detective said in a chilly monotone, "There's a problem and you're gonna clean it up."

"What's that?"

Tanner's dark eyes turned coal black. "I been generous about layin' off Ronnie. He's still small potatoes and most of the businesses he robs carry insurance, but now the kid wants to get bigger. I hear Nemo's tryin' to make a deal with some Commie bastards for marijuana and thinks he can use the Little River Rats to sell it. I don't want any Reds makin' money by messin' up our school kids. You're the one who buys most of his stolen merchandise, and you're gonna stop 'im. But don't kill 'im. I don't allow any homicides in my part of town."

Copperhead answered without hesitation. "I'll take care of it right away."

Tanner continued sitting in Kosofsky's office for an hour; drinking, smoking and making light conversation. Not another word was said about Ronnie Nemo.

After the captain finally left, Bill called Jersey Charlie and told him, "Come over to the bar. I gotta see ya right away."

Fifteen minutes later, Fakish arrived. Copperhead began to explain his dilemma, but was surprised when Jersey Charlie interrupted and said, "I know all about Nemo's plans. He wanted to include me. I told 'im I'd think about it but the minute he left, I got hold of Captain Tanner and told 'im all about it. We gotta keep him happy, so whatta we gonna do?" They sat in silence for a few minutes pondering the problem before Jersey Charlie said, "Ya know who could help us?"

"Who?"

"Blackie Bethel."

"Who's he?"

"He used to be in the Rats. Now he's a fight manager. He was managin' Carl Starling before the guy got his draft notice. Ronnie looks up ta'im and allus talks 'bout 'im, and I'm sure he could come up with somethin'."

Copperhead made some calls and was able to set up a meeting the next day. When Bethel walked into the bar owner's office, Charlie and Bill were surprised he was only in his late twenties. He had a medium build, appeared fit and was wearing a conservative suit and tie. Blackie said, "I can't stay long because I'm on my lunch hour, but I have an idea about how to solve your problem. Let me put it all together and then I'll see you tomorrow night."

Bethel's first name was really Blackburn, but preferred Blackie. He was the descendent of a sea captain from the Bahamas who settled in Key West. He was born in Miami and became one of the original Little River Rats while in junior high, along with the Cash brothers and Long John Fulford. The Cash's and Fulford were high school dropouts, but Bethel graduated from Miami's Jackson Senior High School. After graduation, he enlisted in the Army and was assigned a clerical position in a headquarters company. He learned accounting procedures and after serving his two year hitch and returning to Miami, Blackie was hired by an accounting firm as a bookkeeper.

When Carl Starling decided to become a professional boxer, he turned to Blackie for advice. They shared several things in common. Both graduated from the same high school, although Carl was a few years behind Blackie. Bethel had a Bahamian heritage, and Starling was brought up on the islands. Their partnership clicked, and Blackie guided Carl to an unbeaten record before the fighter was drafted into the Army.

When Bethel returned to Doc's Melody Bar the following night, he revealed his plan to Fakish and Kosofsky. "I'm going to tell Ronnie Nemo I want him to become a pro boxer and I'll manage him."

"Ya really think he's that good?" asked Jersey Charlie.

"I'm gonna offer him something bigger than a pro boxing career. I'll tell him if he wins one pro fight, he's a cinch to be voted in as leader of the Little River Rats. Once that happens, I can arrange for grants from foundations, charitable groups and the government to train everyone in the gang for good paying jobs. Ronnie will be the head of the program and he'll get a good salary and an expense account. I'll also set things up so you two will be part of it."

"What happens if he doesn't win the fight?"

"He'll be all alone and won't have an organization to peddle marijuana. The Rats will be making money from the job training program, and I'll see that they forget about getting involved with dope. This will work, but I'll need some cash for expenses. "

"How much?"

"Not much, a hundred and fifty a week until after the fight."

"Fine," said Bill. "Come by here every Saturday and pick it up."

The next morning happened to be a Saturday. Blackie called Ronnie's house and his father answered the phone. "Whadya want?"

"Is Ronnie in?"

"He in trouble again?"

"No."

"He's not here."

"Know where he might be?"

"Hell if I know."

Immediately after Bethel hung up, his phone rang. It was Jersey Charlie. "I'm at my place on 2nd Avenue. Ronnie just walked in."

Blackie made a quick trip to the luncheonette in his 1962 Chevy Impala. When he walked in, Nemo was eating a cheeseburger in a booth along a wall. Bethel walked up and introduced himself to the twenty year old. Ronnie had heard older members of the Rats speak of Blackie with reverence. He seemed in awe as he replied, "You're one of the original Rats!"

"That's right." Blackie sat down across from Ronnie.

Nemo said, "Long John Fulford and the Cash brothers were somethin' else."

"They were tough and had ice water in their veins, but tried to get big money with guns. They didn't know you can get a lot more with a pencil."

"Whadya mean?"

"Well, take me for instance. I went into the Army. Best thing ever happened to me. I learned bookkeeping. Now, I'm working for an accounting firm. Plus, I manage boxers. You've heard of Carl Starling?"

"I've heard of 'im, but never got a chance to see 'im fight. So you're his manager."

"Carl's in the Army now," said Bethel. "In the meantime, I've got a shot at something worth a quarter million or even a half million bucks. I need a key man, and you'd be ideal."

Ronnie leaned forward and asked with eagerness in his voice, "What do I have to do?"

"First, you've gotta be accepted as leader of the Rats. When I was active in the gang, you'd have to challenge the guy on top and fight him to be number one. Now, it's different."

"Yeah, Bobby Bann made the Rats into what he calls a 'social gang' and made things kinda soft. He's steppin' down and insists we're gonna vote for a new president. Some guys would vote for me, but not enough."

"If you win a professional fight, that'll convince the rest. I hear a lot of them agree Bann has gotten too soft. They'll see you're the toughest, and they'll be told about your plan that will make them hundreds of thousands of dollars."

"What kinda plan ya talkin' about?"

"I know a way to get money from the government and do gooders to set up a school that teaches job skills to gang members."

Ronnie shook his head when Blackie mentioned the word "school." "The guys want nothin' to do with school. You know that."

"What if they were paid to go to school?"

"How much?"

"They'd get fifty a week, maybe more. Since you'd be in charge, you'd get six grand a year in salary plus an expense account and company car. And you don't have to worry about getting arrested. It's all perfectly legal."

"Count me in. When do we start?"

"Right now. I'm gonna take you down to the Fifth Street Gym."

Blackie drove Ronnie to the gym run by Chris and Angelo Dundee. Nemo sparred with a journeyman boxer Bethel knew, and the older gang member saw the twenty year old wasn't afraid of getting hit. Ronnie was used to being slapped and punched after being abused by his father for years.

The experienced boxer landed several solid shots on the novice who took two punches to give one good one. Nemo swung wildly, but threw lots of punches and worked like a dynamo. He launched assault after assault in an upright style, constantly walking forward, but threw no combinations. It was obvious he was a fearless street fighter, but had no idea of how to properly deliver a punch.

Blackie thought, "Kid's strictly a brawler, but he's got a good chin." After the sparring session, he asked Nemo, "Where'd you learn to fight?"

"I've done some street fightin', but nobody taught me nothin'."

"You're a natural, Ronnie, a natural. You've got stuff Carl Starling doesn't have."

Ronnie had a look of disbelief and replied, "Ya ain't kiddin' me, are ya?"

"I wouldn't do that," replied Blackie. He slipped Ronnie a twenty and said, "This is just the start."

"Hey thanks." Ronnie thought, "I can't believe it's happenin' so fast, but it's gotta be true."

After dropping Ronnie off where his Mercury was parked, Blackie drove to Doc's Melody Bar. He picked up his weekly $150 payment and told Copperhead what he had in mind for Ronnie Nemo. "I'm gonna try to get Dick Lee to match Ronnie with Dwaine Simpson."

"Why's that?"

"Ronnie's a brawler who's used to street fighting. Simpson's a counterpuncher who dances around and hardly ever knocks anyone out. What are the odds

Ronnie can last six rounds with him?"

"Pretty good."

"That might be true, but what if Nemo telegraphs his punches, rushes at Simpson with his head down and isn't in shape to last six rounds?"

Bill smiled and said, "I get it. We'll build him up so people bet he goes the distance, but you'll make sure he isn't ready to fight. We'll make a killing."

"He has a lot to learn about boxing, and I'll see to it nobody teaches him a thing. I'll also tell him it would better to do less sparring and more roadwork. I'll tell him to run six miles every morning, but I won't be there watching him and fighters slack off if they're not watched. They forget one day of training is like one day of clean living. It doesn't do you any good. His sparring sessions will be at Fifth Street Gym, so nobody in this part of town will really know what he can do."

"I think you've got it all figured out."

"I know I do. If I get Lee to make the match, you can forget about the hundred fifty a week. I'll take a cut of the gambling action."

"You got it."

Immediately after leaving Kosofsky, Blackie Bethel called Dick Lee and said, "I have a match you have to make, Dick. It'll be a classic."

"What is it?"

"Ronnie Nemo wants to fight Dwaine Simpson. You'll have a puncher against a counterpuncher."

Lee replied, "How many fights Nemo had?"

"It'll be the kid's first."

"I can't go along with that. Simpson's got a lotta experience."

"Ronnie's a great street fighter. He'll be able to take care of himself. Besides, Jersey Charlie wants it to happen."

"Ya mean the guy who sells ice cream sandwiches at our shows and gives part of the money to the Masons?"

"That's the one. He'll buy a hundred ringside tickets if you match Nemo and Simpson."

The promise of selling so many ringside seats convinced Dick Lee to go along. He said, "I'll get Simpson to take the fight. I know what to do." Immediately after hanging up with Bethel, Dick called Dwaine and told him he wanted to match him with Nemo in a six rounder for fifty dollars.

"Ya mean the kid who's in the Little River Rats? No way, I've never seen 'im fight. I don't know nothin' about the way he boxes. He's also a jerk."

Lee countered by saying, "I'll give ya an incentive… no deductions from the fifty bucks."

"Ya must want this fight bad."

"It ain't just me. Blackie Bethel's managin' him, and he's bein' promoted by Jersey Charlie. Jersey Charlie owns a buncha luncheonettes and says he'll buy a hunnert ringside seats if ya fight Nemo."

"Bethel was Carl Starling's manager, right?"

"Yep."

Dwaine paused for a moment before saying, "Okay, I'll take the fight." He thought, "Blackie's not gonna waste his time on somebody with no ability. Besides, fifty bucks is fifty bucks."

Once the match was made, Nemo told Bobby Bann he wanted to see him. Bann had announced he no longer wanted to be active in the Rats and the gang would have to vote on a new leader, but a date for the election still hadn't been set.

They met in the garage next to the house the twenty year old shared with his dad. They wouldn't be disturbed because Al Nemo was sleeping off a drunk. Ronnie brought two cold cans of Regal beer from the house. He handed one to the president of the Rats and said, "I'm runnin' for president, and I want the votin' held right after I fight your buddy Dwaine Simpson."

Bobby Bann asked, "Why you wanna take over the gang?"

"'I know how we can make big money."

"I've heard about what you're up to. Ya wanna make a mint sellin' dope."

"That's one way, and I know others," replied Nemo. This was not true. Ronnie's hopes for becoming rich all rested on his marijuana connection. Even though Blackie promised him a six grand salary, he believed the Cubans were the ticket to the really big money.

Bann shook his head and said, "If you're president, the cops'll be watchin' ya all the time. You'll constantly be settlin' arguments among the members, like I'm always doin'. Ya get 'em involved in dope and you'll never know if ya can trust the people around ya, and may find yaself in a cross fire. Ya wanna be on top, but got no idea of what ya have to do to stay on top. Hell, it ain't easy, and that's why I'm gettin' out. I'll set the election for the night after the fight, but I don't think ya know what you're gettin' yaself into."

Nemo replied, "Don't bullshit me. Ya got a four dollar an hour job, and ya got soft. Don't worry. I got a plan."

"Well, I don't wanna hear 'bout it 'cuz it's gonna lead to trouble I want nuthin' to do with." Bann quickly finished his beer and left.

Nemo spent two weeks preparing for the fight, but his training was far from rigorous. He sparred on only three of the fourteen days. Each sparring session lasted just five rounds, and fifteen rounds of sparring wasn't enough preparation for a professional debut. Blackie Bethel didn't offer any criticism, but Nemo knew he wasn't training properly. Training didn't matter to him because he was dead certain he would win the fight. He had a secret weapon he hadn't told Blackie about. He knew Dwaine Simpson was always in need of money, and was going to pay the veteran fighter to lose. He was so confident of his plan working he revealed it to Doug Murdock, a fellow member of the Little River Rats. He loved telling Doug about his schemes and hearing him say, "You're a genius."

At 5' 9" and 195 pounds, Murdock was much bigger than 5'7" 145 pound Nemo, but had allowed Ronnie to order him around and chew him out in public ever since they'd known each other. After Nemo told Murdock what he intended to do, Doug said, "Jeez, Ronnie, you're a genius! Ya got it all figured out."

Nemo looked at his fellow gang member sternly and said, "Don't tell anyone, or else."

"Ya know I wouldn't do that." Murdock's answer satisfied Nemo, but the smaller man didn't realize his relationship with Doug had suddenly changed. The man he bullied for so long was thinking, "I've had enough of Ronnie. I'm gonna pay him back for those miserable years and make some dough."

Nemo waited until the night of the fight to put his plan in motion. He and Dwaine were alone in the Little River Auditorium dressing room, making their final preparations. Ronnie approached the veteran fighter and said in a low voice, "I'll give ya a hunnert bucks if ya let me win."

"Forget it."

"Make it two hunnert."

Simpson said nothing, but his eyes communicated how he loathed Nemo. The twenty year old boxer hadn't bothered to use a middle man to make a discreet offer. Ronnie's clumsy attempt at buying him off angered Dwaine, but he had enough self control to keep from shouting.

Nemo saw the hostility in Dwaine, but misread it and thought, "He's just playin' hard to get." He said, "Awright, I'll go up to three hunnert..."

Simpson cut him off. He moved his face close to his much younger opponent and said menacingly, "Listen, you little piss ant, I wouldn't lose to ya if ya paid me a thousand dollars. I don't like ya, and there's a lotta other people 'round here who don't. I'm gonna make ya sorry ya wanted to get in a ring with me."

While Dwaine and Ronnie were having their confrontation, fight fans were streaming through the aisles of the auditorium, jostling for seats or heading for refreshments. A dense blue cloud from all the cigars and cigarettes hung overhead. Blackie Bethel was sitting at ringside. His right leg jiggled in excited anticipation of what would unfold that evening. Just before taking his seat, Blackie was approached by Dick Lee. The matchmaker laughed as he told the fight manager, "There's a rumor Simpson's gonna take a dive. What a load of crap! You'd hafta be hard up ta bribe college boy. Anyone bettin' on a fight between a twenty year old who's never been in the ring and a chicken shit who can't punch has to be crazy. It could be the first no hitter in the history of boxing."

Bethel knew Doug Murdock had spread the rumor. It had no basis in reality, but everyone believed it because they all knew Doug and Ronnie were the closest of friends. Copperhead and Jersey Charlie took in so many bets on Nemo the odds of Simpson winning dropped from six to one to seven to five. Bethel was aware of everything going on and as he awaited the fight, he thought, "I could make more tonight than I've ever seen at one time." The pieces of his plan were falling into place.

His bribe offer had been turned down, but Nemo deluded himself into thinking he could beat Simpson. He thought, "Sugarfoot is too soft ta be a fighter. Ya just gotta go after him and not let up." He attacked Dwaine from the very start of the bout, running across the canvas rather than waiting for the lanky blonde to come to him. The shorter man telegraphed his movements and put so much of his bodyweight into punches that both feet sometimes left the ground. The seasoned ring veteran eluded the frenetic but ineffective novice fighter and neither landed any blows during the first two rounds. Ronnie began to connect with some punches at start of the round three, but delivered the blows one at a time rather than in combinations. None were solid hits because of Dwaine's constant motion and ability to roll with the punches. He was willing to wait his opponent out. After two minutes and fifteen seconds, the wild swinging novice ran out of steam. He let his guard down, and Simpson instantly unleashed a right hand just under the heart, followed by a left hook on the chin. Ronnie Nemo didn't see the punches coming. His legs turned to jelly, and he collapsed against the ropes in a jumble of limbs.

As the referee began his count, Blackie Bethel shouted to Ronnie, "STAY DOWN UNTIL EIGHT!"

Nemo groggily replied, "Wha... what time is it now?" just before he was counted out. Simpson had won by scoring a rare knockout.

Ronnie had to be assisted to the dressing room. After he was placed on a rubbing table, the fighter said to his manager, "I heard a bell and thought the round was over, so I tried to sit on my stool. Next thing I know, they took me in here."

Bethel replied, "You didn't hear a bell, you got your bell rung. You were knocked out and nowhere near your corner when it happened. It just wasn't your night."

Ronnie's life was in shatters and his dreams had crumbled when he was knocked to the canvas. He was glassy eyed, but able to hold back his tears as he said, "Looks like I'm not gonna be in charge of the Rats."

"Ah, you never can tell," replied Bethel with an insincere smile. "They saw you didn't chicken out. Let's just see what happens." Blackie Bethel had never really been in his corner. The kid who aspired to be Mr. Big had been betrayed from the very start.

The Little River Rats held a meeting the following night to vote on their new leader. Copperhead allowed them the use one of the rooms in his office and was present for the balloting. Ronnie Nemo showed up early, still hopeful things would go his way. The bar owner greeted him by saying, "Tough luck, but ya showed guts."

"Thanks, Copperhead."

Fifteen Rats were present to vote. All but one chose Doug Murdock. The only ballot cast for Ronnie Nemo was his own. The twenty year old with the big ideas sat expressionless for the entire meeting.

When it was over, everyone left except Bill Kosofsky and Nemo. Copperhead poured the twenty year old a shot of Jack Daniels and said, "Everything comes to an end, and your days as a thief are over."

"Whadya mean by that."

"I mean nobody's gonna buy the stuff ya steal, includin' me. Captain Tanner put the word out on ya. If ya go to another part of town, it'll be dangerous for ya... maybe even fatal. You're no longer protected, and ya better keep your mouth shut. Ya should be grateful we didn't just kill ya." Ronnie didn't know there was no chance of his being murdered because Captain Tanner wouldn't allow it. He believed every word Kosofsky said.

Nemo's voice quavered as he asked, "Wha... what do I do now?"

"Get a job, fall in love, get married, settle down and have a buncha kids."

The life Ronnie Nemo had known was over. He had been reduced to a used up fighter after only one bout. To his credit, he didn't give up, got back on his feet and fought back. He joined the Army, made a career of it, married, got hitched to a mortgage and settled down to a normal, contented life. Losing to Dwaine Simpson turned out to be the best thing that ever happened to Ronnie Nemo.

Blackie Bethel split a large betting haul with Jersey Charlie, Copperhead, Chappie Roberts, Doug Murdock and Captain Tanner. Blackie saw great things on the horizon as he awaited Carl Starling's return from serving with the 82nd Airborne and the resumption of his boxing career. Carl was not the same boxer after he was discharged. He fought six times, but won only two, lost three and had a draw. Starling retired from boxing and became a well known charter boat captain.

By the time Carl Starling's career ended, Bethel had succeeded in obtaining funding for a Little River Rats job skills program. Doug Murdock was rewarded with a salaried position as head of the program. Blackie resigned from his bookkeeping job and stopped managing fighters because he was too busy skimming tens of thousands from grants and donations. He rode the gravy train until a congressional investigation led to the program being shut down. Murdock drifted out of sight. Bethel later became involved with the Golden Gates Estates land scam on the west side of Florida, near Naples. As to Marquez, Oliva and the other Cubans supporting the Castro regime through sales of marijuana, they faded out of the picture with the arrival of Miami's Cocaine Cowboys. It was ironic Blackie Bethel became a grifter, while the two fighters he managed, Carl Starling and Ronnie Nemo, found happiness by making much better choices.

PART FOUR:

DWAINE S PROFESSIONAL BOXING CAREER WINDS DOWN

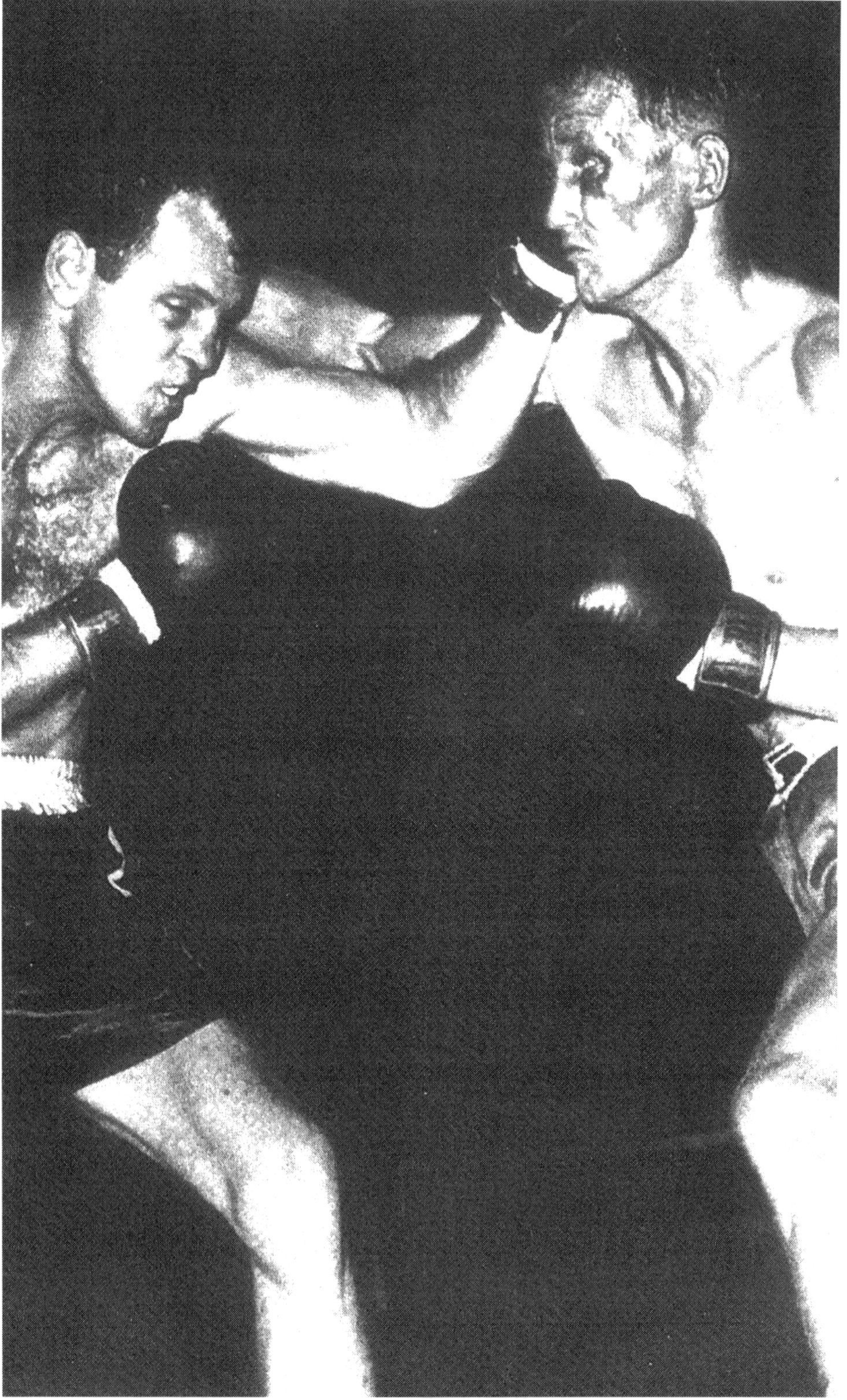

MEETING RHYTHM AND BLUES GREATS AND A BOXING LEGEND

Club Night Beat, the lounge in Miami's Sir John Hotel, was a gathering place for black headliners appearing at Miami Beach hotels. Since blacks were not allowed to stay at those places, they took rooms at the Sir John. After performing their acts at "The Beach," they would head for Club Night Beat to socialize. Many sat in with the house band, Hot Poppa Turner and His Three Daughters.

Sam Rabin, who owned the hotel, staged weekly boxing shows for a solid year. Dwaine fought ten times at the Sir John and would have gladly done it for nothing. He was a rhythm and blues addict, and his appearances on the fight cards came with an added bonus: Choice seats for performances of some of the all time greats. They included Sammy Davis, Jr., Sam Cook, Etta James, The Drifters, Roy Hamilton, Aretha Franklin, The Midnighters and Screamin' Jay Hawkins. He literally had to fight his way in to see them, but it was well worth it.

When first arriving in Miami, Muhammad Ali stayed at both the Sir John Hotel and the Mary Elizabeth Hotel before purchasing a home in Liberty City. This was back in the days when he was known as Cassius Clay. The Mary Elizabeth was Miami's finest hotel for blacks, and Dwaine Simpson spent many memorable nights in its Club Fiesta lounge. He would go there with his black friends who were boxers and basketball players to enjoy great entertainment. Many times, there were very few whites in the place, but he would fit in by donning a pair of sunglasses and explaining, "I'm a black albino with pink eyes." Later, he changed his story to, "I'm a black albino with pink eyes, wearin' blue contact lenses."

Musicians weren't the only legends Simpson came to know through boxing. In April, 1966, Dwaine was matched in a ten round main event held on the island of St. Croix in the U.S. Virgin Islands. He faced Willie Munoz, a cousin of world lightweight champion Carlos Ortiz. The boxing show was held to benefit the territory's Police Athletic League, with the main attraction being a six round exhibition between Ortiz and the legendary Sugar Ray Robinson. Robinson agreed to participate because of his long friendship with Charles Greeneveldt, Chief Criminal Investigator for the Islands.

Dwaine flew in a day early and was pleased to discover he, along with Robinson, Ortiz and Munoz, would be housed at a luxurious seaside resort. After he checked in, members of the PAL drove him back to Alexander Hamilton Airport for the arrival of Sugar Ray's flight from New York. Once the four visiting fighters were assembled, they were welcomed by a committee of local officials and prominent Virgin Islanders and given a musical greeting by a traditional steel drum band. Each boxer was placed in a convertible and became part of a motorcade parading through the towns of Christiansted and Frederiksted. Townspeople gave the boxers such a rousing welcome Dwaine thought, "If the people in Opa-Locka could see me now!"

The fighters also visited the Insular Training School for Boys at Estate Anna's Hope, an orphanage where world champion Emile Griffith was raised. It was a thrill for Dwaine to sign autographs for a large number of young kids.

The main event matching lightweights Simpson and Munoz took place in an outdoor ring set under a stand of shade trees and a green awning. None of this prevented the sweltering heat from taking its toll. Dwaine held his own against his ranked opponent for the first five rounds, but ran out of gas and took a drubbing for another three before the fight was stopped in the eighth and Willie Munoz awarded a technical knockout.

After the boxing show ended, Sugar Ray Robinson took Ortiz, Munoz and Simpson out to dinner. The boxing immortal gave Dwaine words of encouragement about his boxing and his life. As the evening drew to a close, Robinson asked his manager and trainer, George Gainsford, for a photo to give the lanky blue eyed blonde. Gainsford reached into his briefcase and handed Sugar Ray a glossy photograph, but didn't have a pen handy. The former world champion began to look for a ballpoint, but Dwaine piped up and said, "Don't worry 'bout it. I'll have ya sign it later." Unfortunately, the great Sugar Ray Robinson left for New York early the next morning before Simpson could have him autograph the photo.

Dwaine collected his three hundred dollar purse, the most he ever made as a boxer up to that time, and headed back to Miami. He had been TKO'd by Willie Munoz, but had very little soreness, no cuts and no injuries. Meeting one of the greatest fighters of all time was the highlight of his trip to the Virgin Islands. It had been a priceless moment, and his only regret was not keeping quiet until Sugar Ray found a pen and signed the glossy photo.

BOXING IN A FOREIGN LAND CAN BE HAZARDOUS TO YOUR HEALTH

One day late in 1969, Dwaine was called to the phone at work. A Cuban exile who promoted fights named Felix Zabala was on the line. Simpson had heard of him and was willing to listen to what he had to say. Zabala came right to the point. "I am looking for the right opponent for welterweight contender Dario Hidalgo from the Dominican Republic. Are you familiar with him?"

"Yeah, he's had a coupla fights in Madison Square Garden. How do I fit in?"

Zabala replied in a heavy Spanish accent, "Well, I think you are perfect for what I have in mind. You are a tall, blonde haired, blue eyed American with a legitimate and excellent record." It was true that Dwaine fought 135 documented bouts and won ninety percent of them, but records are not always what they appear to be. Dwaine thought, "I don't think this guy looked at who I fought. A hunnert of 'em were four rounders 'gainst fighters no better'n Helen Keller and Little Red Riding Hood. Wonder what his angle is."

Zabala continued his sales pitch and got Simpson's attention when he said, "If you fight Hidalgo in Santiago, his hometown, we will pay you three hundred dollars plus expenses."

Dwaine thought, "Haven't been paid that much since that time in the Virgin Islands. I gotta take the fight. What do I have to lose?" He said to Zabala, "Okay, ya got your man."

Zabala added, "I have to mention I am not allowed in the Dominican Republic because of some promotion problems in Puerto Rico, so I am sending my wife to handle my duties."

"Fine with me."

Dwaine arranged time off from both his jobs and had a pleasant flight to the largest city in the Dominican Republic. He was picked up at the Santo Domingo airport by an air conditioned van. The only persons in the vehicle were Mrs. Zabala and the driver. Simpson thought, "Man, this is class!" He was dressed in a style popular in the States: A white turtle neck and a blue blazer sporting an embroidered U.S.A. emblem. As he rode in the van, he thought, "Here I am, a main event boxer takin' on a national hero. The way I'm dressed, anyone would know I'm somebody."

It was a two hour drive to Santiago along roads so bumpy Dwaine thought, "Maybe this is what goin' over Niagara Falls in a barrel feels like." When they arrived at a small hotel a mile outside the city, he felt as though he had gone ten rounds.

He didn't speak a word of Spanish, so Mrs. Zabala interpreted for him. Through the promoter's wife, he asked the driver to take him to the nearest travel agency. He wanted to book a flight home and make sure he could leave as soon as possible after collecting his purse.

As the van rolled through the town's main street, Dwaine saw a banner stretched high above that read "Dario Hidalgo vs. Dwaine Simpson (Florida Welterweight Champion)." He thought, "Hell, I'm not even the Opa-Locka Welterweight Champion."

It was early December, but the weather was hot and the travel agency was an open air business. As Simpson left the van, nearly one hundred fifty people gathered around. They were attracted by the way he was dressed, and little kids ran up to him just to touch his clothes. The crowd stood outside the business while he booked his return flight. Immediately after Dwaine finished making the arrangements, someone shouted, "KILL THE AMERICAN!"

Others took up the cry, and Mrs. Zabala hurried Dwaine back to van. It was a jarring experience, and she tried to calm him as they rode back to the hotel. "You have done nothing wrong," she said. "Most of the people hate Americans because the U.S.A. sent Marines in here four years ago to help the government in power against rebels. The rebels are Communists, and Santiago is a stronghold for them."

This only made things worse. Dwaine became so frightened he didn't know what to say. He thought, "Here I am, a long way from home, worried about gettin' beat up by a world ranked boxer and maybe gettin' shot by a local resident." He finally asked her, "What should I do?"

"As long as you do not go into town, you should be fine."

After Mrs. Zabala and the driver dropped him off, it was the last time Dwaine saw anyone he recognized except the man he would be fighting. The promoter's wife stayed somewhere else, and he was left to fend for himself. There was a restaurant in the hotel, but his inability to speak Spanish confined him to a tiresome diet of fish, salad, bread and bottled water for breakfast, lunch and dinner. It was three days before he could figure out how to say *huevos* and ask for eggs.

In addition to his problems getting something to eat, the days before the bout were so stressful he had trouble sleeping. He would arise at five in the morning to walk the hotel grounds and do some shadow boxing. Very early on the morning of the fight, he was returning to his room when he heard noise. Five men carrying rifles and wearing ammunition belts across their chests were coming from the hotel. They were laughing and talking in loud voices and didn't notice Dwaine. He had no idea what they were saying and became worried about what they might do if they saw him. He hid in the bushes, thinking,

"If they kidnap me, I'm outta luck. Nobody I know has any money or even wants me, 'specially my ex-wife."

He never left the hotel until two men picked him up late in the afternoon of the fight. They drove him to the baseball stadium where the boxing show was to be held and arrived five hours before fights were to begin. Dwaine couldn't believe how many people were arriving early. He thought, "There's so many of 'em. Why are all these women and children here?"

The primitive conditions of the stadium were shocking. Just as he stepped inside the entrance, he saw a man with his trousers down taking a crap in full view of everyone. He thought, "Guess they don't have restrooms here. Hope there's a toilet in my dressing room." Then he thought, "What am I worried about? I'm part of the main event. I'll prolly have a nice dressing room all to myself."

Two men approached him. They didn't speak English but after they made some hand gestures, Dwaine realized they would be working in his corner. He followed the men to an enclosure behind a dugout.

The three of them walked into a large room that felt like a sauna and smelled like a goat farm. Dwaine saw men changing into boxing gear and suddenly realized he was in the dressing quarters. He thought, "THIS is what a main event fighter gets? Hell no!" He looked for Dario Hidalgo, but he wasn't in the room. Simpson thought, "I'm sure the hometown star is well taken care of." Dwaine didn't see any toilets and thought, "It's so hot in here if I take a leak, the piss'll evaporate 'fore it hits the ground." He also noticed two big swinging doors leading to the street, and was grateful the doors were securely fastened by cradled two by fours.

In addition to the boxers, there were nearly forty adult males and boys as young as five in the crowded room. All of them were eating, laughing and talking. He felt uncomfortable as he undressed because several of the men were staring at his pubic hair. He thought, "Guess they wanna see if I'm a natural blonde." This caused him to change as fast as he could into his boxing attire. He was wearing a red silk robe, red trunks and even red boxing shoes and thought, "I can't fight that great, but I sure look good."

A nice looking ten year old boy without legs approached Simpson in his wheelchair. He reached out to touch the fighter's robe and shake his hand. Just as Dwaine was about to offer his hand to him, five other kids lifted the handicapped youngster from his wheelchair, thrust him into an old wooden locker and slammed the door shut. Dwaine screamed, "NO!" He immediately took the boy with the missing limbs out of the locker, gave him a hug, returned him to his wheelchair and handed him his boxing glove key chain.

The stifling heat and foul odors became too much for him, so Simpson left the dressing quarters an hour before the first fight. He entered the arena and climbed in the ring to test the ropes and the footing of the canvas. He needed tight ropes and plenty of room for his fast stepping, ducking, dodging, running style of fighting. To his dismay, he found the ropes were like spaghetti, and this would force him to stay in the middle of the ring. He also discovered the canvas was soaking wet and had large lumps under it. It would be difficult for both Dwaine and Dario Hidalgo to move around, but the Dominican's fighting style was better suited to the conditions. Simpson could never go toe to toe with any boxer, but Hidalgo was very good at it.

The inspection of the ring abruptly ended when an armed soldier who spoke no English walked up. He pointed at Dwaine and motioned him to return to the dressing room. Simpson asked why by gesturing with his hands and shrugging. The soldier pointed at the stands, then made the sign of a pistol with his thumb and index finger and pointed it at Dwaine. The blonde boxer understood perfectly what the soldier was trying to tell him. "Somebody might try to shoot you."

Dwaine returned to the crowded, hot, smelly changing room but once the preliminary bouts started, everyone rushed out to watch the fights. Simpson was all alone when he was startled by loud banging on the two large swinging doors. He became very worried when a crowd began pushing on them. He remembered all the angry people at the travel agency, and a frightening thought came to him: "They wanna bust in and kill an American!"

Dwaine tried to reassure himself by thinking, "There's no chance those two by fours'll break." Suddenly, the crowd began battering the doors with a large object. He thought, "Omigod, they're gonna break down the doors and kill me!" A second thought occurred to him. "Maybe they'll torture me first." An image flashed in his mind of being dragged into a basement with blood coming from his nose and mouth and getting chained to a wall. The pounding on the doors became louder, and he heard wood begin to splinter. He thought of running from the room, but his limbs wouldn't cooperate because he was petrified with fear.

He was standing perfectly still as the doors came down. Fifty people dropped a huge pole used as a battering ram and poured into the dressing room. Gangs of childlike adults ran by Dwaine without paying any attention to him. All they wanted was to see the fights for free. This didn't make him feel any better, and Simpson was so fearful of appearing in public he remained in the hot, smelly room for two hours until a member of the event staff came for him.

When he climbed into the ring, he found nothing had been done about the soaking wet, lumpy canvas. He wouldn't be able to use his usual boxing style and thought, "Maybe I'd be better off in my bare feet," but decided not to remove his shoes.

Dwaine held his own for the first minute and a half, but the wet canvas made the thin leather soles of his boxing shoes as useless as ice skates. He couldn't run, step fast or move around as usual. An even bigger problem than slippery shoes was Dario Hidalgo's knowledge of how to cut off any escape route. Normally, if an opposing fighter took a step toward him, Dwaine could elude him by stepping out of range. The wet canvas made this impossible, and Simpson was forced to stand toe to toe and try to fight Hidalgo's way. As Dario pounded the lanky blonde with hard punches to the body and head, Dwaine thought, "They musta given him a two by four from my dressing room."

After sustaining cuts under both eyes and losing a front tooth, Dwaine was knocked out midway through the first round. It was a painful way to make three hundred bucks. To add insult to injury, the promoters wanted to pay him in Dominican money, but he insisted on American cash only. It took some haggling with the help of Mrs. Zabala, but they finally came up with two hundred dollars in twenties and a hundred in singles. He thought, "Thank God they didn't load me down with any coins."

Early the next morning, he felt as though Sammy Davis, Jr. had tap danced on his head. His flight was leaving late in the evening, but he was anxious to get away from Santiago as quickly as possible. He told the hotel employees as best he could his flight was scheduled for an early afternoon departure, and they arranged transportation for him.

When his ride to Santo Domingo Aero Puerto arrived, he was surprised to find it was a Volkswagen Bug occupied by the driver and another man. They sat in the front and he squeezed into the back. He was wearing his white turtle neck and blue blazer with an embroidered American shield on the pocket and had stuffed all his money in his socks.

The airport was two hours away, but two men flagged the Volkswagen down after only twenty minutes on the road. They got in the back seat with Dwaine, creating such cramped quarters he had one butt cheek on the door and the other on the seat. The three other passengers rode for ten miles before they got out and paid the driver. Simpson thought, "This is a goddam taxi!" After two more stops to pick up people, he had enough. He pulled fifty dollars from his socks, told the driver "*Vamos to Aero Puerto*" and handed him the money.

They reached a very poor neighborhood just outside Santo Domingo occupied by many armed soldiers. Front doors of houses had been left open because of the oppressive heat, and most of the homes had dirt floors. To Dwaine's surprise, the driver suddenly pulled over in front of a makeshift restaurant, got out of the car and pointed to his mouth.

The taxi driver spent nearly thirty minutes in the restaurant. While he feasted, people gathered around the small car and stared at Dwaine. Within a short time, there were nearly fifty of them. He thought, "Is it my white turtle neck, blue eyes, blonde hair, bruised face or missing front tooth that attracts 'em?" Taking no chances, he quickly locked the doors and rolled up the windows, even though he would be soaked with perspiration in the hot vehicle.

This offended the crowd, and some of them started rocking the car. Dwaine was thinking, "They're gonna turn it over! They'll drag me out, torture me and then kill me!"

When the driver saw what the crowd was doing to his car, he bolted from the eatery, shoved people away from the driver's door, got behind the wheel and took off for the airport. After being let off by the driver, Simpson went through customs. Once that was over, he bought a fifth of scotch and tried to drink it all. He thought, "Well, I'm still alive. Lost my tooth, but still have my head."

He thought about his girlfriend, Judy, who was an airline stewardess. They had been going together for a couple of years. She couldn't stand him when they first met in a dance club. She was the most beautiful woman in the place, dressed in a colorful blouse, mini skirt and long black laced up boots. He asked her to dance and when she said "No," he somehow managed to turn over a table of drinks. She thought he did it on purpose and figured he was someone to avoid. They were from two different worlds. She was used to fine food and drink, while he drank Regal beer, liked meatloaf and Moon Pies and thought Dom Perignon was a Mafia leader. He'd have to come up with an astoundingly good reason for her to date him.

Dwaine persevered, kept returning to her favorite club and persistently asked the beautiful stewardess for a date until she finally gave in. The only reason she went out with him was he told her, "I've only got six months to live." After six months went by, she asked why he was still alive. Was his disease cured?

"No, I haven't paid the doctor's bill, so he gave me another six months to live."

Despite having so little in common, their relationship blossomed. She was there to pick him up when his flight from the Dominican Republic arrived, but it was not a joyful homecoming. She took one look at him and said, "You're drunk, beat up and missing a front tooth." She then began crying.

Dwaine said in a soothing tone, "Don't do that. Everything's okay. Nobody's perfect. Least that's what my dermatologist tol' me."

THE LEGEND OF HOOT GIBSON

Dwaine had finally gotten back on his feet financially early in 1970, when a tall, well muscled man visited him at his job. He said, "My name's Otis Pewitt. Ronnie Pierson said you could help me become a professional heavyweight boxer."

"How big are you?"

"Six four and two twenty."

"Ya ever fought as an amateur?"

"No."

"What sports have ya played?"

"I played football at Hialeah High and Auburn University in Alabama."

"What do ya do now?"

"I teach phys ed at a high school."

Dwaine paused for a moment, rubbed his chin while thinking, then said, "Gonna hafta change your name, Otis."

"Why's that?"

"Otis Pewitt' sounds black. White fighters sell more tickets, and it's easier to get 'em fights."

"What's a better name?"

"How 'bout 'Otis Dee'?'"

"Okay with me."

Otis was a good student. He intently listened to Dwaine, followed his instructions, trained hard, turned pro without having any amateur bouts and won four fights, three by knockout. Soon after that, Simpson received a phone call from Jimmy Mackey. Mackey was a black trainer and promoter who had worked with Dick Lee, but was much easier to deal with than the tight fisted, controlling Lee. Jimmy was holding boxing shows at a kennel club on Stock Island, near Key West. He asked Dwaine, "Say man, could you get Otis Dee to go six rounds with Hoot Gibson on September first? It's a Friday night."

"I'll see what I can do."

After ending the call from Mackey, Simpson immediately phoned Otis and said, "I got a six round fight for ya in Key West on Friday night 'fore Labor Day."

"Against who?"

"Weaver."

"You mean your buddy who's an iron worker and calls himself Hoot Gibson?"

"That's him."

Otis agreed to the fight, and he and Simpson decided to drive to Key West the day before in the heavyweight's 1969 Ford Torino. Weaver Gibson couldn't get off work and wouldn't arrive until the day of the bout.

On the way to Key West, Otis barreled along at twenty over the limit. Dwaine asked, "Why ya drive so fast?"

"It's the safest way. Less time on the road, less chance of an accident. By the way, how long ya known Weaver Gibson?"

"We go back a while. He's from Opa-Locka and went to Our Lady of Perpetual Help Catholic School." Dwaine took a sip from an RC Cola before continuing. "He wound up teachin' boxing there. One time, he asked me to fight an exhibition with him for the kids. There was no ring. They put down some carpeting and we fought in the middle of the gym. Musta been a hundred fifty people there. Weaver isn't much when it comes to punchin', but nobody has more guts. He'll fight anybody." Dwaine chuckled as he said, "Well, Weaver jumped all over me and ran me all 'round that gym. I had to remind him, 'Hey, pal, take it easy! This is just an exhibition!'"

Otis laughed and then said, "We're gettin' close to Key West. Where's our motel?"

"Never been there before," replied Dwaine.

"Oh great, we're makin' good time, but we're lost."

"I know what ya mean," said Simpson. "If ya don't know where you're goin', ya might end up someplace else. Wait a minute! I just remembered they gave me directions when I booked the room."

After checking the directions, they were able to find the motel without any trouble. The two travelers had just checked in and finished unloading their luggage when the phone in their room rang. Simpson picked it up and heard Weaver Gibson's distressed voice on the line. "Dwaine, got bad news. I hurt my arm at work. I can't fight."

"You're not gonna lose the arm, are ya?"

"No, but it'll take a while to heal."

"Look, don't worry about us. Ya take care of yourself, okay."

Dwaine immediately notified Jimmy Mackey that Hoot Gibson wouldn't be able to fight. Mackey replied, "Well, Otis can fight Randy Clark."

"Who's he?"

"Well, he's six two and about 215. He was a high school football star at Coral Gables High, was in the Marine Corps four years and does plastering work. Lotta blue collar workers buy tickets to his fights."

"How come I never heard of 'im?"

"He's only been fightin' professionally a few months and didn't have any amateur bouts."

"I can't put Otis in against somebody I don't know nothin' about."

"Okay, I'll try and get someone else."

Mackey called Simpson's motel room two hours later and said, "Dwaine, we can't find anybody who wants to fight. We gotta do somethin'. How 'bout you fightin' Otis Dee?"

"Hell, I only weigh a hundred fifty six!"

"When I saw you last month, you looked like you're still in shape."

"Yeah, but Otis goes about two fifteen or two twenty."

"We won't worry about the weight if you'll box him. We'll give you fifty dollars."

"Hell no."

"We'll give you a hundred dollars."

Simpson's eyes lit up. He replied, "Bingo. You're on." He hung up the phone, turned to Otis and said, "They can't find anybody to fight ya, so I'm gonna do it." The heavyweight looked confused.

Dwaine realized he had some explaining to do. He said, "Otis, this is no big deal. It'll be just like when we spar. It's up to me to stay away from ya, but I want ya to go out there to win."

When Dwaine and Otis arrived at the Stock Island greyhound track, they were told the referee would be Jimmy Mira. He was the brother of George Mira, an All-American quarterback at the University of Miami and pro football player. The two brothers owned several pizza parlors in Key West. Dwaine sought out Jimmy Mackey and told the promoter, "Didn't bring any equipment with me."

Mackey replied, "I'll see what I can do."

Dwaine walked to the dressing room with Otis. A couple minutes later, one of Mackey's helpers came into the dressing quarters and handed Simpson a pair of boxing trunks and two boxing shoes. The trunks were too big for him and had a big, ugly stain from something spilling on them. The shoes were mismatched. One was a size ten and the other an eight and a half. He was given no robe to wear, no corner men to assist him and not even a bucket to spit into. All he took into the ring with him was a towel. He looked over at Otis, who had a classy robe and two men to work in his corner, and thought, "Hope they don't laugh me outta the place."

Simpson entered the ring first. He climbed through the ropes and began dancing around and throwing punches. Otis entered moments later and when he removed his robe, he looked like a Greek god. Everybody went "Oooohh!" except for one loud voice shouting, "BOY, HE'S A BIG 'UN, AIN'T HE?" For some strange reason, the crowd took the underdog's side and when Dwaine was announced as "Hoot Gibson," they went crazy. Several fans hollered, "YOU CAN TAKE 'IM, HOOT! YOU CAN TAKE 'IM!" He thought, "What in hell's goin' on? Why are they rootin' for ME?"

Simpson began jabbing and moving at the opening bell. Otis started coming after him, but showed his inexperience when he walked into one of Dwaine's jabs. The punch landed on the much bigger fighter's forehead, and he went down on one knee. Simpson walked over, pushed him with his right hand and Otis rolled over onto the canvas. This drew a loud cheer from the crowd. Dwaine was about to plant his foot on the tall heavyweight, when referee Jimmy Mira said, "If you do that, I'm gonna disqualify you." Dwaine went to a neutral corner until Otis got back on his feet and stayed away from Dee the rest of the round.

The smaller fighter in stained trunks and ill fitting shoes continued to excite the huge crowd by eluding the bigger man for the entire second round. This angered Otis, and he went after Dwaine even before round three began. Simpson had just gotten off his stool and was waving to his fans with his back to the ring when Otis ran at him and connected with an overhand right to the back of the head. Dwaine was still in his corner when the punch landed, and dropped to one knee. When he got up, Dee charged at him again from across the ring. This time, Simpson laid face down on the canvas, forcing the much bigger fighter to hurdle him. Once Otis bounded over him, Simpson lifted his head, looked at his friend and thought, "He's got no idea what's goin' on."

Otis charged at Dwaine a third time. Simpson ducked his head as his friend came close, but lifted it too soon and caught Otis with an inadvertent head butt, splitting open skin above an eye. The wound didn't slow Otis in the least, and he again launched himself over Simpson with a leaping stride. Dwaine had nothing left in his tank and was ready to stay on the canvas and be counted out, when two men suddenly ran up to the ring and hollered, "GET UP, HOOT! GET UP! YOU GOT 'IM, HOOT!"

Their enthusiasm fired Dwaine up and he scrambled to his feet, but it was too late. Jimmy Mira stopped the fight and awarded Otis a technical knockout. When the decision was announced, the crowd booed Otis, but gave Dwaine a standing ovation. Chills ran up and down the journeyman boxer's back.

After Dwaine and Otis were back in the dressing quarters, the tall heavyweight said, "Dwaine… I'm so sorry, I… "

Simpson interrupted him by saying, "Ya got nothin' to be sorry for. I'm sorry I cut ya. We both just did the best we could." It turned out to be Otis' last fight. His pro record was five wins, two losses and a draw with four KO's, including his technical knockout of Dwaine. .

A month later, Jimmy Mackey called the lanky blonde and said: "Dwaine, everybody down here tells me, 'Don't even try to hold a boxing show 'less you get Hoot Gibson.' You gotta fight somebody, and I'll pay you sixty bucks. We still have Randy Clark."

"What! Are you crazy? I'm not fightin' any damn heavyweight, 'specially him!"

"Have anybody in mind you can fight?"

"I got somebody in mind... a guy I play basketball with. He's six four and weighs about two fifteen or two twenty."

"Will he box?"

"I'll ask 'im."

"If he'll do it, we'll give you both sixty dollars."

The basketball player's name was Harry Laskey. He had been recruited to the University of Akron on a combination baseball/football scholarship, but ended up starting for the basketball team. After moving to Florida, he became part of Dwaine's Opa-Locka All Stars squad. Harry had a high IQ and was employed as a sales rep for a pharmaceutical company, calling on urologists. He dressed like a banker during working hours, but was a thrill seeker in his spare time. He worried that his strait laced employer might hear about his less dignified leisure activities, so he adopted his alter ego Terry Callahan, or "T" for short.

Dwaine wanted his friend to be in a receptive mood before asking him to take part in a prizefight. Laskey loved to listen to stories about Simpson's coach at Western Carolina, Jim Gudger. They went out for a few beers and while relaxing, Dwaine said, "T, I ever tell ya about what happened durin' halftime of my first varsity game?"

"No, what happened?"

"Coach Gudger was lookin' at the scorebook and said, 'Simpson, ya scored two points. That's two more'n a dead man.' I thought he wanted me to shoot more, so I fired away every time I got my hands on the ball. That didn't make him any happier, and he tol' me, 'Simpson, the way you hog the ball proves it's impossible to play basketball with a pig. Bet you don't know any plays. Name two.' When I said, 'Romeo and Juliet and Hamlet,' he didn't think it was very funny, and I ended up stayin' after practice and runnin' up and down the court for forty five minutes."

Harry was laughing so hard he began holding his sides. This encouraged Dwaine to continue with Gudger stories. "'Nother time, he said, 'Simpson, I'd rather have a dollar bill than you. At least I get two halves out of a buck.' Then there was the time he said, 'Only difference between you and my dog is he drools and you dribble.'"

Now that he had Laskey in a good mood, he thought the time was right to ask if he'd fight for sixty dollars. The basketball player replied, "This isn't one of your jokes, is it?"

"No, it's for real."

"Where's it gonna be?"

"Key West. We'll drive down Friday afternoon, stay over, then fight Saturday night. It'll be a fun trip."

Laskey thought for a moment before saying, "Ya know, there's a urologist's office down that way I've been meaning to solicit. Okay, I'll do it, but I've gotta use the name Terry Callahan. Pharmaceuticals have standards and prizefighting isn't the image they want for a representative." Dwaine immediately went to a pay phone, called Jimmy Mackey and announced, "It's all set. Hoot Gibson will be fightin' Terry Callahan."

Laskey and Simpson had only a week to prepare, but Harry was an excellent athlete and enthusiastic about trying something completely new. He worked hard the entire time, but Dwaine realized the basketball player wasn't conditioned for boxing. There was little chance of him going the entire six rounds, and he might not last more than two.

They drove to Key West in Harry's 1968 Chevy Impala. Along the way, Laskey asked Dwaine to tell him more about his college basketball days. He asked, "Who was the toughest player you ever had to go up against?"

"A woman named Charlene."

"A woman!"

"Yeah, she was on the All-American Redheads when we played 'em my freshman year at Western Carolina."

"I heard of that team. They were a women's version of the Harlem Globetrotters. Didn't they do trick shots and comedy stuff?"

"Yeah, they'd drive from one town to 'nother in a station wagon and played all kinds of men's teams. There was only seven of 'em on their roster when they played us. They were supposed to have red hair, but most of 'em dyed theirs."

"What about Charlene?"

"I think her hair was dyed."

"No, I mean why'd she cause you so much trouble?"

"She scared me to death."

"How'd she do that?"

"Well, I was a five eleven, hundred and thirty five pound freshman and looked like I was twelve years old. It was an exhibition game, and Coach Gudger put me in early to see what I could do. I could really shoot from the outside and hit a coupla quick baskets. Charlene was nearly as tall as me and started pressin' me on defense. She was holdin' her hands up and pushin' in against me when she said, 'Oh! Don't stop!' I lost my concentration. She stole the ball and dribbled all the way down the court for a layup.

Laskey was laughing so hard it was difficult to keep his eyes on the road. Dwaine said, "It only got worse. Next time the Redheads had the ball, we got called for a foul. I was standin' next to Charlene along the free throw lane when she grabbed my hand, winked and whispered, "Hey honey bunny, I want ya ta dribble MY balls." I pulled my hand away and was so rattled I wouldn't dare try guardin' her. She messed my mind up good."

Laskey was laughing hard and gasped, "Stop, stop! Gotta catch my breath." After a moment, he said, "I'm okay now. So tell me what happened."

"Well, Coach Gudger pulled me outta the game and sat me down next to him on the bench. He said, 'What the hell happened to ya? That ole gal owned ya. If ya were a Monopoly spot, you'd be Baltic Avenue.' I was too scared to tell 'im what happened. I never did find out if Charlene actually had balls, and I really didn't wanna know."

Harry chuckled and asked, "Did it take long to get over it?"

"I felt a whole lot better when the Redheads drove out of Cullowhee. I was grateful we didn't play 'em again and never played any more women's teams. I'll never understand women, and my ex will vouch for that."

On the way to the motel, Harry stopped at a urology practice and made a sales call. Dwaine sat in the waiting room until his friend came from the doctor's office with a smile on his face. He had written a large order, earning a two hundred forty dollar commission; four times what he was being paid to fight as Terry Callahan.

After they finally checked in, Dwaine spoke candidly to the first time fighter and said, "Ya outweigh me. It's up to me to stay away from ya. I hafta warn ya if ya start lookin' really bad, I'm gonna move in and hit ya with overhand rights and lefts. If I knock ya down, stay down and let the referee count ya out."Doug agreed that would be the wisest thing to do.

Both fighters had a good night's sleep and were well rested for their match. When they arrived at the Stock Island kennel club, they were surprised to learn of the enormous interest in the fight. It attracted a sellout crowd and was being broadcast over Key West radio station WKWF. A Miami sportscaster named Jim Dooley was hired to provide a blow by blow description from a ringside seat next to the judges. People sometimes confused the sportscaster with a famous University of Miami football player who later became head coach of the Chicago Bears. Both were named "Jim Dooley," but there was no connection between them.

In describing early first round action, Dooley said, "Callahan hits Hoot Gibson with a lethal jab that makes Gibson take a knee, but he's back on his feet after only a count of four. He's moving well and keeping away from Callahan, the much bigger fighter."

As the round went on, the boxer who was a moonlighting drug salesman became exhausted and appeared unable to defend himself. Simpson purposely went into a clinch so he could warn Harry Laskey of what was coming his way.

Before the referee could pull them apart, Dwaine said, "It's lookin' pretty bad. I'm gonna hafta take ya out."

Laskey was struggling to catch his breath, but was able to gasp, "What?"

"Gonna take ya out."

"Well, hit me!"

Simpson threw three jabs at his friend's larger than normal head, and fans with transistor radios heard Jim Dooley describe the action. "Hoot Gibson hits Callahan hard three times. He turned 'im completely around, but the taller man is still on his feet and won't go down. Fans, this is an amazing performance by two fighters who won't be denied."

Dwaine thought, "Never realized T's head was so big. It's gotta be made of concrete and weigh two hundred pounds." He went into another clinch with the pharmaceutical salesman possessing a thick cranium. He said, "Damn, why don't ya go down and get outta here?"

Harry shouted, "HIT ME!"

Dwaine thought, "Don't wanna hurt the guy, so I'll hit 'im with an open hand." He swatted Laskey with an overhand right and then caught him with a left.

Jim Dooley was engrossed in the action and spoke excitedly into his microphone. "Callahan's legs are wobbling, but he still won't go down. He's gotta be one of the toughest fighters to ever appear in Key West. Hoot Gibson is moving in. He hits Callahan with a right to the body, now a left hook to the body and now a hook to the head. The big man's going down! DOWN GOES CALLAHAN! He hits the canvas like his ankles are tied together. It's a knockout for Hoot Gibson!"

Thousands of fans roared in unison, "HOOOOT! YA DID IT, HOOT, YA DID IT!" The noise was deafening.

Dwaine was mobbed as he tried to make his way to the dressing room. His admirers clutched at him and tried to tousle his hair. Suddenly, he was lifted off his feet by a swarm of hands and carried to his dressing quarters. His delirious fans gently placed him on his feet, and Dwaine thought; "A fella could get used to this. It's almost as good as a championship belt."

When he and Harry Laskey were finally alone, Harry's eyes flashed in anger as he said to his friend, "Sonuvabitch, you tried to kill me!"

"Ya kept tellin' me to hit ya," replied Dwaine. "Ya had a chance to get out, but ya didn't take it. Why didn't ya just go down."

"I was waitin' for the ref to blow the whistle and stop it."

"This isn't basketball. Ya gotta protect yourself at all times."

Four weeks later, Jimmy Mackey had another boxing show lined up, and called to ask Dwaine, "Will you fight as Hoot Gibson once more? Can you please find an opponent? I'll give each of you sixty dollars."

"How 'bout Otis or Terry?"

"Nope, they want a new face."

Dwaine immediately thought of Bill White, a friend of his who wrestled under the name "Killer Kodiak." He was 6' 2" and weighed 340 pounds. Bill was interested in the idea of appearing in a boxing match, and Simpson brought him to the Opa-Locka Recreation Center for five days of workouts. White was not as athletic as Harry Laskey, and couldn't do anything more than charge at Dwaine. This made their workouts dangerous. Simpson finally said, "Bill, if ya run into me, I could be seriously injured."

"Don't worry about it. I'm not gonna hit you that way. I'm a professional wrestler. I know how to handle myself. You're gonna win the fight."

"Okay, but let's make sure we both walk outta the ring in one piece."

Much to the disappointment of the many Hoot Gibson fans, Jimmy Mackey called the next day and said the boxing show had been canceled. "What happened?" asked Dwaine.

"Cops caught a guy bookin' bets during your fight with Terry Callahan. Who you think it was?"

"Can't imagine."

"Remember Bill Kosofsky who used to have Doc's Melody Bar across from Little River Auditorium?"

"Yeah, I was in the place a few times. Even sang and played my ukulele there once."

"Well, that's the guy they caught."

"You're kiddin'"

"Nope. Had over twenty grand on him. Now there's a big investigation, and there won't be any more shows 'til it's over."

No one foresaw how long the investigation would drag on. There were no other arrests, and Kosofsky wasn't indicted or prosecuted. His cash was confiscated and he sued to recover it, but it took years and even then he didn't get it all. There were no more boxing shows in Key West for nearly thirty years.

Dwaine thought his days of masquerading as Hoot Gibson were forgotten until the Opa-Locka Parks and Recreation Department hosted a statewide softball tournament for law enforcement officers. The organizers were short of money to pay umpires, so Dwaine ended up calling balls and strikes. During the second day of the tournament, he was umpiring a game involving a team from Key West. He was startled to hear someone holler, "HOOT GIBSON!" He quickly turned around to see who said it.

It was the next player coming up to bat. A young law enforcement officer was excited at meeting his hero and exclaimed, "I can't believe it! You're Hoot Gibson! I saw both your fights in Key West! You shoulda won 'em both. I was one of the guys who carried you to the dressing room. You're the best, Hoot, the best."

Simpson thought, "All those years fightin' as Dwaine Simpson, maybe I shoulda been Hoot Gibson. Or maybe it had somethin' to do with Key West. It could be the water, the conchs or bein' so near Cuba."

CHRISTMAS IN COSTA RICA

It was the week before Christmas in 1970, and Dwaine was worried about how he was going to come up with money to buy presents for his four kids. He received a phone call from Pat O'Malley, a well known corner man who also had the massage concession at the Eden Roc Hotel. O'Malley said, "Dwaine, can you meet me at Wolfie's in Miami Beach this afternoon? I've got somethin' that'll interest you."

"Yeah, I can make it. Is one o'clock all right?"

"That'll be perfect."

Simpson arrived at the deli to find O'Malley sitting in a booth with Jack Garfield. He had known both for a number of years. Jack was secretary treasurer of the Miami Beach Boxing Commission and had signed the letter announcing Dwaine's ten day suspension for fighting five times in ten days. Simpson walked over to them, shook hands with both men and sat next to Garfield. He looked at the man with the boxing commission and said, "Ya know, Jack, ya didn't hafta suspend me back then. I was gonna take a break from fightin' anyway. Ya didn't think I'd keep fightin' every other night, didja?"

"Nothing you'd do would surprise me, but all that's in the past. Pat and I have something that'll really help you out."

"I hope it's not as helpful as people from the government."

"No," said Pat, "it's gonna put money in your pocket, not pull it out."

Garfield lit a Winston cigarette and took a drag before laying out his proposition. He began by asking Simpson, "Are you familiar with a welterweight named Dorman Crawford?"

"No."

Pat O'Malley spoke up and said, "He beat Sandro Lopopolo in Italy. In case you don't know it, Lopopolo was the world light welterweight champ three years ago. Crawford's won his last two fights by knockouts."

"How do I fit in?"

O'Malley began his explanation by saying, "Dorman was born in Costa Rica." He stopped to ask Dwaine, "Would you like anything?"

"Now that ya mention it," replied Simpson, "I could use a sandwich. This is my lunch hour."

Dwaine ordered a corn beef on rye and an RC. The other two men asked for refills of coffee. While Simpson waited for his order, O'Malley continued talking about Dorman Crawford. "As I was sayin', he was born in Costa Rica and even though he's been livin' in Brooklyn since he was a kid, he's got a big following in that country. They're holdin' a fight for him down there in about a week, and need an opponent. Jack and I think you're the guy."

"How much they payin'?"

O'Malley replied, "We can get ya a thousand plus expenses."

Dwaine thought, "That's the most anyone's ever offered me to fight. Guess they don't know I haven't worked out in months." He took a sip of his RC Cola then asked, "Before I give my answer, I want to know what's in it for you guys."

Jack and Pat looked at each other. Garfield let out a loud sigh and said, "Go ahead and tell 'im."

O'Malley said, "It's like this. Jack and I'll each get five hundred for... "

Simpson interrupted, "So what you're sayin' is Crawford's people are payin' two thousand for an opponent and you guys are splittin' the two grand with me."

Garfield interjected, "You get the expense money."

Dwaine paused for a moment, and then ate the last of his sandwich before responding. "Okay, I'll do it. When did you say the fight was?"

"On the twenty sixth," answered Garfield, "the day after Christmas. You'll leave in three days. Let's go over to my office so you can sign the contract."

As they left the restaurant, Dwaine thought, "Isn't it great how things turned out? My kids are gonna have their best Christmas ever."

Simpson signed the contract, was given his expense money and then returned to work. It was payday and he received a check for $163.75. He decided, "I'll sign it over to Ramona. This way she'll have time to buy presents, a tree and everything else."

When he called his ex-wife with the good news, she didn't know what to say. She began to sob with joy on the phone and it took her a minute to respond. After composing herself, she said, "Dwaine, honey, we've had our ups and downs, but you've always been kind and generous. You're a good dad. But sweetheart, what are you gonna do for rent and food?"

"Don't worry. I've got a big fight in Costa Rica the day after Christmas. Tell the kids I'll see 'em when I get back."

"I will. Hope you win."

Jack Garfield called Dwaine the day before he left and said. "Remember when you told me about the language problems you had in the Dominican Republic? I've got good news. The promoters assured me they can provide an interpreter, but it'll cost you a hundred dollars."

Simpson replied, "Go ahead and get the interpreter. I'll pay for that." He thought, "I won't have to eat the same thing every day, and I'll know what people are sayin' 'bout me."

Jack asked, "You won't have any problem making 156 pounds, will you?"

"No problem," replied Dwaine. He thought, "Makin' the weight is the least of my worries. Biggest problem is I'm thirty six and haven't fought or worked out in four months. No way I can go ten rounds. If Jack and Pat or the promoters find out, there goes the thousand dollars." He said to Garfield, "Don't worry 'bout me. I'll be ready to go." After the man with the boxing commission hung up, Dwaine thought, "I'll go as long as I can, and the ref'll stop the fight before I'm injured seriously. For a grand, it'll be worth it. It'll be great to end my pro career with a big payday."

Dwaine's flight from Miami to the Juan Santamaria International Airport in San Jose, Costa Rica was uneventful. He was claimed at the airport by the man hired to be his interpreter and was disappointed to discover Rafael spoke far less English than he was led to believe. Even with the language problem, Simpson was able to enjoy a more varied menu than what he had eaten during his Dominican Republic misadventure. After dinner, Rafael said, "Pickee you up five thirty in morning, okay Senor?"

"Fine with me," replied Dwaine. He thought, "Oh brother, I hafta run every morning. Haven't done that in months." He went to bed early, knowing he would need all the rest he could get.

Rafael and a driver arrived at the hotel right on time and took Simpson to a three quarter mile horse track where he would do his running. Twenty three reporters from newspapers and television stations were waiting to see the American in action. By then, Dwaine was painfully aware Costa Rica was in high altitude and the air was much thinner than Florida. He was dressed in his running gear when he stepped out of the car, and headed straight to the flat dirt oval. He asked Rafael, "How many times around for six miles?"

"Eight times, Senor."

Dwaine thought, "Oh God, how'm I gonna make it?"

He began his run in front of the grandstand. His legs became tired as he ran along the backstretch, but he had to put on a show for the reporters or he'd blow the thousand dollars. He kept saying to himself, "C'mon, pick it up! Ya feel great!" He slowed down as he approached places along the railings where news people gathered, but would move his arms, legs and torso to make it appear he was giving it all he had. Once past them, he stopped moving his arms and legs so much until he had to pass them again. After the seventh time around, he didn't think he could take another step and prayed, "Oh Lord, please help me!" Somehow he managed to complete the eight laps. He walked away from the reporters when done because he didn't want them to see him gasp for air. He saw Rafael talking to them and became worried. He thought, "If he says the wrong thing, there might not be a fight."

Dwaine was leaning against the car that brought him to the track, when Rafael ran up to him. There was excitement in his eyes as he said, "Senor Simpson, I hear TV reporter say on camera, 'Americano run like deer.'"

Dwaine smiled at his interpreter and said, "Thanks." He thought, "Praise the Lord, the money's still safe."

Later that afternoon, Dwaine was driven to the filthiest gym he had ever seen. He thought, "They expect me to train here!" He was about to object, but suddenly thought, "Hey, wise up! If I insist on a better gym, there'd prolly be more people around and they'd expect me ta spar with somebody. I'm too tired for that."

He did some shadow boxing and then began to work on a heavy bag. Rafael came to him and said, "Senor, these men will spar with you if you want."

The American fighter who hadn't worked out in months was drenched in sweat. "No, no, no!" he said to the interpreter. "I'm in perfect shape, right where I want to be."

Rafael thought, "The man from TV say he run fast and he say he is in top shape. He might win."

After dropping the exhausted boxer off at the hotel, Rafael went to see his friend Felipe, who owned a club in San Jose named Lucky's. In addition to alcohol and musical entertainment, the place also offered gambling.

Felipe was happy to see his compadre and said, "Have a glass of your favorite, and it is on me."

The club owner poured two glasses of expensive liquor and offered a toast, "*Feliz Navidad*." They clicked glasses, sipped their drinks and began to talk.

Felipe said, "So, mi amigo, you have been watching over the Americano. How does he look?"

"The man who is on television say he run like deer, and the Americano say he is in top shape."

"The fight is for ten rounds, is it not?" asked the club owner. "Do you think the Americano will last six rounds?"

"I see no reason he cannot."

"Very interesting," replied Felipe. "Here, drink up." He filled his friend's glass again.

All San Jose was abuzz with news of the Americano who would be fighting Dorman Crawford. The most respected sports reporter in Costa Rica had stated on television that "Senor Dwaine Simpson can run like a deer." Many of the local gamblers saw a chance to receive another Christmas present by putting their money on the blonde American lasting six rounds.

The night before the fight, Dwaine and Dorman Crawford were guests at a soccer game between the Costa Rican national team and Hungary. Arriving at the arena, Simpson was introduced to his opponent. He thought, "I'm not gonna try to get him angry with me 'cuz I'm not in shape to wear 'im down." He smiled as he shook hands with Crawford, who said in perfect English, "You're a lot older than I thought you'd be."

"Gonna take it easy on an old man?"

Crawford shook his head and grinned in response. Dwaine thought, "He seems like a pretty nice guy. Maybe he will take it easy on me."

Prior to the soccer match, both fighters were brought onto the field to salute the crowd. Dwaine had no idea of what was being said in Spanish over the public address system. He was surprised when he received louder applause than the man who was boxing in his home country. The warm welcome was an exhilarating experience that caused the lanky blonde to throw his hands into the air, and his celebratory gesture was captured for posterity by newspaper photographers. Simpson thought, "These guys are much nicer than people in the Dominican Republic who wanna kill Americans."

Bill Daly, Dorman Crawford's fight manager from Englewood, New Jersey, was standing among the stadium crowd, and was also surprised at the response to Dwaine Simpson. He asked one of the locals, "Why are they yelling so loud for the guy from Miami?"

"They probably have money on him, Senor."

"To win the fight?"

"No," the local resident replied. "Many people have bet that Senor Simpson will last six rounds."

Daly's ears perked up. He was nearing seventy years of age and though he never managed a world champion, he had at one time been one of the most powerful figures in boxing. He was a prime mover in the International Boxing Guild for fight managers when the organization was used by organized crime to control the sport during the 1950's and 1960's. He earned the nickname "Honest Bill" because of his free use of the words "honest" and "honestly" in his dealings with fighters, often saying such things as, "Honestly, this is the best deal I could get you." Daly's name came up in almost every investigation of boxing by athletic commissions, legislative bodies and the the federal government, but he avoided being imprisoned for his crooked dealings. He had been in the fight game from the age of sixteen and never let an opportunity to make a dollar, legally or illegally, go to waste. Dwaine didn't know Daly was Crawford's manager or that he had crossed paths with Honest Bill before. The notorious manager handled Henry Dominguez when the Texas lightweight gave Tony Mammarelli a brutal beating.

Bill Daly asked the man he was talking to, "Where does a fellow go in this town to put down a bet?"

"The best place is Lucky's. Ask for Felipe."

Bill went to Dorman Crawford and said, "Something came up at the last minute. Gotta leave now. Can you get back to the hotel all right?"

"Sure"

The manager with the sordid past took a cab from the stadium to Lucky's. He walked in, asked for Felipe and was escorted to the gambling area of the club. Daly shook hands with the club owner and asked, "Are you taking bets on the Dorman Crawford fight?"

"Si, Senor. Are you interested in wagering?"

"I might be," replied the fight manager as he lit a cigarette. "What are the odds?"

"Five to two Crawford will win. Seven to one Simpson will last six rounds."

"Do you take traveler's checks?"

"Si, Senor."

After placing a bet on how long the fight would last, Daly returned to his hotel. Immediately after he left, Felipe called his dear friend Rafael. Rafael had helped the club owner out of a tight fix years before, and Felipe never forgot his friend. He knew Rafael would probably be asleep because he had to be up early to accompany the *gringo* during his final workout. When his old friend finally picked up his phone, Felipe said, "I am sorry to disturb you, *amigo*, but this is important."

"What happened?"

"*Caramba*! Nothing has happened yet, but something big could occur for you."

"I do not understand."

"The manager of Dorman Crawford was here. He just bet two thousand American dollars that Simpson will NOT last six rounds."

"But the man on television say he run like deer, and Senor Simpson say he is in top condition."

"I do not care what those men say. The money of the manager talks loudest. Now listen to me, amigo, how much money do you have?

"Almost nothing. I had to spend it on Christmas."

"Do you still have the deed to the farm you no longer work?"

"Yes."

"Bring me the deed first thing tomorrow. I will find out how much it is worth and I will bet that amount the same way I am betting my own money. Senor Simpson will not finish six rounds."

The Gimnasio Nacional was packed to the rafters for the long anticipated Saturday night boxing show. At the conclusion of the four preliminaries, everyone in the crowd began yelling at the top of their lungs for the Crawford versus Simpson main event to start. Many had "invested" in the American fighter lasting six rounds, and they were so sure he would do it they had been celebrating all evening.

Dwaine knew nothing of this. His only concern was how long he could keep up his fancy footwork and stay clear of any powerful blows from Dorman Crawford. He found it reassuring when Rafael, his interpreter, pinned a small cross to his robe and said, "*Vaya con Dios*." Meanwhile in the plush dressing room assigned to the Costa Rican fighter, Honest Bill Daly was reminding Dorman, "Go to the body and get Simpson out quick."

The noise in the large arena almost drowned out the clang of the opening bell, and the clamor grew louder throughout the first two rounds. While sitting on his stool at the end of the second round, Dwaine found it odd some ringside fans were chanting, "*Uno, dos... solamente cuatro mas*!" He had no idea their words translated to, "One, two... only four more!"

Getting up from the stool and walking toward the middle of the ring to begin the third round, Dwaine thought, "I think I've got my second wind. I feel great!" Suddenly, Dorman Crawford landed a paralyzing left hook squarely on Simpson's liver. Dwaine let out a loud grunt, his face twisted up, his eyes rolled back and his legs began shaking involuntarily. He felt such intense internal pain he thought, "If I don't go down, I'll crap my pants in front of all these people." He fell to the canvas.

Dorman looked down at him and said, "Didn't want to hit you in the face, old man." Simpson could only groan in response.

The crowd became enraged as the referee counted Dwaine out. Bottles flew into the ring and shattered. Dwaine was spattered with shards of glass, and decided, "I'm not gonna move. If I get up, I might get hit in the head with a bottle. Why are they so angry?"

Suddenly, a drunken spectator fell from a railing in the uppermost part of the arena, landed head first and was killed instantly. The tragedy diverted the crowd's attention from Simpson and allowed him to escape to his dressing quarters.

He stepped into the room and found two strangers going through his possessions. Dwaine shouted, "WHAT ARE YA DOIN'?"

One of them spoke English and replied, "Drugs, Senor, drugs." After ten minutes of searching, they didn't find what they were looking for and left with angry expressions on their faces. Dwaine thought, "Is everybody here goin' crazy?"

His dressing quarters lacked a shower, so he put his clothes on his sweaty body and waited forty five minutes until he thought it was safe enough to poke his head out the dressing room door. He thought the coast was clear but as he turned a corner leading to the main hallway, he was faced with two hundred people shaking their fists at him and screaming, "*EL FRAUDE*!" Dwaine thought, "Don't know what that means, but I know it ain't good."

He was wondering what to do next when he felt a hand on his right shoulder. Dwaine was startled and quickly turned around to find a man wearing an event staff uniform. The staff member didn't speak English, but beckoned Dwaine to follow him. He escorted the lanky blonde fighter to a car and drove him to the hotel. Simpson thought, "Haven't been paid yet, but it's too dangerous to stick around."

He checked out immediately and took a cab to the airport, which was fifteen miles from the main part of the city. His flight wouldn't leave until four o'clock the following afternoon, but he felt safer spending the night in the Juan Santamaria International Airport than in town.

During his long wait, Dwaine tried to find someone who spoke English. Finally, he ran into Rigoberto Chavez, who often traveled to the U.S. on business and was willing to help the distressed fighter make a phone call to the promoters. Simpson stood next to Rigoberto as the businessman used a pay telephone. When he got them on the line, he asked, "Mr. Dwaine Simpson would like to know about his purse."

The Good Samaritan's facial expression changed from hopeful to grave. He turned to Dwaine and said, "You have been accused by the authorities of losing on purpose. They say you and the fighter named Crawford were friends and the manager for Crawford made a large bet against you. They are holding your purse pending an investigation."

Dwaine exclaimed, "I got hit in the liver! Can't they understand what that's like?"

"I was not there, Senor. I am only telling you what they said."

"I know, Rigoberto. You've been great to me. Thanks for your help."

Dwaine went to the most comfortable chair he could find in the waiting area. He was too exhausted to think and fell asleep in a slumped position.

While Dwaine and Rigoberto were being told the distressing news, Felipe and Rafael were having a joyous Christmas weekend. The two old friends had won seven times the amounts they wagered on Simpson not lasting six rounds. Rafael won so much he decided to return to farming.

Things had not gone well for Honest Bill Daly and Dorman Crawford. They were almost as miserable as Dwaine because authorities were holding both Crawford's purse and Daly's winnings, pending an investigation. They were still better off than Simpson because neither suffered a painful blow to the liver.

Dwaine awoke with the rising sun. He was stiff from sleeping in the chair and needed something to eat. While searching for food, he passed a newsstand and noticed the front page of the local paper had a large picture of him holding his hands in the air. The headline read, "*El Fraude*," the same words the mob outside his dressing room hollered at him. He purchased a copy and began looking for someone who spoke English. Lucky for him, he spotted Rigoberto. "Are you still here?" he asked the businessman.

"My flight was canceled. I was placed on a much later one."

"Sorry to hear that. By the way, what's this headline mean?"

"Oh, that is a nice picture of you. 'El Fraude' means 'The Fraud.'" Rigoberto gave the boxer a look of sympathy before adding, "You seem to have a problem on your hands."

Dwaine blurted out, "Fraud! I never committed a fraud! What's the matter with those people?" All Rigoberto did was shake his head and smile sympathetically.

After Simpson returned to Miami, he went to see Jack Garfield and asked the man who helped arrange the fight, "What're we gonna do?"

"I'll write the people down there and vouch for you. You've had over a hundred professional bouts and never been accused of anything underhanded. I'll also mention Floyd Patterson stopped a light heavyweight named Charley Green in Madison Square Garden with a body shot. They should understand a body shot can stop a fighter just as much as a punch on the chin."

"Thanks, Jack, I feel better already."

"You want anything while you're here? Cuppa coffee? Soda pop?"

"No thanks, I gotta get back to work. Come to think of it, can I have a coupla bottles of pop to take with me? I came back from Costa Rica with no money."

Garfield handed Simpson two bottles of Nehi and three dollars. Dwaine thanked Jack and left his office. As he walked to his tiny Renault Dauphine, he thought, "I ended up with three bucks after my last fight... same as I did after my first fight. Well, guess I'll never make a comeback 'cuz I've never been anywhere. I started with nothin' and I still have most of that."

Two weeks later, Jack Garfield called Dwaine and said, "I got an answer from Costa Rica. It wasn't a total loss. They fined you all but $180 of your purse."

"Bullshit!" blurted Simpson. He quickly calmed down and admitted, "I shoulda known better. When are they gonna send the hundred eighty?"

"They state you must claim your money in person."

"Oh no! I'm not goin' there again! A ticket costs more'n a hundred eighty bucks and besides, I don't wanna take a chance of gettin' arrested on some trumped up charge."

"You're probably wise letting it drop. I'll send you a copy of this letter."

"Thanks, Jack. I appreciate what you did."

After Dwaine hung up, he thought, "All things considered, it didn't turn out so bad. My four kids had a great Christmas."

The fight in Costa Rica was his last appearance in the ring. Whenever asked what his professional record was, he'd reply in a matter of fact way, "I had 142 fights, with 113 wins, 22 losses and 7 draws." He'd never mention one hundred forty two bouts is more than double the average number of ring appearances made by today's prizefighters. He was a man who couldn't break an egg with his punch and would rather run than trade blows. For him to survive risking his physical well being so many times and still retain his faculties borders on miraculous. Dwaine Simpson is now in his eighties and is hale, hearty and as funny as ever.

PART FIVE

EPILOGUE

A REMINDER OF BOXINGS SEAMY SIDE

After his disastrous trip to Costa Rica, it took Dwaine four months to get straightened out financially. He then entered a golden period in his life. The best thing that happened was his marrying Judy, the beautiful airline stewardess. A close second occurred seven years after his Costa Rican misadventure. Miami-Dade County launched a boxing program at a gym in Opa-Locka. Simpson was placed in charge, and it was a life changing career move. He was no longer a journeyman fighter going through one calamitous event after another. Dwaine took all the lessons he learned the hard way and used them to ultimately inspire thousands of young people. He fostered curiosity, ignited a desire to learn, motivated them to think outside the box and instilled a work ethic. The sport that began as a lark for him became his calling, and he found great fulfillment in it. He also experienced tremendous personal growth. His ability to communicate became more polished, and he became an excellent public speaker renowned for entertaining presentations.

In 1980, Dwaine's program was moved to the Tropical Park Gym on SW 40th Street in Miami. The well equipped facility contained a boxing ring, heavy bags, speed bags, fitness equipment and three mirrors for shadow boxing. By then, he had proven to be exceptional at not only teaching boxing for fitness and competition, but promoting self discipline and self respect among his students, many of whom were at risk kids. Simpson's program received the full support of Metro-Dade Mayor Stephen Clark, who had competed as an amateur boxer and believed, "Boxing is a tremendous activity. It keeps the mind occupied and the body healthy."

In his instructions to all the young people he worked with, Dwaine stressed every sport is a discipline requiring mastery of fundamentals. He would often remind them, "Learning the basics is a slow process with lots of repetition but once you have the fundamentals down, you can develop your own style because you'll have the tools you need to go as far as you want." He was assisted by dedicated part time coaches, including Florida Boxing Hall of Famers Dave Clark and James Warring. Doug Laskey, the pharmaceutical salesman who fought Dwaine in Key West, was also one of Dwaine's assistants at Tropical Park and proved to be an exceptional teacher. He still insisted on working under the alias Terry Callahan because of his concern about what Big Pharma might think.

Professional fighters were allowed to train at Tropical Park in return for making financial contributions which enabled the gym's amateurs to compete in out of town tournaments. The professionals became members of a Pro Superstars program Dwaine organized, and he arranged for them to work out before the regular gym hours. Thirty six world champions and twenty four who fought for world titles used the facility. Such famous ring personalities as Alexis Arguello, Roberto Duran, Mark Breland, Trevor Berbick, Evander Holyfield, Gerry Cooney and Wilford Scypion were members of Pro Superstars.

Dwaine found satisfaction in helping elevate boxing from what it was when he fought as a pro. The days of fighters being cheated, abused and thrown on the scrap heap when no longer useful seemed to be over, but that was not the case. Reminders of pugilism's dark side always seem to surface when least expected.

It was March, 1983, and seventy four year old Chappie Roberts was alone in his Fort Lauderdale condo. Life had become harder for him, and his health was starting to fail. He had gone through a heart attack, a hernia operation and multiple cancer surgeries. He was still alive, which was more than could be said for his fellow New Jerseyites Charlie Fakish and Bill Kosofsky, both of whom had passed away within the previous three years. Charlie died because of a freak accident. He woke up in the middle of the night needing to urinate and on his way to the bathroom, fell and hit his head on a night stand. Fakish lay unconscious and bled to death. He lived alone, and his body wasn't discovered for days. He left no heirs and neglected to draw up a will, so all assets went to the state. Bill experienced mental health issues. After having twenty grand confiscated by the authorities in Key West, he had become miserly, secretive and paranoid. He tried to hide his wealth by burying it, but foolishly used cloth bags to protect his paper currency. The bags rotted while in the ground, and the money was destroyed by dampness, worms and insects. The shock was too much for him, and he suffered a fatal stroke.

Roberts was pondering what the future held in store for him, when the phone rang. He picked it up and the voice on the other end asked, "Chappie Roberts?"

"Yeah."

"Chappie, this is Mike Jones. I'm Wilford Scypion's manager."

"I've heard of you," replied Roberts. Jones was a forty eight year old New York City realtor who became well known in boxing circles while managing heavyweight contender Gerry Cooney and lightweight challenger Howard Davis.

"Wilford's going to be training in Miami for a fight with Marvin Hagler. We need sparring partners."

"I can get 'em for ya. Where's he gonna be training?"

"The Tropical Park Gym. Are you familiar with it?"

"Oh yeah."

"How much will you charge to supply sparring partners?"

"Lemme see... there's housing, food, transportation and their pay. I figure five thousand a month."

"I'll go for four thousand a month, and they gotta be left handed fighters."

"When do I get paid?"

"At the end of the month."

"I need money to work with."

"I'll advance you a thousand dollars."

"Okay, ya got a deal."

"Fine, I'll get a check out right away. What's your address?"

The money from Mike Jones arrived as promised. Unfortunately, the elderly trainer became greedy. Rather than the usual rate of thirty five dollars per round, he tried to get away with paying sparring partners fifty dollars a day plus fifteen dollars meal money and housing them in a motel at SW Eighth Street and Tamiami in Miami's Little Havana section. The first four boxers he hired refused to work under those conditions and quit. Chappie then remembered Gene Wells, a black middleweight with a round butter scotch face who resembled Muhammad Ali and had once been part of Ali's training team.

Chappie located Wells in Louisville and after they spoke on the phone, the fighter agreed to fly down that Sunday. Roberts picked him up at the airport and drove him to the motel in Little Havana. Before Gene got out of Chappie's four door Chevy Impala, the little old man handed him fifteen bucks and said, "Here's meal money. Pick ya up at noon tomorra."

The next day, Roberts pulled into the motel parking lot promptly at twelve o'clock. When Wells opened the passenger door and got in, Chappie asked, "Ya got five bucks? I need some gas." The fighter handed a five dollar bill to the aging trainer.

On Gene's first day of working with Wilford Scypion, the round faced middleweight was surprised to learn he would have to switch from his natural right handed stance. Chappie had failed to mention Scypion was preparing to fight a southpaw. Wells had trouble adapting to a different stance and was knocked out in only the second round of the sparring session. He was revived and managed to finish out the day.

Roberts drove Wells back to the cheap motel, where the fighter spent a miserable evening. He tried to find a place to eat, but every restaurant in the neighborhood served only Cuban food, and he didn't want that. He went to bed early, but was too restless to sleep. Thoughts raced through his head, and his mind drifted back to the eight years he fought professionally and was known as "Louisville Gene." He recalled the times he worked as a sparring partner for heavyweights Muhammad Ali and Jimmy Ellis and remembered when he suffered a severely broken thumb and wrist which required two bone grafts. He thought about his son from his first marriage and his second wife back in Louisville. When he told her he was going to Miami to work as a sparring partner, she said, "You're crazy! I won't be here when you get back 'cuz you'll never admit you can't support us by boxing. You shoulda got a job a long time ago."

After a long night with little sleep, Tuesday finally arrived for Gene Wells. When Chappie picked him up at noon, Gene appeared sullen. He had nothing to say to the old man and didn't utter a word until they pulled into the Tropical Park parking lot. When he finally spoke, Wells angrily blurted, "Ya gotta tell these guys I need more money to eat! I haven't eaten all day! There's nowhere to eat but Cuban places, and I don't like Cuban food!"

"What the hell do ya like, Gene?" Something about the way Chappie said it sent Wells over the edge.

The fighter lost control of himself. He spit on Roberts, pulled out an ice pick, started yelling and attacked Chappie. The old trainer used all his strength to battle his assailant, but Gene stabbed Chappie once in the arm and twice in the fingers before the senior citizen was finally able to knock the ice pick from the boxer's hand. Both men bolted from the car. Chappie forgot to take his maroon Chevy out of gear, and it rolled through the lot toward a row of parked cars. Although bloodied, Roberts hobbled alongside it, hollering, "HELP ME! HELP ME! HELP!"

Thirty people inside the gym heard the shouting and rushed to the parking lot. A young boxer jumped in the Chevrolet, jammed the gearshift into Park and stopped the car before it hit anything. Someone shouted, "IT'S CHAPPIE ROBERTS AND GENE WELLS!"

Another person ran to Chappie and asked, "What happened?"

He pointed to Wells and said, "He stabbed me with an ice pick."

James Warring, a world kickboxing champion who was part of the gym's staff, walked up to Wells and said, "Hey man, put that pick down! If you don't, I'll kick you." Gene had seen Warring work out and knew what he was capable of. He let the ice pick fall from his hand to the pavement. The kickboxer asked the troubled athlete with the butter scotch complexion, "What's the matter?"

Wells muttered, "I couldn't take it anymore. I couldn't take it. He put me in a place where they don't speak English. I'm hungry. I want to eat."

By this time, Roberts had gotten behind the wheel of his car. The nostrils of his punched out nose were flared, his shirt was pulled open and blood covered his stubby fingers. He felt the pounding of his heart with his bloodied hand and said, "I don't feel well."

Dwaine Simpson called the police. An officer responded, and filled out a report. Chappie Roberts declined to press charges and went to Miami's VA Medical Center for shots and a closer checkup. Ken Weldon, Scypion's trainer, said to Simpson, "We're through with both of 'em. We don't need that trouble. We'll find someone else with a car and somebody else for sparring." Weldon and Mike Jones got rid of Chappie and put Gene Wells on a plane back to Louisville. He was fortunate to avoid prosecution and receive another chance at putting his life together.

Chappie Roberts survived being attacked by Wells, but his days were numbered. Five years later, Roberts passed away in the VA Medical Center. He was 79.

When all the excitement was over, Dwaine said to James Warring, "I thought times had changed and pro boxing had cleaned up its act the last few years, but I guess I was wrong. Fighters are still being used and thrown away."

THANKS FOR THE MEMORIES

BY

LAURA BROWN

Thanks for the memories,
Of rings and gloves and ropes,
And championship hopes,
To those who treated us like dopes,
I thank you so much.

Thanks for the memories,
For some fun that I had,
At times which I was bad,
Because of Lord Lee,
Who charged one third fee,
I thank you so much.

Thanks for the memories,
When it was time for pay,
He deducted gauze and tape,
And every time I took his bait,
That very ugly ape,
I thank you so much.

THE STORY OF DWAINE SIMPSON BOXINGS CLOWN PRINCE

Thanks for the memories,
I made a hit in town,
In the audience not a frown,
I felt I earned a crown,
For being the perfect clown,
I thank you so much.

Thanks for the memories,
Of trips to foreign lands,
Motorcades and marching bands,
And the time in Costa Rica,
I was accused of cheating them,
I thank you so much.

Thanks for the memories,
I opened Tropical Park,
All these kids showed up,
My heart was all pumped up,
And I gave them joy and spark,
I thank you so much.

Thanks for the memories,
For a lovely lady Judy,
A real rootie tootie,
She didn't like me at first,
But I conquered her with my wits,
And she became my beauty,

I thank you so much.

TRIBUTE TO A SON OF A BITCH

It was early in 2011 and Dwaine was preparing the speech he would give at his induction into the Florida Boxing Hall of Fame. He was not being honored for his performances in the ring, but for his career as a master teacher of boxing. He was trying to make it as humorous as possible. He wanted to stand at the podium and see smiles and laughter, not a bunch of people fidgeting and checking their watches.

He jotted down several one liners from the past on a legal pad. "When I was in college, a professor told me I had the intelligence of an empty ashtray." "I thought I'd get picked for the Hall of Distinction, but wound up in the Hall of Extinction." "My brain has such small capacity you can smell somethin' burnin' whenever I try to think."

As he tried to form perfect sentences using just the right words and arrange his oneliners into a monologue, he recalled names and faces of many people he had encountered in boxing. The first who came to mind was Irish Gene Robinson, the man Dwaine decisioned in four rounds and turned out to be a vicious criminal. Robinson spent over twenty years in prison for shooting two FBI agents. The hardened criminal was released in 2005, but arrested four years later for selling marijuana, oxycodone and firearms. Dwaine thought, "He drew a twenty year sentence at the age of 64, so I guess he'll wind up dyin' in prison."

He next thought of Dick Lee and wrote on his pad, "Dick Lee thought he should be Mr. Boxing in Florida... Not." When Dwaine Simpson first met him, Lee's full time job was Director of Parks and Recreation for Hialeah. After persuading the city of Miami to back his amateur boxing programs, he worked there for twenty years before retiring in 1979 and moving to Orlando. He supposedly continued to be in charge of weekly amateur shows in Miami, but manipulated things so it became a "no show" position. Dick only came around for the event itself. He would drive down from Orlando, make his appearance and pick up $250. The grand a month Dick Lee received for lending his name to the shows supplemented his city pension.

Lee was able to get away with such things because of his tight grip on Florida's amateur fighters. His first step toward seizing control was becoming state chairman of AAU boxing and his hold became tighter when he acquired the Golden Gloves franchise for Florida in 1971. Dick did things his way. He showed little concern about how old the fighters were. In any other state, a fighter had to be sixteen in order to compete, but Dick Lee saw no need for age requirements. If anyone questioned him, he would show them a letter from a thirteen year old boy living on a farm in central Florida. The kid wrote, "I've been learning how to box by punching some of the cows." Lee often cited the letter to prove age limits were unnecessary, and amplified his stance by saying, "If a kid wants to fight, let 'im. If he gets in over his head, we can always throw in the towel and stop the fight."

He also brought in amateur fighters from Puerto Rico, Jamaica and the Bahamas to represent Miami in Golden Gloves competition without bothering to check birth certificates or other identifying documents. Mike McCallum became the first fighter representing Miami to win a national Golden Gloves title in 1977, but was really from Jamaica. Lee's policy of bringing in boxers from other countries made it very difficult for true home grown talent to compete in state and local tournaments.

Dick Lee was inducted into the Golden Gloves Hall of Fame in 1986 and when it was announced the city would be building an arena for the Miami Heat NBA team, he became obsessed with hosting the 63rd Annual National Golden Gloves Finals. Miami Arena was originally under the control of Al Howard, head of the city's parks and recreation department. Over the years, Lee and Howard had become close friends, despite Al being a "college boy" who held bachelor and master's degrees. When the arena opened in 1988, Howard verbally promised Dick he could use the facility rent free to host the 1990 Finals. The eyes of the boxing world would be on Miami, and Dick would be in the limelight. It could lead to his becoming the man at the top of the boxing pyramid. He envisioned a limitless horizon as he waited in anticipation of his destiny being fulfilled.

Miami's political situation drastically changed by the time 1990 rolled around. Parks and Recreation was separated into two departments, Al Howard was no longer around and organizations using the arena had to pay regardless of any promises made. Dick was faced with a $100,000 rental charge for the four days needed to stage the event. Gate receipts were not large enough to cover the rent plus all other expenses involved, so the Golden Gloves national headquarters chipped in thity grand. Lee was forced to pay the remaining $70,000 out of his own pocket, wiping out his life savings.

He also went through numerous personal problems. Dick was married four times, and his last wife, Neri, was a much younger Latin woman. She had entered into a marriage of convenience with him in order to obtain permanent residency in the U.S. In return, she would take care of him in his declining years and share his condo in Hallandale Beach. It was a tumultuous relationship, and she physically abused him. Every three months, police were called to the condo because Mrs. Lee was beating up her husband. Whenever this happened, he'd move in with his two daughters, who shared the same residence. After a couple of months with them, he would always return to the woman who treated him so badly. He suffered from Alzheimers for the last three years of his life and in the end, was reduced from a man with vigor, vitality and zeal into a crumble of skin and bones who couldn't remember how to dial 911. .

In recalling the promoter who played a prominent role in his becoming a professional boxer, Dwaine wrote, "Dick Lee thought he was as tough and smart as anyone in the world and could control amateur boxing in Florida. He didn't understand one person can't control an entire sport. There are too many people involved. Fans pay to see athletes and without athletes, you don't have a sport. Athletes must learn the fundamentals and playing by the rules when they're young, and this requires teachers. Dick was not a teacher. He was a money grubbing organizer who insisted on playing by his own rules."

As he continued to reflect about the man who once managed his pro career, Dwaine thought, "He wasn't all bad, though. He got me into boxing, and it took me from being way below normal to normal. He held shows in many small arenas and gave a lot of boxers a chance to fight professionally. He also taught me a person can dislike someone intensely but still do business with 'em. That has to be worth somethin'. But I can't deny what a mean, controlling, tight fisted bastard he was. He was a financial manipulator who nipped at my finances for years. Do I miss him? Yeah, like I miss a hemorrhoid."

Dwaine decided not to bring up Dick Lee during his speech. It would be better to focus on positive things, such as how great his life had been after his wife, Judy, came into it, how proud he was of his son, Guy, becoming an excellent boxing teacher and how well his daughters turned out. He continued working on his presentation and after an hour went by, was almost finished. All that remained was an explanation of why boxing meant so much to him. He gathered his final thoughts and then wrote, "My professional career formed only twenty five percent of my sixty years in organized boxing, and the most rewarding part was the forty years I spent teaching and coaching at risk kids. It did my heart good to see them learn about respect, self worth and how much is required of them in order to be great because I myself was once an at risk kid. In summary, the things about boxing that make it a wonderful lifetime experience for our youth are the challenge, the excitement, the fears, the overcoming of the fears, the accomplishment, the satisfaction and last but not least THE LAUGHS!."

THE END